ECOLOGY AND ECONOMICS

ECOLOGY AND ECONOMICS
An Approach to Sustainable Development

Ramprasad Sengupta

OXFORD
UNIVERSITY PRESS

OXFORD
UNIVERSITY PRESS

Oxford University Press is a department of the University of Oxford.
It furthers the University's objective of excellence in research, scholarship,
and education by publishing worldwide. Oxford is a registered trademark of
Oxford University Press in the UK and in certain other countries

Published in India by
Oxford University Press
22 Workspace, 2nd Floor, 1/22 Asaf Ali Road, New Delhi 110002, India

First published in India 2001
Oxford India Paperbacks 2002
25th impression 2023

ISBN-13: 978-0-19-566213-9
ISBN-10: 0-19-566213-X

Typeset by InoSoft Systems, Delhi 110 092
Printed in India by Replika Press Pvt. Ltd.

To the memory of my parents
Renu and Sukdev Sengupta

The Indian mind never has any hesitation in acknowledging its kinship with nature, its unbroken relationship with all.

The fundamental unity of creation was not simply a philosophical speculation for India; it was her life-object to realize this great harmony in feeling and in action.

The earth, water and light, fruits and flowers, to her were not merely physical phenomena to be turned to use and then left aside. They were necessary to her in the attainment of her ideal of perfection, as every move is necessary to the completeness of the symphony.

Rabindranath Tagore

PREFACE

The two-way linkage between nature and economy through resource flows and wastes has an important bearing on the enquiry into the well-being of society. Nature's limits in providing support to the living system while sustaining the economic one has led to the emergence of the disciplines of resource economics and environmental economics. In this context most of the issues have centred around the question of sustainability of the current capitalist development process driven by market forces. The conventional neoclassical analytic framework has perceived these issues as imperfect definition of property rights on nature and externality arising from the divergence between private and social costs in the use of nature. Normative analysis applies welfare economics and capital theory based on static or intertemporal dynamic framework of choices. While the analytical apparatus of conventional economics would be useful for this purpose, the validity and significance of the results would depend on the quality of the assumptions as well as the formulation of the concerned economic problems of optimal resource use and pollution. Correct scientific assumptions regarding the interface between nature and economy should be made. This is reflected in the valuing of nature either as a source or sink. It is increasingly recognized that a deeper analysis warrants the internalization of some important interface ecological factors into economic models for a systemic understanding enabling the formulation of sustainable policies.

The new school of ecological economics emphasizes the need for interdisciplinary analysis on these issues, thereby advocating a unified scientific and integrative approach rather than the narrow reductionist approach of conventional economics. This has led to the realization of a need for an interdisciplinary exposure to the students of environmental and resource economics, particularly with respect to the relationship between the economy and the biosphere. The knowledge of some of the basics of the structure and functions of nature is considered necessary to understand the basic problems of environmental economics. While there is vast technical literature on ecology, students and teachers of economics often feel lost as they are unable to determine ecological concepts and laws relevant for economics and how they are immediately or remotely related to economic issues. This book bridges this gap not only for students, teachers and researchers in economics but also for general readers with wider interdisciplinary interest. Although it is usable as a text on environmental and resource economics at undergraduate level, it is aimed as a reference for readers who intend to understand the interconnections between the economy and ecosystems—and thereby between ecology and economics.

Apart from introducing the basic concepts with resepct to earth and its biosphere, this book outlines three main laws or processes relating to the functions of nature—entropy, flow of solar energy, and bio-geo-chemical cycles of nutrients. It focuses on the interlinkages between these laws and economic processes, particularly from the point of view of sustainability of development. The chapters on population growth and human ecology delineate the implications of these scientific laws in terms of carrying capacity of nature, that is, the size of the population and life support to an economy by way of provision of natural resources and various eco-services including degradation of the wastes generated. The analyses and discussions have covered economic issues relating to resource use as well as degradation of land, soil, water, vegetation, biodiversity, energy and non-energy materials, on the one hand, and recycling, disposal of biodegradable and non-biodegradable wastes on the other. The environmental problems discussed range from soil erosion and chemical pollution to desertification, ozone depletion, acid rain, and global warming. In the discussions on ecological laws and their implications for the sustainability of economic processes, illustrations have been taken from Indian scientific experiments and developmental experiences to provide a distinct Indian perspective to the subject. Most of the issues have been illustrated with Indian data along with global data, to familiarize the reader with the Indian subcontinent.

This book has carefully avoided conventional topics of environmental and resource economics, theory and policy. However, the first chapter points to the limitations of conventional neoclassical economics in dealing with the ecological sustainability of economic processes. While highlighting the evolution of ecological concepts in economic thought, emphasis has been laid on the necessity for resolving paradigm conflicts between the two disciplines of ecology and economics. The book demonstrates the possibility of resolution by incorporation of ecological elements in a very simple economic model of sustainable development in a capital theoretic framework. The institutional questions to make the results of such interdisciplinary analysis operational have also been raised in the last chapter.

The World Bank Project on the Capacity Building in Environmental Economics in India provided me the support for writing this book. I am extremely grateful to U. Sankar of the Madras School of Economics, Chairperson of the Environmental Economics Course and Curriculum Committee (EECCC), for requesting me to write such a book. I also thank the EECCC of the Ministry of Environment and Forests of the Government of India and the World Bank. I began the work in 1998 while teaching in the Jawaharlal Nehru University (JNU). However, the major part was completed in April 2000 during my stay in the Indian Institute of Management (IIM), Calcutta. I am indebted to both the institutions for extending to me the infrastructural support for this work.

I have benefited immensely from many discussions and valuable inputs on draft manuscript from Amit Bhaduri at JNU, Jayanta Bandyopadhyay at IIM, Calcutta, Gopal Kadekodi at CMDR, Dharwad, Ratan Khasnobis of Calcutta University, and R.C. Jhamtani at the Planning Commission. Anup Sinha and Uttam Sarkar of IIM, Calcutta provided with useful comments and editorial sugggestions. C.K. Varshney and Sanjay Chandra of JNU and Kanchan Chopra of the Institute of Economic Growth, helped me with the reference material. I remain grateful to all of them. I also thank Aniruddha Mitra and Kaushik Banerjee for research assistance. The burden of all assertions and errors of this book is, however, only mine.

Sukumar Majumdar of IIM, Calcutta word-processed the manuscript of this book very carefully. I thank him for his commitment and painstaking assistance.

Finally, I must thank my wife Sheila for being understanding, supportive, and encouraging through out the project.

I shall consider my efforts meaningful if the book is found useful by its target readership and serves its intended purpose.

Ramprasad Sengupta

CONTENTS

TABLES

FIGURES

Chapter 1

INTERLINKAGES BETWEEN ECOLOGY AND ECONOMICS

Introduction

Human beings are among the innumerable species inhabiting the earth who, like other species, live by developing a relationship with their environment comprising both living organism and non-living substances. However, unlike other species the relationship between man and nature has vastly changed over time due to the development of human consciousness represented by science, technology, values and culture. With the help of science and technology human beings have transformed the resources of nature into products according to their value system for consumption and betterment of their well-being. However, in the phase of capitalist development which began three centuries ago, indefinite accumulation of capital and generation of surplus became the driving force behind the growth of economic activities, with the institution of market providing the mechanics of attainment of social well-being. This has made possible an indefinite growth of demand for natural resources and environmental services to support resource intensive development. Given the size of human population and the aggregate size of world economic activities, such a demand on the biospheric resources was not considered for a long time to be causing any stress or strain on nature's functional system or disturbing the ecological balance. Economics, until the last quarter of the twentieth century, ignored the limitations on the functioning of an economy except diminishing return of land. With population explosion and pace of industrialization of the world, the situation has now vastly changed at the end of the twentieth century. Today, there are ample evidences of the adverse impacts of unmindful expansion of economic activities driven by the forces of capitalist accumulation on the ecological balance for example air and water pollution, desertification, climate change, biodiversity loss, etc. It is feared that too much tilting of the balance may cause the ecosystem to move away from the existing locally stable equilibrium to a new equilibrium which may describe a new eco regime whose characteristics are unknown and, therefore, involve vast uncertainties. The sustainability of the present global pattern of development process has become an issue of deep concern especially due to uncertainty of the human ability to adapt in future with less cost, to the changing environmental condition. In order to arrive at the right policy approach for sustainable development it is imperative to (a) understand the inter-relationship between the structure and function of nature and economy; (b) adapt to some shift of the paradigm of economic analysis for appropriate integration of the interface issues in various sciences in an interdisciplinary framework. The purpose of this book is to explain the interface relationship between ecology and economics for a better understanding of the nature-economy interaction and the concepts and conditions of sustainability of development. For appreciation of the relevant issues, the background for the discussion on nature-economy interaction is delineated in the following sections.

Ecology and economics share the same Greek root 'okois' meaning 'house' or 'habitat'. Ecology is the study of the relationship of the living organisms (biotic elements) with the nonliving materials (abiotic elements) in the surrounding environment. Ecology is the study of the structure and function of nature, including mankind.

Economics, on the other hand, means the study of management of households. However, the historical development of the subject has been as a branch of social science, studying the problems of material well-being of human society. Conventional economics presumes that the well-being of a society depends on the flow of consumption of material goods and services. However, economics has been concerned traditionally with the consumption of only such goods of utility to consumers required to be produced using scarce resources. Economic theories have centred around production of material commodities and services which involve, directly or indirectly, conversion of some *natural resource* with the help of human labour and manmade capital, into final consumable form. The output of such transformation process may be a capital good which would be used as a means of production in the subsequent periods. Natural resources forming the material basis of production would be low entropy, abiotic or biotic substance which after being converted into a consumer or capital good, and subsequent usage would, as high entropy waste, flow back to nature. Nature is used both as a source and as a sink for enhancing human consumption (Ayres and Kneese 1969; d'Arge, Ayres and Kneese 1970). It is assumed that the flow of high entropy wastes as received would be degraded and subsequently transformed by nature for regenerating its low entropy resources as per the ecological laws and principles. (Figure 1.1)

The use of nature as a source and sink of economy involves interaction between nature and economy. The laws governing the function of the economic system and the natural ecosystems

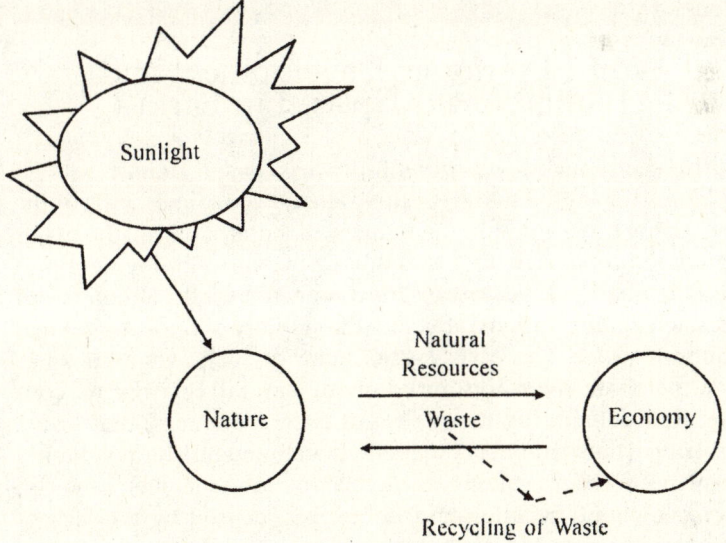

Figure 1.1 Nature–economy interaction.

would have to be compatible for sustaining the balance of both the systems. It is suggested that given the unity of root of the two words, there should exist a unity of purpose and function connecting nature and economy and interrelating the two disciplines of ecology and economics.

However, in practice, these two disciplines began with different sets of assumptions and developed very different principles for the analysis of their respective worlds reflecting conflicting paradigms. Economics has lost the broader perspective within which the function of the human economy has to be visualized. Economic thought, evolved historically in such a moral, material, and scientific environment that it led to economic theories based on questionable assumptions regarding the relation between the economy and nature.

Our discussion focussing on the nature–economy interactive relation emphasizes the interface between ecology and economy should explain the environmental and the resource crisis casting its gloomy shadow over industrial development and urbanization. A transdisciplinary approach is essential for understanding the environmental problem, and for developing policies for environmentally sustainable economic development.

World Economic Development and Limitations of Spaceship Earth

World economic development process has different sets of problems for (a) the mature industrialized economies and (b) the developing economies. In the industrialized economies, the major economic problem is the instability of income, employment and prices of commodities arising from repeated cycles of boom and recession among nations, affecting the stability of the international economic order. The basic causal factor of such instabilities has been periodic over-accumulation of capital relative to consumption demand by the people of such economies, due to the maturity of their capitalist process of development. The developing countries have problems of persistent low income, poverty, unemployment, inflation and debt crisis, caused by the lack of capital resources, access to technology, and over-population. Besides, there is also the global problem of the growing gap

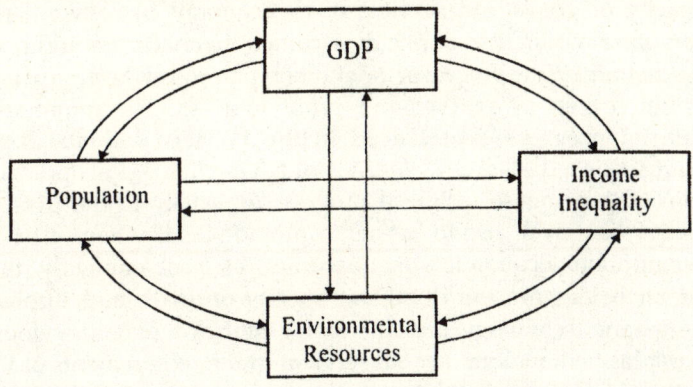

Figure 1.2   A framework of analysis of sustainability of development

between the rich and the poor nations. Conventional economic approach for finding solution to the problems of industrialized countries has been in identifying ways for (a) expanding home market, innovating new products, restructuring, and raising consumption levels by encouraging wasteful consumption, and (b) by ensuring the growth of exports. All these are intended to ensure profitable employment of capital stock which is growing continuously out of reinvestment of retained profit of corporations. For the developing countries, the solution has been sought in finding ways of mobilizing financial resource from home or abroad and adopting appropriate strategy for the deployment of these resources for removal of poverty and unemployment.

The crux of the solution suggested by conventional economics appears to be based on the greater employment of capital stock with the normative implication that the productive capacity or the material base of the production economy should be expanding at all levels. The dominant ideology in economics also insists that the optimal expansion of the production base of an economy can be achieved, only in a market economic system where price guides investment decisions and ensures efficient allocation of resources through the profit-seeking activities of the firms, with the exception of obvious market failures.

The long-term vision of economic progress requires as a necessary condition, indefinite market-propelled expansion of the production capacity of goods and services of an economy. In conventional economics' vision, it is implicitly assumed that nature would pose no constraint to the process of indefinite expansion of the production system driven by market and profit motives. The impressive material progress experienced in the Western industrialized countries over the last two centuries and the technological optimism which the immense technical progress especially in the present century has given rise to, seems to provide justification for such presumption. Economics thus assumes, at least implicitly, that human beings are the dominant species on earth and through science and technology, their increasing control over nature would be established, making her subservient to the requirements of the economy. The assumptions of economics contradict the basic principles of the natural system. Any regime of steady state economic growth under a frozen technology efficiency scenario would imply constant proportionate growth in flows of resources from nature to economy and the corresponding return of wastes from economy to nature. The rate of growth of flow of resource and waste from and to nature respectively, can be less than that of the growth of gross domestic product (GDP), provided, less resource intensive efficient technological production processes, are available. Since the overall material resource requirement per unit of output cannot be reduced to zero, that is, 'something cannot be produced out of nothing', the required flows of resource as well as waste will be growing at a varying higher or lower rate in the development process requiring considerable support from nature for increasing resource supply and waste absorption. In turn, this poses a conflict with the fact that our planet is a finite place like a spaceship endowed with limited amounts of abiotic resources and receiving a finite flow of solar energy per square kilometer per hour. The existing solar energy flow can sustain only a finite maximum rate of regeneration of the biotic resource depending on the existing size of its stock. (Boulding 1966)

Ecology and Economics
Conflicting Paradigms

The source of the conflict between developmental process and environmental constraints can be traced to the failure of conventional economics to recognize the role of entropy law of thermodynamics, while making the basic assumptions of a developmental model. (Georgescu–Roegen 1971a, 1971b; Dally 1971; Ayres 1978)

Entropy is a measure of bounded or unavailable energy in a closed thermodynamic system. Energy exists in two qualitative states—available or free energy over which man has complete command, and bound energy which is unavailable or which man cannot possibly use. The chemical energy contained in a litre of oil is free energy, which can be transformed into heat to do mechanical work, while heat energy contained in hydrogen in sea water is bound energy. When a piece of coal or a litre of oil is burnt, the initial free energy resource is transformed into heat, energy, gases like carbon dioxides, nitric oxides, etc. and some unburnt particulate matter. In such usage the initial energy is chaotically dissipated into disorder. Similarly, the use of non-energy materials, such as iron ore, conforms to the same principles. Iron ore, an ordered structure of low entropy when converted into a steel sheet, would still be of lower entropy than iron ore since it contained a higher concentration of Fe. With the wearing out of the steel-based material over time, its Fe content is dissipated into disorder and after its use, it is thrown away as high entropy waste into nature's sink.

In the economic process the basic material inputs are low entropy natural resources. Energy resource use in the production process, is entropic. The abiotic material resources like iron ore, bauxite or copper would be transformed into ordered structured product like steel, aluminum or copper sheets with low entropy. However, the metallic conversion process has used large amount of low entropy energy and other resources like fluxing and refining materials, etc. which have ended up in a high entropy state. In the aggregate effect the stock of low entropy matter energy has gone down. The use of biotic resources in the production process can also be shown to be entropic, for instance the decrease of biodiversity due to developmental process. Finally, any use of output of the production process for consumption or capital use would involve degradation due to gradual dissipation of the basic constituent elements of the material product into a higher disorder state.

The food consumed by man involves movement along entropy gradient as low entropy food energy after providing energy for functioning of the body metabolism and biomass growth leaves the organism as degraded heat and other body wastes. A living organism requires continuous low entropy energy and nutrient inputs through food, water and oxygen to maintain its internal order and low entropy character. If these life support supplies are stopped, the body of the organism would degenerate into an increasing disorderly state ending in its death and decomposition.

Similarly, the economic system represents a highly ordered complex system with its organic structure comprising innumerable firms and households. The flow of labour services from the households to the firms and that of the produced goods and services from the firms to the households describes the interrelationships among the components of the organic structure of an economy. For the metabolic activities of an economy such as production and consumption to be carried repetitively the economic system, would require continuous inputs of low entropy matter and energy from the ecosystem and in turn release high entropy matter-energy wastes to the ecosystem for absorption. In case of stoppage of supply of low entropy resources from nature, the functioning of the economic system would come to a halt. The economy being a subsystem of the global ecosystem, its function and growth would thus contribute to the increasing scarcity of low entropy matter and energy which constitute the resources of the economic production system. This argument rests on the presumption that our planet is a thermodynamically closed, and therefore a materially non-growing system.

One may, however, speculate that earth does not represent a strictly closed thermodynamic system since energy from the sun received by earth is partly absorbed in the earth's biosphere, terrestrial and atmospheric systems, and partly reflected back (30 per cent) into the outer space. Part of solar energy flow reaching the biosphere is transformed into chemical energy (0.8 per cent) through photosynthesis which flows through various plant and animal life forms along the food chain, contributing to the maintenance and growth of their biomass stock. The economic system uses many biotic resources (low entropy) for food as well as non-food uses (e.g., biomass fuel, agro-based or forestry-based raw materials for industries, etc.). All biotic resources are regenerated although at a finite rate per unit time and therefore most of the biotic resources are renewable in human time scale.

The remaining solar energy generates heat energy which is partly utilized in the processes of evaporation and precipitation and in driving the flow of winds, waves, ocean currents, etc. The climate system and resource flow which provide the crucial life support to the biosphere are essentially driven by the solar energy. The flow of hydro-energy resources as used for non-energy purpose in the economic system are derivatives of solar energy flows and renewables. At any given time and place the availability of renewable resource, whether biomass or hydro-potential, would obviously be bounded. If the economic system uses these resources at a rate higher than their rates of regeneration by nature, there will be depletion of stocks of renewable resources. The harvesting of forest biomass at a higher rate than the rate of regeneration would cause deforestation or, the extraction of groundwater at a rate higher than that of its recharging would result in the depletion of the aquifer reserves. The finiteness of the solar energy flow per unit time thus tends to set a bound on the maximum rate of use of any renewable resource per period on a sustained basis.

Apart from regenerating biotic resources the solar energy flow drives the bio-geo-chemical cycles of various nutrients in the biosphere. Ecological principles indicate how basic elements like carbon, oxygen, nitrogen, sulphur, phosphorous, etc., which are essential for life support, are transferred through food chain from abiotic environment into the living organisms only to flow back again from the biotic to the abiotic environment through the waste disposal process (chapter 4 gives some of the details). Any waste of the economic system which is biodegradable is transformed in the course of the interactive process between organisms and their abiotic environment through the operation of interconnected cycles. In the process of operation of ecological laws and cycles, resources are regenerated and made available at lower entropy, for example, photosynthesis fixes carbon dioxide from the atmosphere possibly released as waste from the biomass burning in the economic system. The bio-geo-chemical cycles combined with the energy flow thus facilitates the regeneration of low entropy resources in human time scale and the degradation of the wastes resulting from economic processes.

If the waste products of economic processes are not biodegradable, they will be broken down very slowly, involving a process of slow chemical transformation through environment interaction over a long period. For example, hazardous chemical and radioactive wastes which are manmade compounds may require thousands of years for degradation. For regeneration of the non-renewable, finite resources like oil, coal and minerals at low entropy the bio-geo-chemical process may work on a geologic time scale of millions of years.

The impression that nature's ability to regenerate low entropy resources by degrading high entropy economic wastes implies a reversal of the second law of thermodynamics is not correct since the processes of regeneration involve enormous use of low entropy solar energy directly or indirectly. In the aggregate effect the entropy law is not violated.

The breakdown of the waste compounds and regeneration of resources, however, requires time. For any ecosystem there are upper bounds on the rate of flow of solar energy along the food chain at any species stage per unit time and on the time rate of movement of basic chemical elements along the pathways of various nutrient cycles. There is indeterminacy in the precise values of the speed of flows or movements of cycles due to varying choices of pathways in the movement of nutrients. The rate at which nature can regenerate and supply resources, however, varies from resource to resource and place to place. The rate at which nature absorbs a waste would also vary from one waste compound to another. The maximum time rate or speed at which nature can absorb a waste or supply a given resource by way of regeneration is often far exceeded by the time rates of its regeneration as required by the development process. The mismatch between the two time rates of regeneration (supply) of low entropy resources or of degradation (absorption) of high entropy wastes as warranted by the ecological process and by the economic developmental process is at the root of the environmental crisis, often manifesting in the short run as a resource crisis. A resource crisis arises if the rate of regeneration of low entropy resources falls short of the required flow of resources from the ecosystem to the economic system, rendering the existing growth process unsustainable. If the rate of generation of high entropy wastes, on the other hand, exceeds the rate of absorption of waste by nature per unit of time, the remaining waste would be deposited in the ecosystem as pollutant. The stock of the pollutant would accumulate in the ecosystem and the accumulating stock would adversely affect the productivity of the natural system, human health, and the regenerative function of nature (see Table 1.1). That resource crisis and environmental crisis are now real life threats for the sustainability of the development process, is indicative of conflicting paradigms of ecological principles and conventional economic principles of development (Meadows *et al.* 1972, 1992).

Ecological Concern in the Evolution of Economic Thought

In the evolution of economic thought, the classical economists were concerned about the sustainability of the contemporary process of explosive industrial growth being experienced in Western Europe in the eighteenth and nineteenth centuries. The early economists predicted the approach of the industrial economy towards steady (stationary) state in the long run. While William Petty, a physiocrat, recognized the role of nature in the creation of value in his argument that labour is the father and land or nature the mother of wealth (see Petty 1899), with Adam Smith the limitation of the market rather than the supportive role of the nature was the restraining factor for the growth process. Among the classical economists Ricardo pointed to the limited availability of good quality land as the factor behind the diminishing returns to land at its extensive margin with the expansion of population and labour working on it. While rationalizing the category of rental income in a capitalist society, his analysis points to the limits to the growth process as imposed by the forces of diminishing returns to land. Malthus, on the other hand, emphasized the limitation of land as imposing a limit on its carrying capacity of population. He predicted the growth of population at the rate of geometric progression while growth of food supply would be at the rate of an arithmetic progression. Hence, the carrying capacity of land would be expressed by over-population, with the restoration of balance brought about by famines, wars and pestilence caused by acute food scarcity (see Malthus 1798).

Table 1.1
Major pollutants, their sources and health effects

Pollutant	Source	Effect
Carbon monoxide	Incomplete fuel combustion (e.g. two-stroke engine)	Affects the cardio-vascular system
Sulphur dioxide	Burning of sulphur-containing fuels like coal in power stations and oil by vehicles	Affects the res-piratory system
Suspended parti-culate matter	Smoke from domestic, industrial, and vehicular sources	Small particles are poisonous and are carriers of carcino-genic tracer elements
Oxides of nitrogen	Fuel combustion in motor vehicles, power stations and furnaces,	Affects the res-piratory system
Volatile hydrocarbons	carbonaceous fuels, (two-stroke engines, industrial processes, disposal of solid wastes)	Carcinogenic
Oxidants and ozone	Emissions from motor vehicles, photochemical reactions of nitrogen oxides and reactive hydrocarbons	Causes increased sensitivity to infections, lung diseases, irritation in eyes, nose and throat

Source: Government of India, CSO (1998).

Although neoclassical economists like Jevons was concerned with the limiting factors like the availability of coal and wrote on the coal question, his construct of economics as mechanics of utility and self-interest maximization led to the evolution of a reductionist paradigm in which economics had been subsequently discussed and analysed as a specialized discipline in isolation from natural sciences. The existence of a continuous mutual influence between the economic process and environment, has been ignored by the economists and issues relating to resource and environmental quality neglected until the middle if not the third quarter of the twentieth century.

Karl Marx postulated that everything that nature offers man is a spontaneous gift. Marx's production scheme describing the functioning of the economy is represented as completely circular and self-sustaining with no threat of constraint of scarcity of low entropy resources. Marxian ideas on the interrelated issues of ownership of wealth and resources, social relations of production, equity and just distribution and political economic sustainability of the capitalist process, have facilitated our understanding of the interrelation of issues of ownership, equity in distribution and environmental sustainability. However, Marx and his followers have so neglected allocative efficiency problem and the role of nature in economic processes that in spite of highlighting the issues of just distribution, their ideological rejection of rent and interest as a necessary price and insistence on a labour theory of value only, has been responsible for much of the environmental destruction in the communist countries.

In the twentieth century issues relating to resource and environmental control were first addressed in the writings of Harold Hotelling and A.C. Pigou, respectively. Hotelling developed a model of efficient resource use over time, enabling the understanding of how resources are to be exploited over time and the conditions under which conservation or depletion would occur. He shows how a higher rate of interest or rate of discount would imply a faster rate of rise of prices of the resource and depletion of the deposit. In the case of renewable resources, the level of rate of interest would influence the kind of plant species which will be regenerated, that is, high rate of discount would lead to more of investment in fast growing plant varieties and mono-culture while affecting biodiversity. (see Hotelling 1931). After the oil shock of the 1970's enormous literature developed on the optimal pattern of exploitation of natural resources essentially developed as an extension of the capital theory (see Dasgupta *et al.* 1979; Dasgupta 1982; Conrad *et al.* 1987; Pearce *et al.* 1990).

A.C. Pigou (1920), on the other hand, addressed for the first time explicitly the problem of market failure arising from waste disposal and pollution. The public good character of nature's sink service which is unpriced is pointed out as the fundamental source of the problem of externality. Pigou elaborated how costs and benefits that are not included in market prices affect the manner in which people relate with their natural environment. As a follow up of Pigou's work a vast literature on environmental economics has developed as an extension of applied welfare economics or public economics (see Baumol *et al.* 1975; Pearce *et al.* 1990).

The discussion in environmental economics has mostly centered around three sets of issues: (a) valuation of environmental damage and benefits due to generation and reduction of pollution; (b) determination of the optimum level of pollution and degradation of nature; and (c) choice of instruments for environmental pollution control at the optimum level under alternative situations of market imperfection, property rights regime, and uncertainty. The results of the analysis of the optimum level pollution or degradation, hinge crucially upon the valuation of environmental service or damage which is of a public good or bad character. However, the methods of valuation which are often used and discussed reflect inadequately the impact of economic processes on ecosystems: The valuations are based either on subjective judgment of individuals surveyed in a scheme of contingent valuation or simulation of market for the environmental service with the help of the data of the related variables in a rather contrived manner. Moreover, such valuations ignore the fact that their relevance may be restricted to a limited range around the historically existing level of environmental quality while future environmental dynamics would pose a 'non-linear' problem with the possibility of drastic change. Use of extrapolated values over a larger range may be conflicting with what physical or ecological sciences would warrant. The biological and ecological behaviour suggest non-linearity in their description through functional forms and existence of threshold in certain range of the concerned variables. For instance, this may get reflected in the sudden hike in the marginal cost of damage of the stock as a toxic pollutant reaches a threshold value. The guidance by the optimality calculus based on marginalism on the basis of the estimated environmental valuation functions of commonly used methods may therefore turn out to be seriously misleading in some instances. A precautionary approach to policy based on the understanding of ecological implications of economic processes may be a safer strategy in such a situation than the approach based on the marginalist principle. In order to be able to discriminate among policy situations warranting optimality versus pre-cautionary approach, it is necessary that ecological consequences of economic processes and policy are understood. The analysis of conventional environmental economics as a mere extension of applied welfare economics lacks this ecological perspective and consequently ignores the deeper implications of the inter-dependence between economics and ecology.

Finally, institutional questions are also quite important in the context of both resource and environmental management. The use of open access common resources has been a source of serious problem of over use of resources and environmental degradation in developing countries. The issues of allocation of property rights on local or global commons followed by reliance on market-based instruments or private bargaining for environmental control and resource use have been subject of debate and discussion in environment and resource economics. An important issue in this context is whether the problems of the environmental sustainability of the development process can be resolved within the overall market institutional framework with economic policy intervention. The nature of the struggle between the rich and the poor would depend on the characterization of the institution of property rights of the society. The struggle between man and nature and between the rich and the poor has important interdependence determined by the institutional environment. Social and institutional policies may have important role in resolving some of the important conflicts. Reliance on commons institution based on a model of cooperation involving participatory management has emerged as an important option. Some of the analytical constructs in this context that have emerged in the literature can be viewed as an extension of the modern institutional economics dealing with law, institutions, environment and economy (see Dasgupta and Mäler 1993, 1997; Baland and Platteau 1996).

Need for New Eco-principles

For defining the condition of sustainability of development process it is important to situate the human economy in the context of functioning of the concerned ecological system. The inter-dependence between the economic system and the relevant natural ecosystem underscores the biophysical limits of the input of resources in the economic system and the flow of wastes from the economy to the ecosystem. Together they define the condition of sustainability which requires that these limits are not violated as the costs of violation are considered to be too high. Such an analysis of economic development from the sustainability perspective would require the formulation of operational criteria for sustainability to take due account of scientific laws to resolve the paradigmative conflicts of ecology and economics (see Dahl 1996).

Development is dependent not only on technological solutions but on human values pertaining to the notion of human well being. Appropriate technological interventions are needed to relax the constraints imposed by ecological principles on the functioning of the human economy. The development of knowledge base for technological change has to take due account of the ecological principles governing the ecosystems. The economic and social policies should support appropriate technological change and induce changes in values for environment protection and promoting sustainable development.

The theoretical contributions in resource and environmental economics during the last twenty to thirty years though significant, are limited in explaining problems in sustainability of the development process. Developed within the paradigm of conventional economics, the theories are mainly extensions of capital theory, public economics or institutional economics and employ analytic methods assuming the partial equilibrium framework with *ceteris paribus* assumption and applying marginal analysis. Such an analysis mostly addresses short- or long-term issues on human time scale based on certain ecosystem postulates. While by parametrization one can generate a spectrum of results of such economic analyses for a range of values of the factors specifying the ecosystem, it is inadequate to understand the complete ecological implications of economic processes.

Nature–economy interactive relations necessitate the adoption of holistic perspective, interdisciplinary research and analysis for systemic understanding of the interactive relationship between the economic and the ecological factors. Ecological and economic systems, in fact, exhibit the characteristics of living systems and are not always well understood using the classical reductionist science approach. A systems approach of analysis would be useful for the analysis of the totality of interplay of all the ecological and economic factors and of other interactive factors from relevant disciplines. It is proposed that the system dynamic approach in economics should adopt transdisciplinary integrative synthetic approach, explaining systemic behaviour tracing the dynamic causal sequence of interaction of factors along the feed back loops of closures and the initial equilibrium condition. The systems dynamic approach is appropriate for sustainable development where the economy–biospheric interaction is integrated and would illustrate aspects of the dynamic sequence of low entropy resources flowing into the economic system, converted into products, and rendering a level of well being to the individuals or society, leaving the economic system as wastes and entering nature's sink as wastes. The dynamic sequence would trace how wastes lead to degradation of natural assets resulting in the loss of their productivity and capacity to act as a support system to living organisms (by affecting regeneration rate of natural resources) as well as to human economy. Biodiversity resource loss in the sequence would affect the resilience of ecosystems due to non-linearity in the ecological subsystem. Local problem of unsustainable agriculture or a global problem of climate change can be understood by transdisciplinary integrative synthetic analysis of the positive system behaviour rather than by adopting the classical reductionist approach with partial equilibrium framework using the method of marginalism. This methodological approach is being utilized for developing environmental policies in the emerging branch of ecological economics as distinct from environmental economics (see Costanza *et al.* 1997; Common and Perrings 1992).

The developments in environment and resource economics emphasize that economic analysis make correct postulates of the natural system and adopt a unified science approach for addressing the present-day problems of development (see Boulding 1970). The incorrect assumptions of conventional economics about nature as an unlimited source and sink imply neglect of the environmental constraint and need to be replaced by assumptions consistent with the entropy law and the laws governing the bio-geo-chemical processes of the earth. In addition, there is necessity to modify some basic concepts of economics like capital, real income and development, integrating the qualitative and quantitative environmental attributes of the development process. For example, a resource measure of soil or water or forest should consider the qualitative attributes along with quantitative measures. The qualitative–quantitative integration would enable the economist to make appropriate valuation of environmental attributes, define and estimate measures of green income or savings which would exhibit the impact of the qualitative degradation or improvement of environment, in the accounting measures as depreciation or appreciation of assets (see Dasgupta, Kristrom and Mäler 1997; Dasgupta and Mäler 1999; Markandya and Richardson 1992).

A unified approach of environmental science and economics raises the issue of time scale in the development process and the preservation of environmental resources. The ecosystem operates in a geologic time scale where the problem of survival due to resource or environmental crisis is absent. The problem of sustainability of economic processes arises in the context of operation in human time scale which is at variance with the geologic time scale. The mismatch of time rates of change of economic and ecological variables can be illustrated in land use. With change in land use due to developmental activities in human time scale and planning horizon, forest and wet lands are irreversibly lost, while these resources perform important ecological functions in purifying air and water; conserving soil, and controlling climate change in geological time scale. The loss of landscape due to developmental activities is an amenity loss. Accumulation of pollutants in excess of absorptive capacity of a local ecosystem causes degradation of the environment, resulting in qualitative loss of environmental services, crucial in determining the quality of human life on a human-time scale.

As development process conflicts with ecological sustainability which in turn constrains all economic development processes, it is important to examine the feasibility and scope of economic development without violating the resource constraints and environmental quality. However, such an interdisciplinary analysis of sustainability would require the understanding of the interactive relationship between the functioning of an economy and ecosystem. A model of sustainable development would require not only interfacing with ecological factors as parameters, but internalizing them by appropriate endogenization. The task is difficult as economic models are developed mainly in the partial or general equilibrium framework with policy motivation guiding the framework and employment of marginal analysis. The ecological models are positive behaviouristic dealing with the totality of function of the interrelated ecosystems. Economic theory and analysis are concerned with human well-being in human time scale. Unlike economics, ecological functions and laws are not anthropocentric and the ecological models do not assign special role to human beings. Besides, many of the economic behaviouristic issues are defined in static logical framework, while the ecological processes are essentially dynamic. For the analysis of sustainable development, issues have to be in an appropriate ecology–economics interdisciplinary framework, which integrates human well-being and ecological equilibrium. The necessity of holistic and unified science approach in economics has warranted the adoption of systems approach and careful choice of length of time horizon of decision-making and of treatment of ecological factors as exogenous or endogenous. We discuss in Chapters 2, 3, 4 and 5 some of the ecological aspects which have important interfacing with the functioning of human economy and society.

Scheme of the Work

Chapter 2, defines the basic concepts of ecology, relevant for understanding the structure of nature. Chapter 3 and Chapter 4 are devoted in explaining the two basic ecological laws and functions: (a) solar energy flow and (b) bio-geo-chemical cycles— their respective life support roles in providing food, regenerating economic resources, and degrading the various wastes of economic system. Chapter 5 discusses the population growth of species in general and the special problem of human population growth in particular, including the concept of carrying capacity of nature. Chapter 6 continues the discussion on human ecology by elaborating the limits of nature as a source and as a sink for supplying raw materials and absorbing wastes, respectively. In the discussion on human ecology of Chapter 5 and 6, the interrelationships are traced among the size of population, GDP as proxy for the level of economic activity, income inequality and environmental resources, particularly in the context of a developing economy. These interrelations as indicated in Figure 1.2 span issues of economic and environmental sustainability which are mutually interactive. All chapters illustrate Indian problems. Chapter 7, comes back to the issue of sustainable development of human economy, defines the relevant concepts, and derives the scope and conditions of sustainability. It concludes by commenting on the policy approaches for sustainable development and emphasizing the role of institutional factors in the context of the ecology–economy relationship.

Chapter 2

THE BIOSPHERE AND THE ECOSYSTEMS

Earth, Life and Biosphere

The resource base of material processes of production is nature. It is important that resource is available in accessible form in nature for human exploitation. If the basic material elements are available in a diffused form or qualitatively unusable, an apparently abundant resource becomes scarce and a serious constraining factor for development. While 70 per cent of earth surface is covered by ocean water, fresh water constitutes only 3 per cent of world's hydroresources, which is unevenly distributed over regions, across the globe. Soil quality in terms of minerals, nutrients and moisture content widely varies from place to place. Good quality of land is highly limited in supply in many regions of the world. The combination of soil quality and water, along with the climatic condition, determines the pattern of vegetation and the potential of primary productivity of sunlight. These basic natural endowments with implications for potential economic development, exercise determining influence on the functional life support role and waste absorptive capacity of natural ecosystem. The assessment of the resource endowment of an economy and life support or carrying capacity requires an understanding of earth's structure and processes and concepts such as of biosphere, organisms, population, community, ecosystem, etc.

Earth is composed of three major parts—lithosphere, hydrosphere and atmosphere. The lithosphere consists of all the soil and rock covering 29 per cent of earth. The hydrosphere, refers to all the water of earth, including oceans, lakes, rivers, tanks, etc., covering about 71 per cent of earth's surface. The atmosphere is composed of gases and particulate matter in varying composition over several layers and temperature ranges, and extends up to 240 miles up from earth's surface. The troposphere is the lowest and heaviest portion of the atmosphere extending up to 7 miles up from the surface of the earth, contains 99 per cent of all water vapour and 90 per cent of the air, and is responsible for the climate of the planet. The stratosphere is the portion of the atmosphere which lies between 7 miles and 30 miles up from the surface of the earth. The ozone layer of the atmosphere which functions as a protective shield from ultraviolet radiation, is located in the lower range of the stratosphere extending from about 12 to 15 miles up from the surface of the earth. Lastly, the ionosphere which is composed of ions, is located beyond the stratosphere and extends up to 240 miles up from the surface of the earth. Outer space begins from where the ionosphere ends (see Hanks 1996).

Life exists in all the three spheres of the earth from 7.5 miles below the earth's crust up to 6 miles above sea level. Life forms range from micro organisms like bacteria and fungi, moss and lichen to insects, birds, fish, plants, trees, reptiles, mammals and human beings, adding to a total of 36 million known species. The number of living species is always changing with a large number of species becoming extinct every year while new species emerge through various genetic mutation processes. According to the gradual aggregation theory, the number species today is only 1 per cent of all the species that have ever existed on earth since the day about 3500 million years ago when biological evolution began.

Each of the living organisms interact not only among themselves but with their nonliving environment for exchanging energy and nutrients essential for their existence. The life support systems for organisms are discussed in Chapter 3 and Chapter 4 in which we analyse energy flow and bio-geo-chemical cycles, respectively.

The biosphere has two components: (a) biotic component and (b) abiotic component. The biotic component comprises all the living organisms of the planet. A living organism would have characteristics such as intake of energy from sunlight to maintain its internal order, growth in size and complexity until maturity for which it taps the abiotic environmment for nutrients, multiplication through reproduction by sexual or asexual means at their maturity, and response to stimuli of light, heat, touch or chemical changes induced by the external environment and maintaining homeostatis[1] (see Cunningham 1994, Ch. 2). Although organisms of different species like fishes, rabbits or birds have different habitats, most are found at the junction of the three spheres of the earth, i.e., where land, water and air meet as the organisms need to use, mix and manipulate the various elements of soil, water and air for their life support. These life support systems are complex and interactive. It is often difficult to understand their precise function and how all of them together constitute an integrated self-organized and controlled system working on a geologic time scale, much larger than the human time scale of 80–100 years.

Ecosystem

The biosphere consists of innumerable ecosystems such as forest, ocean, pond, etc. each of which has interdependent biotic and abiotic components. This interdependence of biotic and abiotic elements has an inbuilt mechanisms to stabilize the ecosystem within certain limits. The ecosystem's self-regulating and self-perpetuating mechanism characterizes the ecological balance of the system which behaves like a superorganism. As an individual organism grows in size and complexity until maturity, an ecosystem too develops through its successional stages such as a fallow land gradually turning into a mature forest as it is not interfered with through external disturbances including human activities. Every ecosystem has a characteristic climax community representing the converging state of maximum complexity and

---

[1]The human body, is a marvellous system of self-regulating process. Its subsystems at cellular, tissues or organ level have feedback mechanism to maintain a stable and well balanced whole. Our body moderates internal temperature by shivering when it is cold and by sweating when it is hot. The hormones of the endocrine glands balance each other to regulate the functions of a body and maintain a harmonious equilibrium which we call "homeostatis". (see Cunningham 1994).

stability attained by it through natural growth and evolution. Many modern ecologists contest this view and consider the biological community to be a mere chance association of species who could adapt to the environment in a place and time. The history of landscapes over thousands of years, reveals that a forest landscape of today had different species composition and other abiotic characteristics at different times. The shortness of human time scale and horizon is responsible for the deterministic interpretation of ecosystem dynamics and its tendency of convergence to a state of harmonious equilibrium.

Our planet has the right combination of gases, temperature, water and other resources making life possible. Despite sun getting hotter over last several billion years, earth's temperature has remained remarkably constant enabling the biological system to self-maintain and self-perpetuate. According to Gaia hypothesis (Lovelock 1988 and Koromondy 1999), such a fortunate situation has not emerged in our planet by way of a mere accident. The hypothesis visualizes earth as a superorganism. The atmosphere, climate, oceans and the crust of the earth are regulated at such a state comfortable for life because of the role and behaviour of the living organisms. The homeostatis of the earth is maintained by the active feedback processes operated automatically and unconsciously by the living organisms. Such a holistic view characterizes the planet as an integrated system and imputes meaning to life. Hence, human beings, as part of biota, are supposed to behave so that the homeostatis is not disturbed and all life forms can self-perpetuate. If, however, the human beings with their science, technology and drive for indefinite accumulation of wealth through growth of capitalist production disturb the homeostatis of the integrated system, it is possible that environmental conditions would change, making the possibility of life on earth as it exists, remote.

Are the different ecosystems of the biosphere independent systems? While an ecosystem like forest, lake or river-basin represents by itself an integrated system, it is not, however, a closed one. Every ecosystem has to receive energy flow in the form of light or primary chemical energy from outside the system and must have a way of disposing of the heat through transpiration of living organisms in some other ecosystem. An ecosystem may gain or lose materials to other ecosystems. The ecosystem of a downstream river gains water, nutrients as well as living organisms from upstream ecosystem and loses them to the sea when it reaches there. Ecosystem maintains stability of composition of its biotic and abiotic elements in spite of such gains or losses, although the individual elements would vary over time. Ecosystems of any region of the biosphere would influence one another to varying extents depending on the extent of relative openness of the ecosystems. Besides, the ecosystem concept is used in both real and abstract sense. Ecosystems are real like a pond, a grass field, a river, a forest, a tidal estuary, an open ocean, or a city with their respective geographic specifications. An abstract ecosystem is a conceptualized scheme developed on the basis of real ecosystems and does not have any particular size.

Particular national or regional economy would physically comprise a large number of real ecosystems of varying sizes covering the geographic area influencing one another. The Indian economy comprises ecosystems of diverse characteristics ranging from forests in plain terrain, forests in mountainous terrain, inland wetlands, coastal wetlands, river basins, mangroves, coral reefs, desert, wastelands, agricultural fields, urban sprawls, etc. Ecosystems of a country or global economy can be classified on the basis of the rate and source of energy flows. Such classification will facilitate the understanding of how human economic activities alter natural ecosystems, highlighting the issues of sustainability of regeneration of resources for the development process.

Components of Ecosystem: Biotic Environment

The biotic components of an ecosystem are of two kinds: producers and consumers. The producers are autotrophs (i.e., they nourish themselves) who convert solar energy into chemical bond energy through the process of photosynthesis. They convert inorganic substances, such as water and carbondioxide into organic substances like carbohydrates. All plant species in lithosphere and hydrosphere are such primary producers of energy. They produce their own food and supply food to all other species through food chain (see Hanks 1996; Kupchella *et al.* 1998).

The consumers in biotic communities are heterotrophs who obtain their energy for sustenance and growth by consuming other organisms ranging from microorganisms and bacteria to all animals including human beings. They are classified into four major groups on the basis of the food source:

(a) Herbivores (e.g. cows, sheep, goats, rabbits, elephants, etc.) obtain their energy by eating plant biomass only and are primary consumers.

(b) Carnivores (e.g. wolves, tigers, vultures, spiders, frogs, etc.) obtain their energy by eating primary consumers and other carnivores. Those carnivores which derive their energy indirectly from the producers by way of eating the herbivores only are secondary consumers, while those who derive their energy from other carnivores only are called tertiary consumers.

(c) Omnivores (e.g. bears, racoons, human beings) are consumers who derive energy from both producers and other consumers.

(d) Saprovores or decomposers (e.g. fungi, bacteria, etc.) live on dead organisms by decomposing them and deriving energy.

Consumers classified as (a), (b) or (c) are large consumers or macro-consumers that ingest other organisms or particulate organic matter by feeding on them. The decomposers do not consume food in the ingestive manner of herbivore or carnivore; instead they consume through absorption when the micro-organisms break down the complex compound of dead protoplasm by releasing the enzymes produced in their bodies and absorbing some of the decomposed organic products. The decomposers release some organic elements (like vitamins or antibiotics) which are either stimulatory or prohibitory to other organisms.

The producers and consumers of the different trophic levels of a region (as indicated by the hierarchical positions in the food chain) and their interconnections constitute the biotic component of an ecosystem. An example of food chain connecting the different species of plant and animal life forms may be grass → mouse → snake, or grass → bird → fox, or grass → sheep → human beings' where → represents the relationship "used as food by". The weight of all the organisms existing in such an interrelationship at any point of time in an ecosystem is called biomass or standing crop. However, it is not the size of the biomass but the level of activity of the biotic subsystem as reflected in the growth of the biomass per unit of time which is relevant for the sustainability calculus of the food system.

Abiotic Environment

The productivity of a biotic subsystem and its richness in the ecosystem depend on the nonliving or abiotic component. The abiotic segment has three components:

(a) Inorganic substances like carbon, nitrogen, water, phosphorous, sulphur etc. which are involved in the material cycles of the ecosystem and are discussed in the sections on Inorganic Substances.

(b) Organic substances, e.g. carbohydrates, proteins, lipids, humic substances, etc. that link the abiotic and the biotic subsystems of biosphere.

(c) Climate regime, temperature and other physical factors characterizing the living environment and conditions of existence for living organisms.

Inorganic Substances

Air, water and soil constitute the abiotic component of the biosphere, each consisting mainly of inorganic substances in various compound forms which are available either in particulate form in soil, or as dissolved in water or gaseous molecules in the air. Carbon, oxygen, nitrogen, hydrogen, silicon, iron, manganese, phosphorous, sulphur, etc. are examples of the basic inorganic substances whose compounds are constituents of the abiotic environment. However, of the large number of inorganic elements, some are essential for life support and are called biogenic substances or nutrients. Some nutrients like carbon, hydrogen, nitrogen, phosphorous, and calcium known as macro-nutrients are required by living organisms in large quantities and are available in abundant amounts in nature. Other nutrients essential to plants and animals in small amounts are, on the other hand, called micro-nutrients for example metal ions like iron, calcium, magnesium, potassium, magnesium, or nonmetallic elements like sulphur etc. There are still other nutrients which are required in infinitesimally small amounts for living organisms are called trace elements such as aluminium, manganese, iodine, etc. A lack of micro-nutrient or trace element can affect the productivity of ecosystem as much as that of a macro-nutrient would cause. For example, if the human body does not get enough iron, it will become anaemic or if a plant does not get enough magnesium it cannot produce enough chlorophyll for photosynthesis, or in the absence of molybdenum micro-organism would be unable to transform nitrogen in the air into nitrates which they release for use by plants. Macro-nutrients are found in almost all organisms while the micro-nutrients or trace elements are found in varying amounts in different species. The following Table 2.1 shows the relative amounts of inorganic chemical compounds that are required for living organisms.

Any individual inorganic chemical element can exist in combination with other elements in the form of compounds. Some of these compounds cannot be used by the individual organisms in reduced forms to gain access to the required essential elements. For example, plants need carbon, only in the form of the carbondioxide CO_2 compound and none of the thousands of the other carbon compounds are of any use. Similarly plants need nitrogen in the form of soluble nitrate (NO_3) or ammonia (NH_3). The nutrient cycles of ecosystems ensure the regeneration of the required compounds for the biotic system. Economic activities interfering with the functioning of these cycles, would pose serious problem of adequate availability of the basic elements in the required compound form thereby impeding sustainability of the functional processes of ecosystem and the economic system (see Odum 1975).

Organic Substances

All life forms are composed of various chemical organic compounds. Living organisms convert inorganic elements and organize them into organic chemical compounds which build organisms and keep them functioning. Living organisms composed of four major types of organic compounds— carbohydrates (i.e., sugar and starches), proteins (enzymes, etc.), fats (lipids, etc.) and nucleic acids (DNA, RNA, etc.)—are available in widely dispersed form in the nonliving environment. As

Table 2.1
Relative amounts of different nutrients in living organisms

Macro-nutrient constituting more than 1% of dry organic weight	Micro-nutrients constituting 0.2 to 1% of dry organic weight	Trace elements constituting less than 0.2% of dry organic weight	
Carbon	Calcium	Aluminium	Selium
Hydrogen	Chlorine	Boron	Silicon
Nitrogen	Copper	Bromine	Strontium
Oxygen	Iron	Chromium	
Phosphorus	Magnesium	Cobalt	Tin
	Potassium	Fluorine	Titanium
	Sodium	Gallium	
	Sulphur	Iodine	Vanadium
		Manganese	Zinc
		Molybdenum	

Source: Kupchella and Hyland (1990), p. 54.

organisms decay they widely disperse and the products of the disintegration processes—called organic detritus—are an important constituent of the abiotic environment. Organic compounds of the abiotic environment are predominantly organic detritus of plant and play an important role in determining the soil characteristics and other features of an ecosystem. As end product of the decaying process of organic matter humus or humic substances are formed. Humic substances are resistant to further decay and remain as a structural part of the ecosystems for some time and are dark, yellow-brown and amorphous particulate matters visible in soils and sediments constituting the organic components of soil. They are also found suspended or dissolved in the waters of streams, lakes, etc. Humus contributes important properties to soil favourable for the growth of plants though excess humus is harmful for plant productivity (see Odum 1975).

Climate Condition and Limiting Factors

The third category of abiotic component of a biosphere, namely, the climate condition exercises a determining influence on the kind of organisms in plant and animal would be present in a given region of biosphere. Climate, with its components of temperature, rainfall, moisture and the chemical nature of soil determine the conditions of adaptability of various organisms on land. In hydrosphere, temperature, salinity of water and other chemical attributes of water body (for example dissolved oxygen), will determine the range and survival of living organisms. Across the biosphere, a number of gradients of climatic factor exists. For example, temperature gradient from arctic to tropics or from mountain top to a valley, moisture gradient from dry to rainfed wet areas and so on. The abiotic conditions of the physical environment such as the positions on the various gradients of the climatic factors, and the availability of energy and nutrients create environmental pressures on the living organisms. Organism adapts to environment pressures within tolerance limits.

The biotic composition of an ecosystem is explained by its climatic and the abiotic resource conditions, the geographical qualitative specificities of the concerned area of landmass, water body or atmosphere, and the solar radiation condition in the particular region in the grid of latitudes and longitudes of the earth where the ecosystem is located. Biodiversity of ecosystems is determined by the climate, geography along with the structure and function of the concerned ecosystems of a region. It is for this reason that diverse plant and animal species are found along temperature and moisture gradients. Deciduous trees are found at higher altitudes as they require low temperature and can survive in low-moisture conditions. It is for the same reason that elephants are found in Africa and not in Norway or Finland and kangaroo is found in Australia and not Canada. Light and temperature are the major limiting physical factors for both terrestrial and aquatic ecosystems. Major chemical limiting factors for terrestrial and aquatic system are availability of water on land, dissolved oxygen in water, nitrogen and phosphorous. The acidity of water or soil in pH scale is also crucial for the viability of living organisms. Soil becomes acidic if the pH level drops below 7.0 units. As it rises about 7.0 it becomes alkaline or basic. For most organisms the tolerance range of pH is narrow, between 6.8 and 7.2 (Hanks 1996).

Economic activities have adversely changed the conditions of abiotic environment resulting in the extinction of many species.

Acid rain occurring due to nitric oxides and sulphur oxides emissions from economic activities into the air with the subsequent precipitation through rain have resulted in acidic land and aquatic system. High acidity in a lake beyond the concerned tolerance level kills phytoplanktons. Aquatic species dependent on phytoplankton will starve, if phytoplanktons die. In such a situation the local aquatic food chain would collapse and the lake will die. High acidity of soil would create stress on soil organisms essential for the recycling process of nutrients. Leaching of toxic wastes dumped into land fills in different soil horizons, may result in the death of the bacteria causing nitrogen crisis for soil thereby seriously affecting the viability of plant life in the ecosystem.

The limiting factor principle states that neither too little nor too much of a favourable physical, chemical or climatic factor of the abiotic component of an ecosystem is desired for the survival of an organism in an ecosystem. Population growth of a species increases its density per unit of area in the ecosystem which upon exceeding a critical level creates a condition of stress for it. As a result the population gradient is likely to become negative beyond a point and the species would have the, problem of survival beyond the higher threshold value which defines the upper limit of the tolerance range. We discuss these issues relating to population of species and carrying capacity of an ecosystem in greater detail in Chapter 5.

Soil

For the economic system, soil and water of the abiotic environment of an ecosystem play a crucial role in determining the conditions of agricultural production. Soil is the surface of the earth's crust. It is the product of: (a) weathering and breaking down of parent rock materials containing various nutrients, (b) decomposition of organic matter, and (c) activities of the biotic community in the ecosystem. Soils differ in quality from ecosystem to ecosystem.

Most of the organic and inorganic substances are found in the biotic and abiotic components of an ecosystem due to their free movement between organisms and their abiotic environment. Humic substances are an exception as they are not found in the biotic compartment of the system. The physical structure and chemical composition of soil determines the presence of nutrients and quantity of water retained in the soil. Hence food chain is determined by soil quality which determines the plant types which can grow and the types of animals dependent on the plants will be present.

The process of weathering of the parent rock material produces pieces of various size ranging from gravel to sand to silt to clay which determine permeability of different soils. Soil permeability would determine the rate of water percolation through the soil particles, water retention volume in the soil and the duration of water retention for use by plants. Water moves quickly through gravel but very slowly through clay soils.

During the process of soil-formation, several layers are formed which constitute the soil profile. At the top, the first layer of soil called top soil is formed with particularly modified parent material. It is followed by subsoil as one moves downwards, which consists of more unmodified parent materials in the subsequent layers. While the top soil is a nutrient rich mixture of fine organic material and disintegrated rocks in the forms of gravel sand, silt or clay, the subsoil comprises materials leached from the top layer. The top soil is critical for determining the nature of vegetation and animal life forms. The rate of top soil formation depends on several factors including nature of the parent material, topography of the area, climate of the region and the biotic community inhabiting the topsoil layer. The chemical or nutrient composition of soil depends on the nature of parent material of the concerned region of the earth's surface, and the organic material that was decomposed. The amount of moisture in soil is important for plants to derive adequate nutrient from the abiotic environment. Apart from water, the chemical characteristics like pH level of soil determine the accessibility of nutrients by plants, for example, if the pH level of soil is 8, calcium is available for plant use, while iron would not be so available.

Soil quality and its chemical processes again depend not only on its abiotic content but on the biotic community which uses soil as its habitat. Most of the living organisms living in the layers of soil are microscopic like bacteria or fungi, though larger organisms like worms, mites, beetles, various kinds of larvae, etc. too inhabit soil. All these organisms play a crucial role in the formation of healthy soil by degrading the dead organic materials and releasing the nutrients derived from such decomposition in their basic elemental form in soil so that plants can use them.

Soil is a stock changing in quantity and quality over time. Soil formation is a continuous process. Soil is classified as young, mature and old based on the rate of accumulation of organic materials. A young soil horizon gains more organic materials than it loses resulting in the development of the top soil. A mature soil balances the gains and losses of organic material over time. An old soil loses more of organic material than what it gains and nutrients are leached from such soil resulting in the thinning of top soil profile. Land with good quality soil is a scarce natural resource. Agricultural productivity is highest in young soils which are nutrient rich. Only 24 per cent of the land area of the world is endowed with young soil, adequate water and appropriate climate for agriculture. The United States of America has 38 per cent of good soil of the world and therefore a highly productive agriculture system. The soil quality is unevenly distributed across the land surface of the world. Agriculture has used fertilizer and irrigation to increase soil productivity where soil is not endowed by the ecosystem with adequate water or nutrients. The variation in the soil quality has warranted variation in the methods of agriculture and product-mix. However, the use of inorganic fertilizer, pesticides and some of the agricultural methods, as adopted for example in the cleared rain forests in the western manner, has adverse feed back effect in terms of productivity of the ecosystem and become counter-productive. This issue will be elaborated upon in Chapter 6 when we discuss the conditions of sustainable agricultural development.

Energetics of Ecosystem

Energy is an important common denominator of all ecosystems. Energy flow determines the generation of biomass and chemical energy in different forms in the ecosystem. The source and availability of energy determines to a greater or lesser extent the extent of biodiversity and the kind of organisms constituting the biotic composition of an ecosystem. Energy flow drives the bio-geo-chemical cycles which ensure the recycling and regeneration of the abiotic component of the ecosystem. Both these functions contribute towards the regeneration of resources and their supply which are relevant for economic activities. Ecosystems are classified in terms of source and intensity of energy flow into two kinds: ecosystems designed by nature, and those designed by man. Ecosystems derive their energy from two major sources: the sun (solar radiation), and chemical fuels (like biomass, fossil. fuels). An ecosystem is defined as solar powered or fuel powered on the basis of the major source of energy for the ecosystem— sunlight or chemical fuel (see Odum 1975).

Nature designed ecosystems are all solar powered. However, such ecosystems are further classified into two categories: (1) unsubsidized solar powered ecosystems, and (2) naturally subsidized solar powered ecosystems. Unsubsidized solar powered ecosystems depend on sunlight as their only source of energy, for example, ecosystems like open ocean, mountain-range forest, grasslands or large deep lakes where very little energy is available from other sources to supplement solar radiation. The photosynthesis process provides them most of the chemical energy from sunlight. Since solar energy reaches the surface of the earth in a very dilute form, the unsubsidized natural solar powered ecosystems are characterized by scarcity of energy, low power-density per square metre of surface area, low productivity in terms of primary production per square metre as given by the process of photosynthesis. Energy flow varies between 1000 K Cal to 10000 K Cal per m^2 of surface area, the average being around 2000 K Cal per m^2 of surface area in such an ecosystem. Such a system would be sparsely populated by organisms adapted to energy scarcity conditions and which are efficient in utilizing the available scarce energy and other resources. Although these ecosystems do not provide adequate biotic resources which can meet directly human needs, all of them together provide important basic life support service for our planet by purifying large volumes of air every day, recycle water, and control the climate by regulating the flow of wind or currents of the ocean. A small portion of human need for food and fibre is obtained as a byproduct of such systems. However, these ecosystems provide immense indirect support to vegetation elsewhere by their influence on climate.

Naturally subsidized solar powered ecosystems are supplemented by other auxiliary forms of energy as supplied by nature itself, for example, tidal estuary, coral reefs, rain forests, river streams, etc. Auxiliary energy is provided by tidal waves in coastal estuary, rain and wind in the rain forest and river current and waves in a river ecosystem. These tidal waves, river current and wind flows are expressions of solar radiation energy as converted into mechanical form and facilitate recycling of mineral nutrients, transportation of food, nutrients and wastes, thereby allowing the organisms of these ecosystems to concentrate on efficient conversion of sunlight into organic matter. Such ecosystems experience inflow of energy in the order of 10,000 to 40,000 K Cal per m^2 (20,000 K Cal per m^2 being the approximate mean of the range) (see Odum 1975). The productivity of such systems is quite high and is reflected in not only high life support capacity, but often in excessive production of organic matter that is substantively exported to other ecosystems. The coral reef is in fact an example of a very rich nature designed nature subsidized ecosystem.

The ecosystems, designed by human beings, are of two kinds: (1) man subsidized solar powered ecosystem, and (2) fuel powered ecosystem. The man subsidized solar powered ecosystems have been obtained as a result of modification of some of ecosystems of the nature by human activities, for example, agricultural system or aquacultural system. Solar radiation is the major source of energy and its flow in the system has been through photosynthesis. Human intervention has channelised the primary productivity of such systems into primary products like food and fibre which would meet some of the basic economic needs of human society. However, these ecosystems have been substantively subsidized by energy resources like human labour, animal labour, and fossil fuels, which have been involved in cultivation, irrigation, fertilization, pest control, etc. The supplementary energy flows into the system enhance its productivity per unit of surface area and are as much important as solar radiation. Advancement of technology in agriculture has found efficient ways of optimising the net productivity of biomass considered to be useful for human consumption. Though the evolving of high yielding variety seeds through gene technology brought about the Green Revolution in many countries, including India, the new varieties were not more efficient in the photosynthetic process of converting solar radiation into biomass (chemical) energy, but were better suited to benefit from fuel subsidies. Many of the new varieties were dwarf plants with small root systems and just enough leaves and stems to capture the maximum of usable solar radiation for grain production. Such high yielding varieties were genetically programmed to produce grain at the expense of non-edible tissues and required external support from the fuels and other forms of energy subsidy for their survival. Such fuel subsidization of agro-ecosystem has adverse externalities raising problems of sustainability of the process of agrarian development. We shall come back to this in Chapter 6.

Ecosystems subsidized by nature and those subsidized by fuel are roughly similar in their energy intensity and productivity. The total annual energy flow into an agro-ecosystem would lie in the range of 10,000 to 40,000 K Cal per m^2 or 20,000 K Cal per m^2 approximately on an average of its surface area. The most productive agricultural system would have similar energy intensity level as the most energy rich photosynthesis system. The main difference between these two types of ecosystems is in the distribution of the energy flow. In agriculture most of solar radiation flows through photosynthesis into human consumables like food and fibre, whereas any nature designed ecosystem with or without natural subsidy tends to distribute the energy flow through photosynthesis into various plant species and products so as to optimize biodiversity for survival and perpetuation.

The fuel powered man-designed ecosystem derives energy from the main source of fossil fuels or nuclear fuel, for example, the urban–industrial system or fabricated infrastructural system like highway corridors. Major energy flows in these systems are those of fuel energy through the various urban–industrial or infrastructural activities which are high value adding as well as highly energy intensive economic activities. Human beings dominate these ecosystems; and the other species living there are dependent on man for the supply of energy. The supply of food, water and other natural resources for human beings and other dependent species are mostly imported from other ecosystems. Fuel energy and resources are supplied to these systems by other ecosystems where they were lying as deposits in the lithosphere and had been obtained as a result of geo-chemical transformation of photosynthetic products over millions of years. Such urban-industrial ecosystems are the most energy intensive ecosystems with, the annual energy flow in the range of 100,000 to 3,000,000 K Cal per m^2 surface area, the average being around 2,000,000 K Cal per m^2 as per crude estimate. While these ecosystems depend upon other ecosystems for the supply of food, fuel, water and other types of life support, they themselves produce huge amounts of wastes and pollutions which cause excessive damage to the supportive ecosystems which are not able to fully absorb the wastes generated over time.

The dependent and open nature of urban ecosystem has serious implications for sustainability of mankind. Every hectare of surface area of urban ecosystem requires several hectares of agro-economic system to supply food and fibre and many more hectares of nature designed ecosystems for general life support including absorption of wastes generated from the economic activities of the urban system. The greater the difference of the total energy flow per unit of surface area between an urban ecosystem and a solar powered ecosystem (purely natural or cultivated), the greater is the amount of surface area of the solar powered ecosystem that will be required to provide life support to a unit of surface area of urban system. Increasing land use changes on large scale have severely limited the carrying out of the functions of the solar powered ecosystem. Planning for sustainable land use and development points to the need to take account of the positive and negative externalities arising from the functions of the different types of ecosystems. The non-market character of many of the life support ecoservices are by and large at the root of the apparent neglect of these concerns in our planning for urban development in many countries. The sustainability of development requires a balanced composition in the distribution of land surface area among alternative types of ecosystems in terms of energy intensity and their primary productivity.

Biodiversity

The biotic component of an ecosystem contains great diversity of a wide range of species of plants and animals in a square kilometre of forest or ocean with few species dominating a particular ecosystem. A few common species are associated with large number of rare species. For example, a hardwood forest, may contain 50 species of trees of which half a dozen or less would possibly account for 90 per cent of the timber. Similarly, if a sample of vegetation of a grassland is taken, it may contain 30 grass species, while it is not be surprising that one grass species has a share of 25 per cent in the total standing biomass, one third of species have a share of 85 per cent and the remaining two thirds have only a share 15 per cent of the total. The distribution can be even more skewed when one analyses samples of animal life, particularly of small organisms. However, such a distributive pattern does not mean that the uncommon species are not important for determining and maintaining the characteristics of an ecosystem. Another feature of biodiversity is that diversity has a relationship with the size of organism. Diversity is greater in small organisms than in large organisms; for example, there are larger variety of mites than mammals in a forest. Besides, the extent of diversity also depends on the condition of existence of living organism. Diversity is reduced where the condition of existence is severe or geographically isolated as in the arctic or in an island.

Human activities, reduce and exercise selective pressure on biodiversity. Economic activities in the primary sector like agriculture, fishery, forestry, etc. try to modify ecosystem. Economic objectives involve the transforming of a crop species to the dominant species in an agricultural field. Even in such a situation diversity tends to persist. When herbicide or weed control measures are not applied, even a grain field will demonstrate that one food crop is associated possibly with 10 other species of herbaceous plants with a share of about 7 per cent of aggregate standing biomass. In view of the natural tendencies for diversification, it is not surprising that whenever control on the growth of other non-target species in the field is exercised, a large amount of energy is required as subsidy to the field to prevent such natural growth. Given the interdependence, elimination of some of the species may so alter the condition of the existence of even the protected species (as in the case of agricultural crop or floriculture, etc.) that the latter may require direct or indirect energy subsidy from outside the ecosystem for survival and growth, like high requirement of energy in the form of mechanical or chemical inputs work in an agricultural field.

Human impact on biodiversity is a major point of conflict between economy and ecosystem. The economic system has given rise to new limiting factors like pollution and wastes which are inorganic and non-biodegradable and are flowing into the ecosystem. Sewage and industrial waste pouring into a stream or chronic overdose of insecticides in agriculture or forest affects the species composition of the ecosystem. The new limiting factors might be destroying the conditions of existence of many a species, and the diversity will decrease accompanied by population boom of the surviving species in the ecosystem. The biodiversity index, is in fact a measure of level of pollution due to the impact of economic activities on the ecosystem.

For the construction of a biodiversity index two aspects of biodiversity are taken into account: (a) variety component of species, and (b) evenness component or the distribution of relative abundance. The variety component is given by the absolute number of species in the domain of life forms for which the index is being defined. The evenness component is determined, on the other hand, by the evenness of distribution of importance across different species as given by their respective availabilities in terms of measures like the amount of standing biomass. Maximum biodiversity in a domain is given by the combination of the maximum number of variety of species with perfectly even distribution of the weightage of importance as given by, say, standing biomass. The following two alternative indices of biodiversity can be used to measure the extent of diversity incorporating both the aspects of diversity.

Let n be the number of species and p_i be the share of the ith species in the total biomass stand. As

$$\sum_{i=1}^{n} p_i = 1 \text{ for all } n, \tag{2.1}$$

p_i^2 will tend to zero as n becomes larger and larger and p_i's become approximately equal in value for different i. The measure $D = \sum_i p_i^2$ called Simpson index would thus give a measure of biodiversity. On the other hand, $\log p_i$ becomes large negative number as the fraction p_i becomes smaller and smaller. Thus the negative of average of $\log p_i$, that is

$$H = -\sum_i p_i \log_e p_i \qquad (2.2)$$

called Shannon index would yield an alternative measure of biodiversity. In order to obtain a normalized value of diversity with the maximum and the minimum of 1 and 0, respectively, we end up with the choice of the following measure: $\overline{D} = 1 - D$, $\overline{H} = \dfrac{H}{\log_e n}$, the minimum will correspond to a situation where n = 1, $p_i = 1$ and the maximum will correspond to a situation where n tends be indefinitely large and p_i's are approximately equal tending to zero (see Odum 1975).

It is, however, the short or medium-term objectives which have induced human beings to maximise the yield of the desired species using their knowledge base and providing energy subsidy. Such optimization has often led to mono-culture and the removal of lot of other species from the surroundings. Biodiversity should· be considered as a resource with high option value. Some of the biotic species with no use value as of today, may be considered to be of immense value for medicinal or industrial or other purpose in future with the expansion of knowledge base. With the tremendous potential of biotechnology to contribute in the 21st century to eco-friendly development process, and the emergence of new innovated products of great welfare significance, biodiversity would have a high preservation value.

The major problem of analysis of preservation of biodiversity arises from the absence of a workable cost-effectiveness framework within which, at least in principle, basic issues can be raised and discussed. Most of the current discussions of endangered species completely lacks theoretical underpinnings that could guide policies. The main underlying issue would be the determining of the basic priorities for maintaining or increasing biodiversity and rank the options of biodiversity preserving project. The recent work of Metrick and Weitzman has developed interesting approach to handle this problem (see Metrick *et al.* 1998). If the unit of analysis is at species level, the overall value of a species would be sum of the two components which contribute to the objectives or rationale of preservation of: (a) the direct utility of the species, and (b) diversity added by the genes of the concerned species. The latter is the basis of option values while the former contributes not only to the use value but also to survival. A project for preserving a species or biodiversity would improve the survivability of the species. The latter would be measured by the difference in the probability of survival between the absence of undertaking such measure and the presence of undertaken measures. The expected gain of taking preservation measure would be the sum of direct utility (U_i) and diversity value in term of distinctiveness (D_i) multiplied by the improvement in the probability of survival (Δp_i). This gain is to be weighed against cost of preserving ith species (C_i) which is measured in terms of opportunity cost of enhancing protection to the ith species. Thus

$$R_i = (D_i + U_i)\frac{\Delta p_i}{C_i} \qquad\qquad (2.3)$$

would yield the benefit to cost ratio which may guide the ranking of alternative biodiversity projects.

The resolution of the problem in quantifying factors—utility of a species, distinctiveness of a species, change in survivability of a species, and cost of enhancing the survivability is possible through several proxies to representing these factors, for example, taxonomic classification of a species along with log of length of size of a typical member may be used to indicate direct utility associated if largeness and popularity of the fauna or animal species (charismatic megafauna) are the major determinants of direct utility. Biodiversity conservation can be analysed by relating the proxies for the dependent variable like priority or magnitude of effort in preservation with the various dummies or proxies that capture the essentials of the four determining factors behind priority ranking. More empirical enquiries into actions for biodiversity preservation have to be carried out as Endangered Species Acts are passed and enforced in various countries for better quantifiability of the fundamental factors behind the choices in biodiversity preservation.

Biodiversity of an ecosystem is an important issue of economic choice because of its amenability to benefit cost analysis. The species matrix which assigns variety and weightage of importance adopts itself to the strength and variety of energy and other material inputs available in the given geographic and climatic conditions. Nature maximises biodiversity given the constraints of resources, climate and geography but not at the cost of reducing energetic efficiency of the ecosystem. Biodiversity is in fact correlated with the stability and resilience of an ecosystem which would have positive relationship with the well being of the existing species structure including the humans.

By stability, ecologists mean reversion of the structure and function of nature to the original system after an experience of exogenous shock which is different from physicists' way of defining the equilibrium after any perturbation. In an ecosystem with low biodiversity and concentrated specialized structure, there is efficient exploitation of the energy and the nutrients which are relatively abundant than in a situation of higher biodiversity and dispersed structure. However, a low diversity and high energy ecosystem will have a tendency to boom and burst as the ecosystem is not replenished with the nutrients fast depleted by the boom as seen in the growth and decay of algal blooms in a lake or rise and fall of yield of an agricultural land producing only one crop. In a tight energy and resource situation, with high biodiversity, on the other hand, most of the energy and nutrient resources will be stocked in the biomass of the diverse species. As a result the rate of withdrawal of such energy or resources from the ecosystem would be relatively moderate, allowing the required balance between regeneration and withdrawal of the resources, resulting in a more stable system. In an unstable situation, an ecosystem may permanently evolve into new eco-regime giving rise to problems of uncertainty regarding future state of primary productivity and possible survival of certain species. As the sustainability of economic development would require stable behaviour of ecosystem, biodiversity becomes a very important condition of sustainable development, apart from being as such a valuable resource with high option value. The positive contribution of biodiversity to the resilience of the ecosystem should also be counted as an indirect utility or use value.

Ecological Regions of an Economy

Soil, water, energy flow, climatic condition, vegetation and biodiversity are crucial in determining the renewable resource flow for an economy. The level and composition of this flow determines not only the ecological resource endowment of an economy, but also its development potential including its structural pattern. A vast country like India may not geographically represent a homogenuous ecological region and does in fact represent a wide range of agro-climatic and agro-ecological conditions. This leads to the imperative of different agro-economic strategies for the development of the different regions. The role of basic ecological factors characterizing the different agro-ecological regions of India is illustrated in the Annexe on India's Agro-Ecological Regions along with its tables, maps, etc. (see National Bureau of Soil Survey and Land Use Planning, ICAR 1992).

Chapter

3 ENERGY FLOW IN THE ECOSYSTEM

Energy Flow and Economic Process

Food security is one of the fundamental concerns of man with each human being requiring food energy approximately 2200 kilo calories (kcal) per day along with some quantities of protein, fat and nucleic acids for supporting body functions. The total solar energy required to supply the food requirement is determined by the mix of plant and animal food sources in the human diet. Since only plants can directly access energy and nutrients from the abiotic environment of nature they constitute the first link of the food chain. Substantial solar energy loss takes place along the food chain from one trophic level to another. Human beings tap energy and nutrients from diverse plant and animal food sources through energy intensive process. In addition, they depend on biomass for non-food energy and supplies of industrial raw materials, materials for construction, medicines, etc. Given constant solar energy flow to earth, species compete with each other for appropriating the limited photosynthesis output for their survival. Since biodiversity is necessary for maintaining and preserving the resilience of the ecosystem, appropriate access to photosynthesis output among species is imperative for sustainable development process. Hence, understanding the process of solar energy flow in ecosystem and its role in biotic resource generation attains importance in the planning for sustainable land use and biotic resource development.

Energy is understood in economics as any fuel commercial or non-commercial, which is required as utility input in production activities, as fuel input in the household activities of cooking, lighting, etc., or as fuel input for providing the motive force for the personal or public transport equipment. In the energy balance of an economy, food energy flow does not figure as an energy item. Food and agriculture are represented as part of non-energy sector, though requiring energy inputs for their production as a supplement to solar energy. While ecological processes of solar energy flow play the major role in the productivity of the primary sector of the economy, they do not figure in the economic balance relation as ecological services like solar energy flow are not marketed. As the capitalist economic accounting system cannot internalize any factor into economic analysis unless there is an expenditure flow supporting the role of the factor, the ecology-economy interactions are not taken into account by the methods of conventional economics. As a result, although energy economics is concerned with the GDP-elasticity of energy use and the cost of supply of energy, etc. where energy is inclusive of the conventional commercial energy and non-commercial rural energy resources; such definition of energy is inadequate for analysing the ecological sustainability of developmental processes. For a holistic analysis of sustainable development issues it is imperative that the totality of energy flow of ecosystems, including human subsidies, are related with human well-being. This chapter focusses on the energy flows in an ecosystem and their interface with the economic processes.

Concept of Energy and its Role in the Biosphere

A living organism maintains its internal order and the entropy level of its internal system by trapping matter and energy drawn from outside environment to continuously replace the dead tissues with the new. While an organism secures nutrients to construct and maintain its physical structure, it requires energy to run the basic life processes. Without continuous input of energy an organic system will stop functioning and the organism will move along a positive entropy gradient until it dies.

Nutrients and energy, the two basic requirements of life process, are distinct in terms of their availability. Nutrients circulate in the ecosystem through exchanges between its biotic and abiotic components but energy does not circulate in the same manner. Carbon, nitrogen, water and other materials which are major physical constituents of a living organism, circulate many times between living and nonliving entities in the biosphere. In contrast, once energy is used by a given organism, it is converted into the degraded form of heat. In such degraded form it cannot power life processes and is soon lost to the ecosystem. The rice or wheat when consumed is converted into body heat after its content has been used up by the body system and cannot again be used by organism for the same purpose. The one way flow of energy is a universal phenomena and it is the result of operations of laws of thermodynamics of physics. The manner of energy flows through the biotic component of the biosphere and the rate of (nutrients) circulation between the biotic and the abiotic environments have determining influence on the composition and dynamics of the biotic component of ecosystem, including human ecosystem. Energy flow and the operation of nutrients cycles in ecosystems are delineated in this chapter.

Energy can be described as ability to do work, which can be used to move an object physically against an opposing force over some distance. Energy can also be described as stored work. For example, if a piece of stone has been moved away from the centre of the earth, work has been done against the gravity of earth which is equal to the force applied to the stone and multiplied by the distance moved. The stone has acquired potential energy which is converted into kinetic energy (energy of motion) when the stone falls down. In the strict physical sense mechanical work always involves movement of one body relative to another. Similarly, fossil fuel, either coal or hydrocarbons, is a chemical energy resource which under certain conditions can be converted into heat energy (e.g. fossil fuel is burnt to raise steam from water in a boiler). Heat energy can be transformed into mechanical energy in kinetic form with the help of a mechanical device (e.g., steam is used to drive a piston which in turn pushes an object and drives a wheel resulting in the movement of an object over distance). The different forms of energy—potential, kinetic, chemical, mechanical, electrical, etc.—are expressed in terms of the capacity of doing work or in terms of amount of heat (in calorie or gram-calorie unit) into which it would be converted. A calorie is the amount of heat necessary to raise 1 gram or 1 millilitre of water 1 degree celcius starting from 14.5°C.

Energy, in order to be harnessable for doing work, must flow from its source. The usefulness of energy in doing work is directly related with its distribution within closed system. The more uniformly it is distributed, correspondingly it would be less harnessable. Where energy is unevenly distributed within a system, for example, in the form of heat, it can travel from high temperature (burning fuel) to low temperature (water) and in the process be used to raise steam to drive a piston and wheel. The first law of thermodynamics states that energy can be transformed from one form into another when it flows, but is never created nor destroyed by any process or event. The total amount of energy in the universe or in any closed system remains the same, although the proportions of energy forms may vary during energy flows within the system. A closed system is a system that does not exchange matter or energy with its surroundings.

The second law of thermodynamics states that whenever energy flows or gets transformed from one form into another, some heat is inevitably produced which tends to disperse rapidly within a system and is the least useful form of energy. As soon as heat is dispersed and evenly distributed within a system, all energy driven activities are halted. Since, the dispersed heat energy is unavailable for utilization, no spontaneous transformation of energy from one form into another is 100 per cent efficient. The ratio of unavailable to available energy for doing work, called entropy, is an index of disorder of a system. Entropy increases when energy is transformed from one form into another for doing work. The laws of the thermodynamics hold true even when energy flows through the biotic and abiotic environment. Living organisms and ecosystem use energy after transforming it from high to low utility state to maintain their highly organized low entropy state. Ecosystems adapt and organize themselves according to the available quantity and quality energy. The universal principle of one way energy flow applies to all environments and organisms and exercises influence on the process of generation of resources for human use.

Solar Energy Flow

Solar light energy is transformed into chemical bond energy through photosynthesis by plants. Chemical energy is transformed into mechanical and heat energy form in cellular metabolisms. These conversions and sequences describe the energetics of organisms and ecosystems. The unidirectional energy flow can be shown schematically as follows:

$$
\text{Sun} \xrightarrow{\text{radiant energy}} \text{Producer}
\begin{cases}
\xrightarrow{} \text{chemical energy} \\
\xrightarrow{} \text{heat energy}
\end{cases}
\text{Consumers/ decomposers}
\begin{cases}
\xrightarrow{} \text{mechanical energy} \\
\xrightarrow{} \text{heat energy}
\end{cases}
$$

Besides providing food energy to the biotic component of the biosphere, solar light energy contributes to the climate regime which defines the conditions of existence of living organisms.

Sun is a thermonuclear reactor which releases considerable radiant energy in the form of electromagnetic waves. The radiation covers a wide range of waves from high frequency short wave, for example, x-rays and gamma rays to long radio waves. The length of the wave, that is, the distance between the crests of the waves, determines the energy content of the electromagnetic wave, with the amount of energy decreasing with the increased length of wave, for example, ultraviolet rays (uv) are short wave high energy waves while the radio waves are long and low energy waves. About 99 per cent of the total solar light energy is contained in short waves in the range of 0.136 to 4.0 microns (1 micron = one millionth of a meter) ranging from uv to infrared rays. The visible range of radiation for human being is only a portion of this range with wave length between 0.38 to 0.77 microns with half the share of 99 per cent.

The total solar light energy that is directed towards the earth and reaching its outer atmosphere is only one over fifty millionth of the suns' total radiant energy. This energy reaches the outer atmosphere at a constant rate, referred as solar flux, of which about half of the total flux reaches earth's surface. It represents the total amount of energy of all wave lengths that crosses a unit area of surface of outer atmosphere of the earth per unit of time. According the available meteorological data its value is estimated to be 1.94 gram calorie (gcal) per square centimeter per minute.

The total radiant energy received at the outer atmospheric surface of the earth over a year is estimated to be 13×10^{23} gcal. The solar flux at a given place varies seasonally with latitude, and during the course of the day due to earth's rotation around its axis. Solar flux is depleted exponentially as it passes through cloud, water vapour, dust and gases of the troposphere. In the northern hemisphere it has been estimated that about 42 per cent of the radiant energy is reflected back into the outer space, of which, about 33 per cent from cloud and 9 per cent from the suspended dust particles of the atmosphere. An additional 10 per cent of the solar flux is absorbed by ozone, oxygen, water vapour and other gases. Only 48 per cent of the total solar energy actually reaches the *autotrophic* layer of the earth's surface. However, radiant energy absorbed in the troposphere is radiated in all directions in the infrared wave lengths. The energy income component of the earth has thus two components—direct solar radiation and the indirect infrared radiation which would amount to about half of the total solar flux targetted towards our planet. About 30 per cent of the energy reaching earth's surface is reflected into the space, the extent of energy reflected back into the space being highly variable from place to place and surface to surface (snow or sand reflects most of the light). Out of the balance energy, more than 69 per cent is converted into heat energy and less than 1 per cent is used by autotrophs for producing food through photosynthesis. Solar energy which heats the lower air, soil, surface water, influences the climate, the weathering process and the physiological responses of the organisms. Table 3.1 gives a rough estimate of the distribution of the use of planet's solar energy reaching the biosphere.

Light energy reaching the earth interacts with matter in one of the three ways—reflection (bounces off), absorption (taken in) or transmission (passes through). The absorption of light energy in the visible spectrum of wave length by a material object results in colour. The wave lengths of visible light that are used by the plants to run the process of photosynthesis are blue and red. When matter absorbs light energy and heats up, heat is radiated into the environment. Any surface or object above 0° Celcius will experience change in temperature (thermal flux) as a result of heat radiation. The thermal flux or variation in temperature of the immediate environment defines the condition of existence of all living organisms in the biosphere and acts as a selective pressure on the biotic system. Thermal flux as induced by solar energy will define the limiting factors for many species, given their adaptive behaviour, e.g., animals in desert are adapted to wide temperature variation between day and night. Human interference or change in natural climate condition may cause thermal flux values to violate the survivability condition of organisms affecting the biotic composition of the specific ecosphere.

Table 3.1
Energy use in the biosphere

	(distribution of share in %)
Reflected	30.0
Converted into heat only	46.0
Converted into heat used in evaporation and precipitation	23.0
Converted into heat used in driving the flows of winds, waves and ocean currents, etc.	0.2
Converted into chemical energy through photosynthesis	0.8
Total	100.0

Source: Hanks 1996, Table 2.4 on p. 73.

The energy flow through organisms is a one way flow with the conversion of solar energy to chemical bond energy being the starting point. Green plants absorb solar light, available in very diluted form, through chlorophyll pigment in the leaves which absorbs blue and red wave lengths of sunlight and produces concentrated energy in chemically bonded form of the organic compounds of carbohydrate, water and oxygen. Oxygen is released into atmosphere and water is transpired by trees into atmosphere, while carbohydrate forms the plant biomass. The rate of energy fixation by photosynthesis is based on Eqn. 3.1 (see Koromondy 1999).

$$6CO_2 + 12H_2O \xrightarrow{\text{673 Kcal of light energy and chlorophyll pigments}} C_6H_{12}O_6 + 6O_2 + 6H_2O \qquad (3.1)$$

where H_2O = Water, O_2 = Oxygen, CO_2 = Carbon dioxide and $C_6H_{12}O_6$ = Carbohydrate. Carbohydrate is the food produced by the autotrophs, the source of food energy of all organisms. The productivity of the photosynthetic process is measured in terms of energy fixed in the form of carbohydrate by autotrophs per unit of earth's surface area per unit of time. Photosynthesis can take place in plants on land and water. In the water bodies of ponds, lakes or oceans the phytoplanktons, algae and various water plants function on the photosynthesis process. Plants contain not only carbohydrate but several nutrients as photosynthesis cannot take place in the absence of nutrients. The gross primary productivity varies across ecosystems depending on the availability of sunlight, water and nutrients in soil and water. Hence, in deep sea or open ocean, or in desert, the primary productivity of ecosystems is very poor because of lack of light or nutrient or water.

Ecosystem's productivity in primary production depends on the chlorophyll availability per unit of area in the system. The distribution of chlorophyll on plants is not uniform across different ecosystems due to variations in the availability of sunlight, for example, higher concentration of chlorophyll per cell of biomass is present in a shaded system enabling higher efficiency of light utilisation than in a brighter light adapted ecosystem. However, productivity ultimately depends on the concentration of chlorophyll per unit of area, and the relation between chlorophyll in an area and the photosynthesis rate. The ratio of grams of organic matter produced by photosynthesis per unit of time to the gram of chlorophyll under light producing outputs is the assimilation ratio. Efficiency of light utilization by a chlorophyll area and the assimilation ratio are inversely related. Consequently efficiency of light utilization is high in shaded system, but the assimilation ratio and photosynthesis yield from light to carbohydrate are low. The high efficiency of shaded system in light utilization is more than offset by the low assimilation ratio as a result of which primary productivity of ecosystem with weak light condition becomes lower. Besides, the chlorophyll area is also influenced by the age factor of the plants reflected in photosynthesis yield.

Autotrophs carry out two kinds of photosynthesis in higher variety of plants—called C_3 and C_4. These are described by, the number of carbon atoms found in the first stable compounds in their respective path ways. The productivity implication of these two types of plants are different with C_4 plants being two to three times more productive than the C_3 plants. Most cultivated crops meeting human needs are C_3 plants like wheat, rice, potatoes, etc. While C_3 plants have peak productivity of photosynthesis in medium light and temperature as well as adequate water availability, C_4 plants like corn, sugarcane, etc. have peak production in higher light and temperature condition and efficient utilization of scarce water. The evolution of these different biochemical pathways as represented by C_3 and C_4 plant types has been induced by selected pressures due to conditions of availability of light, water, temperature, etc. Scientists are trying to find out genetic variation of plant species which can have C_4 plant type chemical pathways to address the growing needs of human population.

Primary productivity per unit of area widely varies across ecosystems of various geographic regions. A hectare area of crop land, forest land, lake, open ocean, mountains or desert, will show substantive variation in the photosynthetic output per unit of area in a year (see Table 3.2). The efficiencies of gross energy fixation in various ecosystems as measured by the percent of electromagnetic waves reaching the chlorophyll area of the plant that is captured and converted into carbohydrate would vary in the range of a fraction of 1 per cent. Under favourable condition, the efficiency of gross production would be 1 per cent while the average is 0.2 per cent approximately for the biosphere. Some portion of electromagnetic wave length reaching the leaves would not, be absorbed. The balance light energy which is not converted into chemical bonded form, would be converted into degraded energy forms of heat or reflected as low energy long wave light into the space.

The net primary productivity of an area in ecosystems is the amount of carbohydrate produced through photosynthesis in excess of the plant respiration cost which is available for consumption of the heterotrophs in the food chain. The estimate of efficiency of net primary productivity measured as net energy fixed in excess of respiration cost of autotrophs as a ratio of radiant solar energy utilized by the plant, is expected to be 0.5 per cent under favourable circumstances and 0.1 per cent on an

Table 3.2

Ranges of net primary productivity

$(K\ cal/m^2/yr)$

Ecosystem	Low	Medium	High
Forest	1.0 to 1.3×10^3 Boreal forest (China) Woodland (Kenya) Chapparal (Mexico)	4.0 to 6.0×10^3 Mangroves (Burma) Temperate deciduous forest (Mexico) Broadleaf forest (China)	7.9 to 9.0×10^3 Tropical seasonal forest (Brazil) Tropical rain forest (Brazil, Zaire, Indonesia)
Grassland	0.5 to 1.5×10^3 Stressed sub-tropical and montane formation (China, Sahel, Andes)	1.5 to 2.5×10^3 Temperate grassland (China, Turkey, Argentina)	2.5 to 3.5×10^3 Tropical grass-land (Brazil, Sudan, India)
Cereals	0.15 to 0.3×10^3 (Upper Volta, Nigeria, Zaire)	0.45 to 0.6×10^3 (Pakistan, Mexico)	0.75 to 0.9×10^3 (Vietnam, China, Indonesia)

Source: Koromondy, 1994, pp. 29.

average for the biosphere. Table 3.3 shows the variation of net primary productivity across ecosystems. Table 3.4, on the other hand, illustrates how the solar energy is utilized in primary production in Upper Lake in Bhopal and shows the photosynthesis efficiency and its variation in different seasons (see Prasad 1990).

For economic well being, the primary productivity of ecosystem is of vital importance for food supply, and for the supply of industrial raw materials, fuel wood, etc. Tables 3.5–3.8 illustrate productivity of woody biomass for the plantation of *Prosopis juliflora* and *Pinus patula*. The former plantation (commonly known as Mesquite in English and Vilayat babool in Hindi) is an excellent source of fuel wood particularly in semi-arid zone and marginal lands, because of its high yield, fast growth, excellent burning quality and drought resistant and nitrogen fixing character. Table 3.5 shows the component-wise biomass

Table 3.3
Estimated gross primary production
of biosphere and its distribution among major ecosystems

(annual basis)

Ecosystem	Area $10^6 km^2$	Gross primary productivity $Kcal/m^2/yr$	Total gross primary production $10^{16} Kcal/yr$
Marine			
Open ocean	326.0	1000	32.6
Coastal zone	34.0	2000	6.8
Upwelling zone	0.4	6000	0.2
Estuaries and reefs	2.0	20000	4.0
Sub total:	362.4		43.6
Terrestrial			
Deserts and tundras	40.0	200	0.8
Grassland and pastures	42.0	2500	10.5
Dry forests	9.4	2500	2.4
Boreal coniferous	10.0	3000	3.0
Forests			
Cultivated lands with little or no energy subsidy	10.0	3000	3.0
Moist temperate forests	4.9	8000	3.9
Fuel subsidized (mechanized) agriculture	4.0	12000	4.8
Wet tropical and sub-tropical (broad leaved evergreen forests)	14.7	20000	29.0
Sub total:	135.0		57.4
Total for biosphere (round figures—not including ice caps)	500.0	2000	100.0

Source: Odum, 1975, pp. 81.

production of the species *Prosopis juliflora* at different ages in units of tonnes per surveyed hectare with spacing of 1.3 × 1.3 metre based on the data of a plantation near Gandhinagar in Gujarat in 1979. Productivity is the measure of the girth at breast height (GBA) which is a function of the age of the plant. The table shows the measures of yield of total biomass and utilisable biomass per hectare. Table 3.6 shows the amount of total standing

Table 3.4
Energy flow during primary production in the
Upper Lake, Bhopal

Items	Winter	Summer	Monsoon	Post-monsoon
1. Average daily solar radiation received at water surface (cal/m^2/day) 10^3	1840	2700	2680	2000
2. (a) Change in O_2 content *in situ* in water body (g/m^2/day)	16.87	9.07	11.2	13.34
(b) Estimated loss due to respiration per day	0.80	0.37	0.56	0.69
(c) Total estimated gross O_2 production (g/m^2/day)	17.67	9.07	11.2	13.34
3. Item 2 expressed as gross carbohydrate output (2) × 0.937	16.55	8.49	10.49	12.49
4. Energy required to produce (2) at 3.68 calories per mg of oxygen	17670 × 3.68	90700 × 3.68	11200 × 3.68	13340 × 3.68
5. Energy fixed in water as carbohydrate assuming the average heat of combustion of carbohydrate at 4.1 kilo cal per gm	17.67 × 4.1	9.07 × 4.1	11.2 × 4.1	13.34 × 4.1
6. Photosynthetic efficiency expressed in percentage (a) ratio (4)/(1)	3.53	1.23	1.53	2.45
(b) ratio (5)/(1)	3.93	1.37	1.70	2.73

Source: Prasad, 1990, p. 136.

energy in million calorie unit and the solar energy conversion efficiency for the concerned plant species at different ages. The utilizable biomass has a share varying between 74.3 per cent and 82.6 per cent for the survey data as presented in the Tables 3.5

Table 3.5

Component-wise biomass production of *Prosopis juliflora* at different ages for plantations in Gujarat

					(tonnes/ha)
			Age in months		
Component	18	24	30	36	48
Wood	4.15	8.09	13.32	23.74	32.56
	(21.1)	(19.5)	(19.27)	(20.71)	(21.91)
Bark	0.80	1.52	2.03	4.13	4.97
	(4.1)	(3.7)	(2.94)	(3.6)	(3.34)
Branch	9.68	22.56	35.24	61.0	75.72
	(49.1)	(54.5)	(50.99)	(53.2)	(50.94)
Utilizable	14.63	32.17	50.59	88.87	113.25
biomass	(74.3)	(77.7)	(73.2)	(77.5)	(76.19)
Leaf	1.99	3.80	5.08	3.00	6.05
	(10.1)	(9.2)	(7.35)	(2.6)	(4.07)
Fruit	–	–	0.12	22.75	29.33
			(0.17)	(19.8)	(19.73)
Root	3.07	5.42	13.32	–	–
	(15.6)	(13.1)	(19.27)		
Total biomass	19.69	41.39	69.11	114:62	148.63

Notes: Figures in brackets represent percentage share of total biomass.
Source: Gurumurti K. *et al.* (1984), p. 887.

and 3.6, and the peak energy efficiency in primary production of 1.87 per cent is found to be attained at the age of 36 months. These features make *Prosopis juliflora* excellent candidate for short spacing short rotation forestry for meeting the fuel wood demand of India. In terms of yield and utilizable biomass it performs better than Eucalyptus, particularly for short maturity rotation.

A study on *Pinus patula*—a tropical tree of Latin America and Africa which is now being planted widely in Nilgiri and Palni Hills in Tamil Nadu where the species has naturalized itself—also shows the growth of net primary production of biomass with the aging of the plants. The results of the study are given in Table 3.7. As this plant species has important industrial use, findings of such a study are very useful for land use planning for providing the support in the form of biomass throughput into the industrial system. Table 3.7 gives the dry weight of standing biomass per hectare for the different ages with componentwise break up for the

Table 3.6
Total standing energy content of *Prosopis juliflora* at different ages
for plantation in Gujarat

(10⁶ kcal)

Component	Age in months				
	18	24	30	36	48
Wood	15.73	29.53	46.64	101.52	123.82
Bark	3.85	5.81	8.10	19.57	21.65
Branch	33.67	82.58	129.20	229.84	275.85
Energy in utilizable biomass	53.25	117.92	183.94	350.93	421.32
Fruit	–	–	0.40	–	–
Leaf	7.9	14.38	23.95	12.16	24.45
Root	11.24	17.81	37.86	92.49	101.57
Energy in total biomass	71.68	150.11	246.15	455.58	547.34
Solar energy* conversion eff.	0.59	0.92	1.22	1.87	1.68

*This is determined by the formula

$$\frac{\text{Standing energy per ha at a period of time}}{\text{Total solar energy received per ha per period}}$$

Source: Gurumurti K. *et al.* (1984), p. 890.

study taken up for the Tamil Nadu region in various years between 1968 and 1981. The weight varies with the measure of the trees. The estimates given are aggregated over the GBH distribution. With solar radiation information, the data on net primary productivity of solar energy flow through photosynthesis for this target plant species would reflect the conversion efficiency of solar energy. Estimates of standing biomass are net productivity figures per acre—after subtraction for respiration cost. Estimate of gross productivity of solar energy flow requires inclusion of energy produced, used in respiration by the plantations. The net productivity figures of the table refer to non-photosynthesizing biomass only, that is, the biomass of the tree net of its leafy portion which carries out the photosynthesis function for the plantation.

Table 3.8 shows the variation of productivity of woody biomass of forestry in India, across the states representing different

Table 3.7
Total standing biomass of Pinus patula plantation
in Tamil Nadu

(kg/ha)

Items	Age in years				
	3	5	9	11	13
No. of trees/ha	644	967	1167	900	1033
Components:					
Wood	1347	4016	97722	69252	70689
Bark	436	925	8584	9490	10493
Branch	1141	3455	20873	13381	20495
Twig	1351	3467	9081	8478	13450
Needle	1901	4981	10810	8076	14049
Core	5	123	212	4153	3182
Standing dead	–	–	24297	19884	12913
Total above ground biomass	6181	16967	171579	132714	145271
Root	1088	2070	22478	23623	25858
Total biomass productivity	7269	19037	194057	156337	171129
Non-photosyn-thetic above ground biomass excluding needles (kg/ha/yr)	1427	2397	17863	11331	10095
Non-photosyn-thetic root bio-mass (kg/ha/yr)	363	414	2440	2147	1989
Total non-photosynthetic biomass	1790	2811	20303	13478	12084

Source: Sharma et al. (1984), p. 928.

ecoregions, with productivity being measured in terms of dry
tonnage of woody biomass per hectare per year. Information of
net productivity of solar energy flow in generating biomass is
important for planning of land use for biotic resource generation
for developmental purpose. The conversion efficiency of radiant
energy for different plant species, their variation over space and

Table 3.8
Annual above-ground woody biomass productivity of
forestry plantations in different locations and
different categories of land

		(t/ha/yr)
	Type of Plantation/Location	*Productivity*
Karnataka	Farm forestry	7.2 to 8.2
	Forest Department	1.5
National	Farm forestry	4.2
	Forest Department	2.6
	Eucalyptus plantation	6.6
States	West Bengal	6.4
	Gujarat	4.1
	Tamil Nadu	3.8
	Himachal Pradesh	1.6
	Andhra Pradesh	1.2
National mean	All plantations	3.2

Source: Ravindranath N.H. *et al.* (1995), p. 232.

reasons are crucial for the planning for sustainable resource use
and regional developmental strategy.

Energy Flow along Food Chain

What happens to food energy generated by the autotrophs? The
net primary production of energy by autotrophs is available for
the use of herbivores of an ecosystem without depleting the
initial stock of biomass at autotroph level. However, only a
proportion of this total amount of net primary production is
consumed by herbivores. Decomposition accounts for a small part
of net production. The balance net primary production is stored
as energy in the growing stock of plant biomass which may be
exported to other ecosystems for different uses, for example,
timber harvested for furniture or house construction. Figure 3.1
illustrates how out of autotroph's gross production of 111 gcal/
cm^2/year in a lake, an amount of 23.0 gcal (i.e., 21 per cent) is
used for respiration and the balance net primary production of

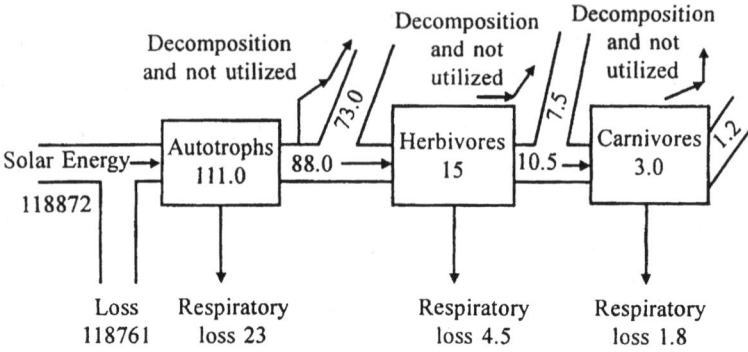

Figure 3.1   Energy flow through the ecosystem

Note: Data is in gcal/cm^2/yr.
Source: Koromondy (1999), p. 96.

88 gcal/cm^2/year is available for the use of the herbivores as food. After accounting for 3 gcal per cm^2/year for plant decompositon and 70 gcal per cm^2 per year for non-use, a balance of 15.0 gcal per cm^2 per year actually flows for consumption by herbivores. (see Table 3.9)

Out of the total energy consumed by herbivores by grazing on autotrophs, a substantive part of it is used for respiration by these consumers for their survival. The respiration cost as a proportion of total food available would be higher for herbivores than for autotrophs due to higher level metabolic activities of the herbivores. With a 30 per cent share of energy intake as respiration cost and a small share of 3 per cent accounting for unassimilated energy or decomposition, the balance amount of assimilated energy, that is, 10.5 gcal/cm^2/year is available as food energy for carnivores. Only 3 gcal/cm^2/year is consumed by the carnivores as food energy while the balance 7.5 gcal/cm^2/year is not used as food by carnivores and is stored as energy in the stock of herbivore biomass.

At the higher trophic level of carnivores, a large part of energy consumed is used for respiration due to the higher energy need of the metabolic activity. The share of decomposition or unassimilated energy accounts for negligibly small share of the total intake. In the example given, respiration cost is shown to be

Table 3.9
Energy flow of lake in Minnesota, USA

	Energy flow gcal/cm²/yr	Efficiency or Loss%
Incoming solar radiation		
producers autofroplis (SR)	118872	
Gross production (GP$_A$)	111	GP$_A$/SR 0.09
Respiration loss	23	20.8
Net production (NP$_A$)	88	NP$_A$/GP$_A$ 79.2
Decomposed	3	3.4
Not utilized	70	79.5
Herbivores		
Gross production (GP$_H$)	15	GP$_H$/NP$_A$ 17.0
Respiration (R$_H$)	4.5	30.0
Net production NP$_H$	10.5	NP$_H$/GP$_H$ 70.0
Unassimilated	0.5	4.76
Net utilized	7.0	66.6
Carnivores		
Gross production (GP$_C$)	3.0	GP$_C$/NP$_H$ 28.5
Respiration (R$_C$)	1.8	60.0
Net production (NP$_C$)	1.2	NP$_C$/GP$_C$ 40.0
		decomposition trace
		neg.
		not utilized 1.2
		100.0
Total loss via respiration	29.3	26.39
Total loss via decomposition	3.5	3.15
Total loss via non-utilization	78.2	70.45

Source: Based on data provided by Figure 7.4 of Koromondy (1999), p. 96.

about 60 per cent of energy intake, that is, accounting for 1.8 gcal/cm²/year, leaving the balance of 1.2 gcal/cm²/year as entirely unused food energy; if the conerned carnivore represents the highest level in a food chain or food energy available for use by carnivores at a still higher trophic level (e.g. snakes in the grazing food chain: phytoplankton → zooplankton → frogs → snake; birds in the grazing food chain: phytoplankton → small fishes → bird). Energy utilized at this stage will be accumulated as part of stored energy in the carnivore's biomass.

The secondary productivity or net community productivity is the total energy stored at different trophic levels beyond autotrophs, and is roughly equal to all energy transferred from the autotrophs after subtracting respiration cost and decomposition, the unused stored energy in autotrophs and heterotrophs defines the harvestable resource for economic system, given the possibility of its use as a resource. The unused energy in the flow along food chain accumulates as energy stock stored in the current period, harvestable in future. Ecological steady state is achieved if the standing crop of different trophic levels remains unchanged over time which is achieved if gross primary production and community respiratory cost are equal and if exports and imports of energy of the ecosystem are either nonexistent or exactly balance each other. Birds feeding on small fishes of a tank represent a case of export of energy from the tank ecosystem and import of energy to the adjacent terrestrial ecosystem. If unutilized energy flow as embodied in biomass is diverted for economic use it is an export from that ecosystem.

The energy flow in the grazing food chain has two important features. First, the flow of energy is one way. It is not possible for the energy assimilated at higher trophic level (say carnivore) to flow back as food to the previous lower trophic level. Energy captured by autotrophs cannot flow back to solar input, what passes on to herbivore cannot flow back to autotrophs for assimilation, what flows to carnivore cannot revert to herbivores. Secondly, there is progressive decrease in the energy available for doing work at each successive or higher trophic level as energy is dissipated as heat at each trophic level. Even if full utilization of net produced or assimilated energy occurs at each stage, the solar radiation rate of energy of 118872 gcal/cm^2/year would result in 56 gcal/cm^2/year at the end of the chain in the given example.

Unidirectional energy flow, degradation of energy at every conversion stage, assimilation or transfer are evidences of the operation of the laws of thermodynamics in ecosystem. Despite accumulation of biomass due to non-utilization, energy content of the accumulated stock would degrade unless the organism containing the energy stock continuously accessed fresh energy to prevent its disintegration.

The grazing food chain, in addition to the detritus food chain, is another energy flow pattern based as the organic matter of the dead organism whether plant or animal. Consumers of dead matters called as detritus consumers decompose and derive energy from dead organisms. A detritus food chain begins with organic matter of dead plant and animal. The primary consumers in the chain are of two types: (a) small animals like soil mites, millipedes on land or various worms in water, (b) micro organisms like fungi and bacteria. While fungi thrive mainly on dead plant materials, bacteria decompose and consume energy from dead animal materials. These detritus consumers are consumed by secondary detritovore consumers and so on, for example: dead leaves → fungi/bacteria/small aquatic animals → small carnivores like small game fish → large carnivore like fish eating birds. Most of the creatures involved in the detritus food chain are small and are rarely visible. As the detritus consumers decompose the dead organism and release basic nutrients in usable compound form while consuming energy contained in the dead materials, the detritus food chain plays an important role in sustainability of the ecological processes. Both the food chains—grazing and detritus contribute to—the sustainability of the ecological processes. In a mature temperate forest, only a small portion (about 10 per cent) is consumed by the grazing herbivores while the balance 90 per cent of net energy produced follows the detritus path. The availability of huge quantity of dead organisms, etc. results in the abundance of detritus consumers which is food for detritovers.

The energy flow model of the interlinked grazing and detritus food chain (see Figure 3.2) shows a large proportion of energy produced in the grazing food chain flowing to the detritus food chain. The dominance of a food chain in terms of share of flow ends on the nature of the concerned ecosystems initiating the energy flow (see Figure 3.2). The detritus food chain often links two ecosystems with primary production occurring in one ecosystem and secondary production through heterotrophic utilization occurring in the other ecosystem, for example, aquatic organisms in an woodland stream are supported by a food chain that begins with dead leaves, twigs and detritus falling in from the forest. Mangrove forests contribute substantially to aquatic organisms through the detritus food chain.

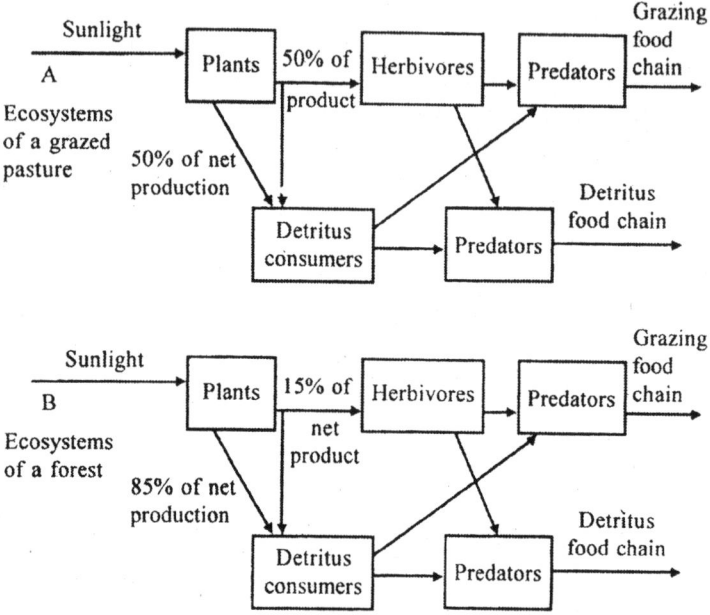

Figure 3.2 Energy flow model interlinking grazing food chain and detritus food chain.

Source: Based on Figure 3.3 of Odum (1975), p. 69.

The number of species in a detritus food chain is much more than in a grazing food chain, with the grazing food chain involving hundreds of species, and the detritus food chain involving thousands of species. The decomposers in the detritus path obtain energy from dead organisms of all trophic levels without affecting the entropy condition. The metabolic activities of the organisms in the detritus chain cause degradation of chemical bond energy stored in the body of the organism into heat.

Food webs are formed with the interlocking of many food chains in an ecosystem with most organisms being part of several food chains. The intricacies of food web are difficult to grasp as a number of species can occupy the same trophic level in a web of an ecosystem. A single organism according to its diet can occupy more than one trophic level. Omnivores feed on autotrophs and heterotrophs in the food web. Figure 3.3 illustrates predator-

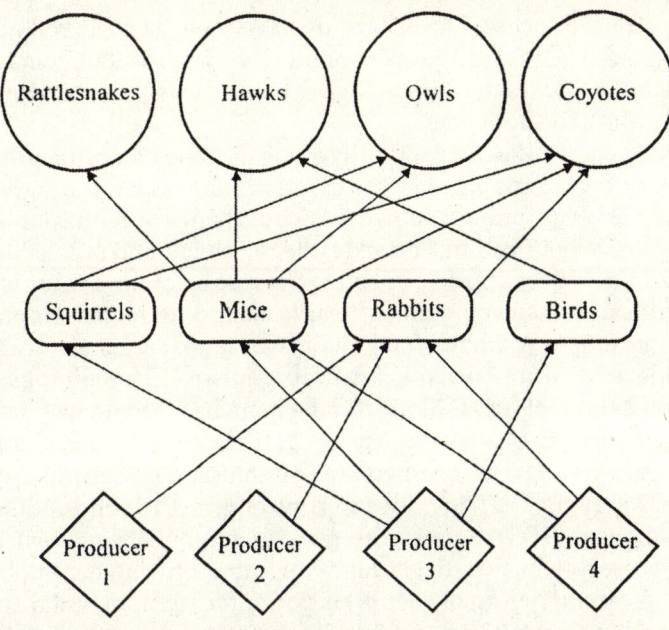

Figure 3.3   Food-web

Source: Based on Figure 2.13 of Kupchella and Hayland (1998), p. 41.

prey related food web. Removal of any one species would have a disastrous effect on the ecosystem, for example, removal of mice at the level of herbivores may cause extinction of snakes, thereby affecting the diversity and balance of the ecosystem.

Given the energy flow along the food chains and the food webs, the biotic component of an ecosystem is characterized in terms of distribution of the organisms, their biomass weight and energy across trophic levels. The frequency distribution of organisms over the trophic levels shows that the numbers decline for higher trophic level for small producers (grass, phytoplankons), if they form the lower base of the pyramidic structure. The structure would be an inverted pyramid if the producers are large (trees). Such a characterization of ecosystem overemphasizes the importance of small producers. In the case of distribution of biomass across trophic levels, the quantum of biomass as dry weight will increase or decrease with the size of the producers. Such a characterization of ecosystem would overemphasize the large size producers. The energy distributions (as absorbed and assimilated) across different trophic levels show that energy availability always declines at higher trophic level irrespective of the size of the producers.

While energy flows entropically along the food chain, materials entering organisms increase in concentration as they progress along the chain and is known as food chain concentration or biological magnification. Pesticides, heavy metals and radioactive materials are examples of materials subject to biological magnification causing serious health hazard at higher trophic level once they enter the food chain. These materials are water soluble and stored in the fat of organisms. The biological magnification of DDT along food chain has been most well documented. The pesticide use of DDT to control mosquitoes and agricultural pests, resulted in DDT entering the detritus food chain. Spraying DDT in water to control growth of mosquitoes also allowed DDT to enter the grazing food chain as well as aquatic ecosystem, resulting in high concentration at higher trophic level. A careful design of chemicals policy for environmental and human health protection is therefore important.

Solar Energy Flow and Ecological Economics

The discussions in the preceding sections have thus pointed to the crucial role played by the ecological process of solar energy flow in generating food and non-food biotic resources that support human life and the economic system. Agriculture and plantation have been essentially biotic generation of plants of selected varieties in a given land area through the photosynthetic process with energy subsidy provided by man to the concerned ecosystem. The agrarian products are used as food for human consumption with or without some industrial processing. The non-food agricultural products are used as industrial raw materials (like food processing, jute, cotton, paper, bio-chemicals, etc.) and their by-products may have direct human use (for example, use of agricultural waste like crop-ends as fuel or for rural house construction). Similarly, the economic products of forestry, animal husbandry, fishery, etc. are essentially harvested portion of net biotic productivity at certain stages of energy flow along the food chain. However, the concerned ecosystems yielding these products receive varying degrees of energy subsidy through human technological intervention. Besides, the solar energy flow provides life support to ecosystems by also driving the bio-geo-chemical cycles which will be explained throughout the various sections of Chapter 4. As it will be seen, these cycles perform the crucial function of recycling the various nutrients of the ecosystem and also contribute to the degradation of the wastes arising from an economy. It is in fact the solar energy flow and the bio-geo-chemical cycles driven by it along with the applicability of the principle of entropy in the use of matter and energy in economic processes which would define the conceptual framework of any interdisciplinary construct of models of ecological economics.

Chapter

4   BIO-GEO-CHEMICAL CYCLES

Why are Bio-geo-chemical Cycles Relevant in the Economic Context?

The interactions between the biological and the geo-chemical processes of the earth driven by energy flow result in the cyclical movement of the basic chemical elements thereby enabling their repeated use as nutrient for organisms and as a resource for economic system. This chapter focuses on the regeneration of resources made possible by the movement of nutrient elements between the biotic and the abiotic environment. These cyclical movements of chemicals also facilitate the transformation of economic wastes (particularly the biodegradable ones) into resources for use by human beings. However, as in the case of energy flow, services provided by nature through the operation of the bio-geo-chemical cycles are neither marketed, nor priced, with the result that economic transactions and accounting system completely neglect such flows and cycles. With the realization that the economic system cannot take nature for granted, the problems of value and accounting systems are now taking account of interaction between, in addition, the integration of bio-geo-chemical cycles and economic processes. Given the nature of these cycles, their pathways and interlinkages with other cycles, human interferences with ecological processes would hamper sustainability of resource regeneration and development process. This chapter describes the major nutrient cycles, providing major life support to organisms and some important renewable resources to the economic system.

Concept of Bio-geo-chemical Cycles

Of the basic constituents of matter and energy of our biotic and abiotic environment, energy has a unidirectional flow, while materials move in circular pattern passing back and forth between organisms and their abiotic environment and such material cycles are termed as bio-geo-chemical. The word 'bio-geo-chemical' is broken down as: bio = living organism, geo = geological environment (involving earth, water, air), chemical = chemical forms or combinations of elements and process. The material elements move in cycles in the form of chemical compounds in local and global environments between the biotic and abiotic components of the biosphere. Through chemical processes, transformations in these compounds occur, with solar energy as the driving force of the physical movement of the chemical compounds through the ecosystems. The bio-geo-chemical cycles are superimposed on energy flows of the ecosystem to demonstrate the relationship between the two basic ecological processes and highlight the role of energy flow in driving the cycles.

Among more than 110 basic chemical elements, approximately 30 in varying amounts are required for living organism. The nutrients are unevenly distributed in the biosphere in its reservoir and exchange pools. The reservoir pool and exchange or active pool are distinct from each other, depending on the amount of element available and its rate of release. In the reservoir pool the chemical element is either available in a non-usable form or inaccessible due to remote location for organisms. In the exchange pools the elements are located in easily accessible forms for organisms. As a result, chemical elements in exchange pool though in smaller quantities are rapidly exchanged with biotic organisms of the ecosystems. In such a process, the nutrients will have several pathways in the exchange and reservoir pools. Energy flow and weathering process ensure flow of materials from the reservoir pool to exchange pool. Some nutrients may follow pathways such that the nutrient element gets trapped in a location which is cut off from both reservoir and exchange pool, and leaves the cycle. Such outflows are downhill loss for the nutrient cycle. The occasional release of previously trapped nutrients in earth flowing into either of these two pools result in an uphill gain for the nutrient cycle.

Hence certain levels of indeterminacy exist in the pathway of a particular chemical element. The distribution of flow of a chemical element along different pathways would vary from geographic region to region depending on the biophysical environmental conditions. How much and how long an element stays in a pool is its residence time which depends on the rates of release and available quantities of the compound from that pool. If a compartment holds 1000 units of a compound and exchanges (that is, releases and receives with other pools) 10 units per hour, then the residence period of the compound would be 100 hours. How much and how fast the chemical elements are exchanged between the pools and move through the system is however relatively unknown. Only indications are available for the rough range of speed of movement of the basic elements along the bio-geo-chemical cycles which could be global cycles, especially if atmosphere or hydrosphere is the reservoir pool. While the impact of a nutrient cycle would be important in the local context of resource regeneration in an ecosystem, the global circulation pattern would benefit or negatively impact any part of the world. Major material cycles are discussed below, illustrating all the conceptual classification of cycles.

There are three major types of cycles—hydrological, gaseous, and sedimentary. While the hydrological cycle is concerned with the movement of a compound, H_2O, water the other two types of cycle—gaseous and sedimentary are concerned with the movement of basic chemical elements. In the gaseous cycles the reservoir pool of the concerned element is located in atmosphere. These are perfect cycles, they exhibit very little change in the distribution and total amount of the chemical element over repeated circular movements and adjust quickly to changes in the total system. Carbon, nitrogen and oxygen cycles are gaseous cycles. In the sedimentary type of cycles the reservoir pool is located in earth's crust or lithosphere from which elements are released through the weathering process. These cycles are not perfect as some part of the supply are lost to the cycle; for example, chemicals trapped in deep ocean sediments are not accessible to organisms. Phosphorous, sulphur, and iodine cycles are sedimentary. These cycles have a tendency to stagnate because their elements are relatively inactive and unavailable and hence make for easy disruption of the system. Six nutrient cycles are discussed in the following sections. They are diagrammatically presented in Figures 4.1 to 4.6 which are based on similar figures of Hanks (Hanks 1996) and Koromondy (Koromondy 1999).

Hydrological Cycle

Water is a chemical element of immense ecological significance for biosphere. It is the medium for all cellular chemical reaction and is essential for all organisms. Water constitutes on the average 70 per cent of the body weight of organisms. Water is an agent of geological change causing erosion in one place and deposition elsewhere. It is an agent of nutrient distribution over the biosphere as it carries these elements in the form of dissolved salts or gases. Water plays a significant role in energy transfer and energy use in the planet. The large amount of energy involved in converting ice into water or vapour, makes water a major factor in ameliorating wide changes in temperature which would otherwise have accompanied the variations of incoming solar radiation, thereby facilitating favourable conditions of existence for organisms.

The major pathway of hydrological cycle is the interchange of water between earth's surface and the atmosphere via precipitation, evaporation and transpiration. Solar energy is the driving force of the hydrological cycle. Solar energy causes evaporation from the entire surface of the earth that is soil, water and organism. Vegetation returns water to the atmosphere by transpiration. A mature oak tree in full leaves moves four to five tonnes of water from soil into atmosphere through transpiration, every day. Organisms absorb water for their biological activities and excrete water in the form of liquid or vapour which is evaporated into atmosphere.

Water stays in the atmosphere in the form of clouds and water vapour. It returns to the earth's surface from atmosphere by precipitation in the form of rains, sleet, ice, snow and fog. The water cycle is a steady cycle as the total evaporation and transpiration is balanced by the total of all forms of precipitation. There is, however, an imbalance between the two for ocean and land separately. On land, there is excess of precipitation over evaporation, the balance being run off from land to ocean. According to estimates, 20 per cent of the annual rainfall takes place over ocean with the balance 80 per cent falls on the terrestrial system (see Koromondy 1999). In the ocean excess evaporation over precipitation would approximately balance the run off from land. Even on land precipitation and evapotranspiration are unevenly distributed depending on interaction between atmospheric circulation and the continental and island topography as well as the pattern of vegetation.

Water, which falls on land by way of precipitation is moved downwards into the soil by gravitational force until it reaches the underground level where soil is completely saturated with water which is called the water table. Such ground water provides 95 per cent of fresh water excluding icecaps, and recharges aquifers. Streams, lakes, tanks, ponds or wetlands constitute surface water. Precipitation on land as surface runoff is carried into rivers and flows towards ocean constituting another surface source of water. The ice caps of mountains melt due to solar radiation and supplement other sources of surface water. Figure 4.1 shows the hydrological cycle.

The total annual precipitation on earth is an impressive quality of 5.2×10^8 km^3 of water, while its source, atmospheric water vapour constitutes a very small amount relative to precipitation. The division of the annual precipitation by the stock of water vapour source, yields a turn over rate of 35 times a year or a residence period of water of 11 days in the atmosphere. The atmosphere is the exchange pool while the hydrosphere is the reservoir pool for the cycle. Of the total estimated water resource, 97.5 per cent of all water on earth is salt water leaving only 2.5 per cent as fresh water. Nearly 70 per cent of fresh water is frozen in Antarctica and polar ice caps, while most of the remainder is present as soil moisture or lies in deep underground aquifers as ground water inaccessible for human use. As a result, less than 1 per cent of the world's fresh water, or about 0.007 per cent of all water on the earth is readily accessible for direct human use. This is available in lakes, rivers, reservoirs and ground water accessible at reasonable cost.

About 110,000 km^3 of water falls as rain every year in all the continents. Most of this flow evaporates into atmosphere or is

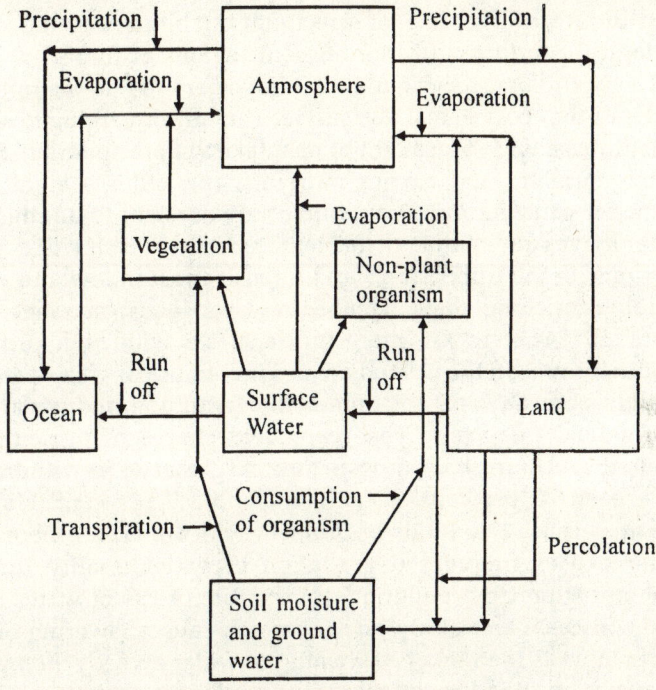

Figure 4.1   Hydrological cycle

absorbed by the plants. About 42,700 km^3 of water flows through world's rivers. The basic mechanism of hydrological cycle is that the rate and amount of evapotranspiration is considered to be as critical as the rate and amount of precipitation. The ratio of these two factors is a major determinant of the distribution of ecosystem types over the surface of earth. Each of the types of major ecosystems—e.g. a given type of forest, grass prairie, desert, etc.—would correspond to a certain range of this ratio of precipitation to evaporation, the precise value depending on temperature, rainfall and the volume of plant biomass. This ratio in a desert with little plant coverage, would possibly be in the range of 0.2 or less, while for a moist forest region it may be in the range of 1.0 and more may be depending again on temperature and the density of plant biomass. The agro-ecological zoning of a country is also determined by and large by the distribution of the rate of precipitation. The Annex illustrates how geographic distribution of the rate of precipitation influences the agro-ecological conditions of the different regions of India.

The hydrological cycle plays an important role in the nutrient cycles of the ecosystems. The surface run off converging to ocean constitutes about 35 per cent of its intake via precipitation. Since water dissolves and carries nutrients, run off is a significant agent for carrying nutrients from one ecosystem to another. As water moves downhill with nutrient loads, the run off will deplete nutrients in the uphill areas and deposit them in lowland areas thereby enriching them. Hence, low wet lands, marshes, and continental shelves are more nutrient rich with high primary productivity than the upland areas. Human use of water consists entirely of freshwater for domestic, agricultural, industrial and commercial purposes. The respective shares of agriculture, industry and municipal bodies in the total global water withdrawal have been 70 per cent, 20 per cent and 9.9 per cent. Human activities cause two kinds of problem with water: (a) the use of water causes frequent degradation of water quality due to contamination from pollution; (b) the rate of use of water from land sources, particularly ground water, causes lowering of the water table as the rate of harvesting of water exceeds the rate of regeneration. Besides, activities like paving of land, draining of wetland, compacting soil, and clearing of forests cause lesser percolation of water and greater run off of water towards the sea. Lowering of water table interferes with water cycle. If the over use of ground water and change in land use due to developmental activities result in the increase in run off of water from land surface, there will be increase in water flow to seas and oceans. The availability of freshwater in ground water form which is accessible for human consumption would be adversely affected by such disturbances in the development process. The discussion of use of water as resource and water pollution will be taken up in Chapter 6 in order to obtain the conditions of sustainable use of water and sustainable pattern of development.

Gaseous Cycle: Carbon Cycle

Carbon, the basic element, is an essential constituent of all organic compounds—carbohydrates, fats, proteins and nucleic acids. It constitutes about 49 per cent of dry weight of all organisms. The carbon cycle involves a gaseous phase—particularly of atmospheric carbon dioxide—although C is contained in CO and CH_4 as well. Carbon moves from CO_2 of the atmosphere into autotrophs through photosynthesis which fixes CO_2 in plants in the form of organic compound. The organic compounds containing carbon, flow to heterotrophs and decomposers through the grazing or detritus food chains. Carbon partly returns as CO_2 to atmosphere through cellular respiration process of the organisms. The process of decomposition of organic bodies releases CO_2 into the atmosphere through oxidation of carbon elements of the body. The carbon cycle is thus driven by solar energy flow through production and consumption of food energy and decomposition of organisms. The carbon cycle is presented in Figure 4.2.

An uphill gain of carbon to this circular flow is possible from volcanic eruptions, burning of fossil fuel due to human activity or weathering of sediment rocks containing carbon by way of oxidation. A downhill loss of carbon from the circular flow is possible in either of the two major ways: (a) the organic matter may

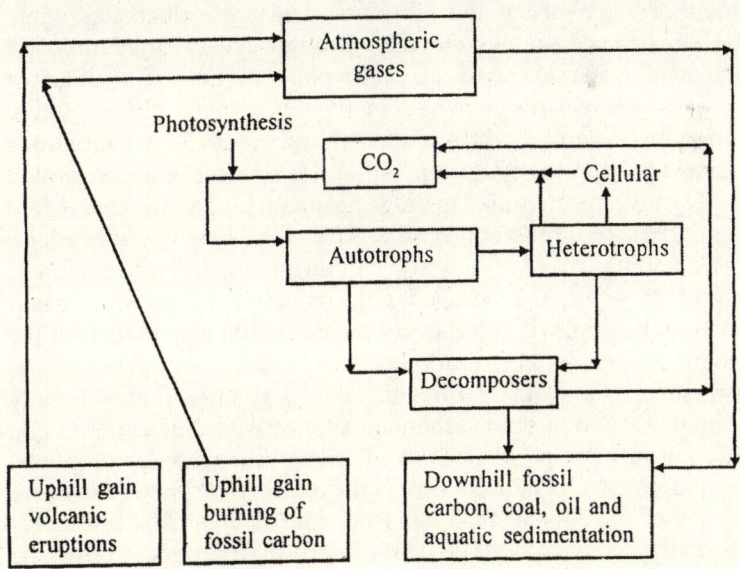

Figure 4.2   Carbon cycle.

be trapped in sedimentary rocks as deposition and transformed into fossil fuel through geochemical transformation processes over geologic time scale and, (b) CO_2 absorbed by aquatic bodies and may be lost in the aquatic sediments not available for the cyclical movement. CO_2 enters the water body from atmosphere or through plant and animal deposit. When carbon dioxide dissolves into water, carbonic acid is formed and the latter combines in a series of chemical reactions with calcium and forms the stable compound of carbonate ($CaCO_3$). These calcium carbonates are not soluble in water and would be deposited as sediments at the bottom of a lake or ocean. Carbon trapped in such deposits is not available for circulation.

The rate of carbon fixation through photosynthesis in the circular movement of carbon is not uniform between day and night, over different seasons, and over the places with varying latitude. Since photosynthesis is intense during summer, rainy season and the spring, CO_2 is present in less quantities in the atmosphere. In winter when the decomposition of vegetation releasing CO_2 is high, photosynthesis process is less intensive and CO_2 is present in high quantity in the atmosphere. The carbon level in the different pools or segments of the biosphere constantly fluctuates while carbon balance and its stability through cyclical operation not achieved instantaneously at every point of time. The different process components involved in this cycle have different time rates; for example, while photosynthesis may be a continuous process, carbon sequestration would not be a continuous process. A CO_2 molecule may stay in the atmosphere for 5 to 10 years before being fixed through photosynthesis process. However, over a long period of time the distribution of carbon among different pools and segments would be restored approximately to its equilibrium level, unless there is significant human interference to disturb the balance. The broad distribution pattern of carbon within biosphere, estimated to be valid over the long run, is given in Table 4.1. Only a small portion of total carbon is really active in the carbon cycle and constitutes the sources of all biotic resources for economic development. Only 0.2 per cent of the total carbon of our biosphere contained in atmosphere, ocean water and all organisms turns over annually. Photosynthesis is 40 to 90 billion metric tonnes in absolute unit per annum. The geologic component of the total carbon of the earth is as large as more than 99 per cent which is not active.

Table 4.1
Carbon in the biosphere

	(billion metric tonnes)
Atmosphere	692
Organisms	3432
Living	592
Dead	2840
Fossil fuel	5000
Ocean water	35,000
Ocean sediments	10,000,000
Total organic	8432
Total inorganic	10,035,692
Grand total	10,044,124

Source: Koromondy (1999), p. 124.

Economic activities have caused some disruptions in the carbon cycle. The over-harvesting of plant biomass leading to deforestation has reduced the chlorophyll area and the quantum of photosynthesis. Burning of over harvested plants (i.e., harvested in excess of regeneration) along with the reduction in the rate of photosynthesis have contributed to the rise in the level of CO_2 concentration in the atmosphere. Besides, the burning of fossil fuel in production activities has caused a rising trend in CO_2 emission and CO_2 concentration in the atmosphere. As a greenhouse gas, CO_2 is the largest contributor to global warming. Although use of fossil fuel is a factor contributing to the uphill gain of carbon in the cyclical turnover, the process of global warming itself has also caused disturbance in the carbon cycle.

Nitrogen Cycle

Nitrogen is a primary constituent of fats and protein and is therefore an integral part of all organisms. Its gaseous cycle is crucial in providing life support to organisms. Nitrogen makes up 79 per cent of the atmosphere in contrast to carbon which has a share of only 0.03 to 0.04 per cent in the atmosphere. Unlike carbon, autotrophs and most of the other organisms cannot use nitrogen in gaseous form as available in the atmosphere. The atmospheric nitrogen has to be fixed into an inorganic compound before it can be tapped for biological processes. In nature, this fixation occurs mainly as a bio-chemical process. It has been estimated that on an average 7.6 million metric tonnes of nitrates are obtained through non-biological process in the nature (electrochemical and photochemical fixation) every year. The biological fixation process, on the other hand, yields an estimated amount of 54 million metric tonnes per year. However, human activities also effect nitrogen fixation in the order of 50 million metric tonnes through highly energy intensive industrial process of synthetic fertilizer to meet the requirements of modern agriculture.

Nitrogen fixation from atmosphere is carried out by various bacteria, algae and micro-organisms in our terrestrial and aquatic systems. Nitrogen fixed by these organisms is converted into forms (nitrate) usable for plants. Nitrogen then flows from autotrophs into all heterotrophs and decomposers through the grazing and detritus food chains. The nitrogen fixers are classified into two types: symbiotic nitrogen fixers and free living nitrogen fixers. Symbiotic nitrogen fixation takes place mostly in the soil of the terrestrial system. Nitrogen fixers are associated with roots-nodules of specific plants and are host specific in nature, for example, the bacteria of the Rhizobium group lives in specific relationship with leguminous plants (peas, clover, beans, etc.) with each strain of Rhizobium being highly host specific, that is, particular strains of Rhizobium being associated with particular strains of legumes.

Free living nitrogen fixers, comprise bacteria, algae and various micro-organisms. Nitrogen fixation by such organisms takes place both in the soil and the aquatic systems. Nitrogen fixed from atmosphere is released as ammonia in the local soil or aquatic environment. Ammonia is further converted into nitrite and the nitrite into nitrates by bacteria, each of these chemical changes in the steps being carried out by a different species of bacteria. Autotrophs can access nitrogen only in nitrate form from the local environment. However, of the two ways of nitrogen fixation, symbiotic nitrogen fixation is quantitatively more important than by free living form, and exceeds the latter by at least hundredfold.

The other source of nitrogen in the ecosystem is the dead organic matter which is broken down by the decomposers. In this process nitrogen in the form of ammonia, recycles into nitrates. No part of nitrogen in dead organism or metabolic waste products is lost in gaseous form. While some of the nitrates would be accessed and absorbed by autotrophs, large part is converted into gaseous molecular form as nitrogen as well as nitrous oxide (NO) and nitric oxide (N_2O) by the denitrifying bacteria in the biosphere. Table 4.2 shows the distribution of nitrogen in the biosphere while Figure 4.3 outlines a circular flow of nitrogen.

Table 4.2
Nitrogen in the biosphere*

			(10^6 metric tonnes)
Atmosphere	3,800,000	Ocean water	20,000
Land organisms		(dissolved N)	
Living	12	Living	1
Dead	760	Dead	900
Inorganic N (Land)	140	Inorganic N (Ocean)	100
Earth's crust	14,000,000	Sediments	4,000,000
Total Organic:		1,673	
Total Inorganic:		21,820,240	
Total N:		21,821,913	

*Of the total nitrogen content in the biosphere it is only a small portion which is active in the cyclical motion. However, the cyclical movement of nitrogen of even such small proportion is quite crucial for life support of living organism and resource regeneration for human economic systems.
Source: Koromondy (1999), p. 139.

The biological involvement in the nitrogen cycles is quite extensive and complicated, but quite ordered. The nature of the involvement is highly specific as certain organisms will be active only in certain phases of the cycle. As nitrogen is an essential input for plant life, the nitrogen cycle is important for supporting agriculture and forestry and other biotic resources necessary for economic activities. Human activities disturbing the nitrogen fixers (soil or aquatic) or denitrifiers, would seriously disturb the nitrogen cycle. The preservation of the community of decomposers, soil micro-organisms and nitrogen fixing bacteria is extremely important for the ecofriendly regeneration of biotic resources for human well-being.

Agricultural activities themselves disturb the nitrogen cycle as nitrogen is removed from the terrestrial systems. Agricultural crops require and absorb nitrogen from soil. When the crops are

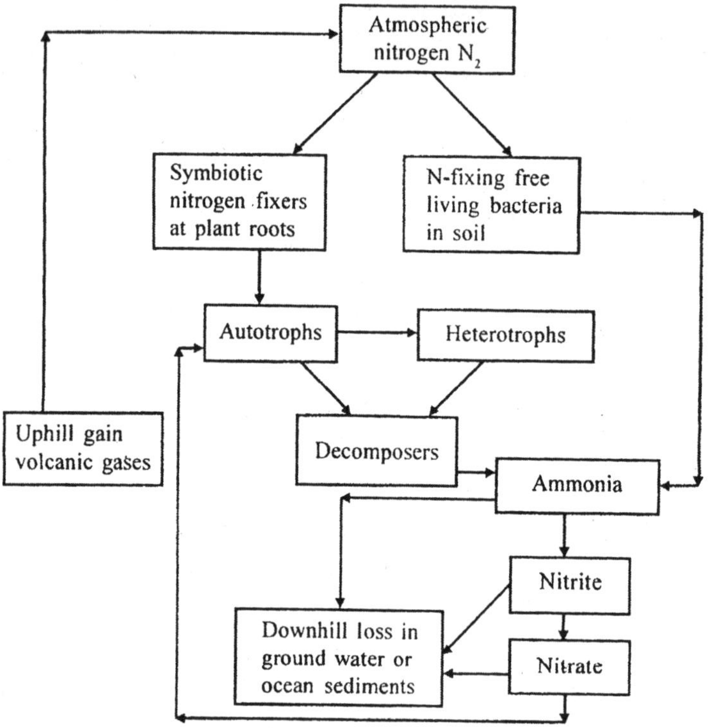

Figure 4.3 Nitrogen cycle.

harvested nitrogen leaves the terrestrial system, the soil of the agricultural land becomes poor in nitrogen content after raising a few crops. In order to compensate for such nitrogen loss, synthetic fertilizers are added to soil in modern agricultural practices. Two problems are faced in this context—first, synthetic fertilizer has to be dissolved into water so that it can spread in soil and reach the plant roots in soluble form. As a result, large amount of water is used along with the fertilizers. Unfortunately, given the practice of water use a large amount of nitrogen is washed off and carried into the water system by run off leaving the terrestrial system and reaches the ground water, lake or river water system leading to nitrogen pollution in the aquatic system. Secondly, the substitution of natural supply of nitrogen through the nitrogen cycle by that of chemical fertilizer is wasteful from energy use perspective. The nitrogen fixing organism requires only some external supply of energy in the form of a carbon compound to effect nitrogen fixation. The energy requirement is quite low for nitrogen fixers in comparison with the order of energy requirement in the process of industrial nitrogen fixation which requires high temperature and pressure condition (like 400^0C temperature and 200 atmospheric pressure) for the necessary reaction. Sustainability of agriculture and biotic resource development would thus emphasize the dependence on natural supply of nitrogen or its augmentation to the extent biotechnology can permit through provisions of bio-fertilizers. Bio-fertilizers are cultured bacteria or microbes equipped with nitrogen fixation property, which under specific conditions make nitrogen available in a suitable form to autotrophs. Preservation of biodiversity is important because of the high option value of various organisms for use as free or symbiotic nitrogen fixers in future.

A range of economic activities like fossil fuel burning, deforestation, industry waste, human sewage discharge, deforestation, mining, run off from agricultural land, etc., generate nitrogen wastes when released in the natural environment. Such addition of compounds has often disturbed the nitrogen cycle and caused nitrogen pollution such as acid rain and entrophication of water bodies.

The global annual nitrogen fixation has been estimated at a total of 92 million metric tonnes with the break up as given in Table 4.3. The nitrogen fixation amount is replaced by denitrification, inclusive of downhill losses of 83 million metric tonnes whose sourcewise break up is as given in Table 4.3. The

Table 4.3
Global cyclical balance of nitrogen (Delwriche)

(10^6 metric tonnes)

Nitrogen fixation		Denitrification	
Biological	54	Terrestrial	43
Industrial	30	Marine	40
Photochemical	7.6	Sediments	0.2
Volcanic	0.2	Excess fixation	8.6
Total	91.8	Total	83.2

Source: Koromondy (1994), p. 65

table shows excess nitrogen fixation of the order of 8.6 million metric tonne. This imbalance growing over time due to increasing industrial nitrogen fixation emission would affect the aquatic ecosystem. As industrial nitrogen emissions and the fossil fuel burning are not balanced by additional denitrification, the excess fixation causes increasing nitrogen pollution of the aquatic system.

Oxygen Cycle

Atmospheric oxygen is a basic requirement of life on earth as organisms (with the exception of a few bacteria) draw oxygen from atmosphere for their cellular respiration and release it as CO_2 into the atmosphere. The respiration process breakdown carbohydrate to release carbon which provide energy for the metabolic functions of the organisms. Autotrophs require oxygen for photosynthesis process of food production and carbon fixation and derive it from CO_2 drawn from the atmosphere. After the photosynthesis process oxygen is released back into the atmosphere in the form of gaseous oxygen (O_2). Minor uphill gain to the cycle takes place through volcanic eruptions releasing oxygen into the atmosphere. Downhill loss also occurs through the absorption of atmospheric CO_2 by the ocean and transformed into calcium-carbonates in sediments in the ocean bed (see carbon cycle). The oxygen cycle is outlined in Figure 4.4.

The atmospheric oxygen also provides an important life support service to organism without entering into the biotic system. The ozone compound (O_3) is formed in the stratosphere with the interaction of gaseous oxygen molecules (O_2) and solar radiation. The ozone layer absorbs most of the harmful ultraviolet radiation from the sun and acts as a sheild for the biosphere. The organisms habiting the biosphere are not adapted to ultraviolet-radiations. However, the stratospheric ozone layer has thinned down overtime. The depleted zones of ozone layer are called ozone holes and are found above the Arctic and Antarctic. Industrial activities accelerate the process of ozone depletions disturbing the natural phase of the circulation Oxygen (O_2) → Ozone (O_3) → Oxygen (O_2). Some chemicals of chloraic compounds like chlorofluorocarbons (CFCs), hydrochlorofluorocarbons, carbontetrachloride and methychloroforms release chlorine when they break down in the atmosphere. Chlorine interacts with the

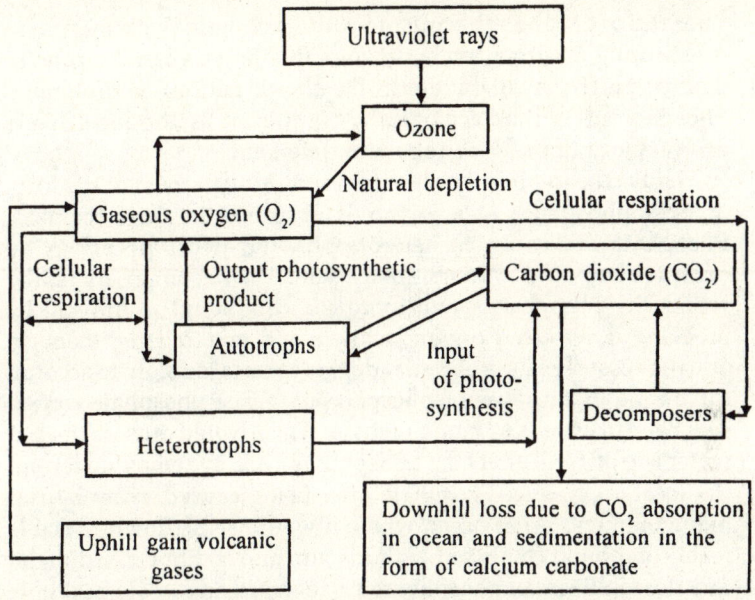

Figure 4.4 Oxygen cycle.

ozone and produces in the process gaseous oxygen which depletes the ozone layer. Chlorine can stay for 40 to 100 years and carry on such destructive process.

Ozone compound can be formed in the troposphere due to biomass or fossil fuel burning, causing NO_x emission. While ozone in the stratosphere is life protector and, therefore, a resource, ozone in the troposphere is a pollutant as it causes respiratory diseases in man and destroys the photosynthetic tissues of the autotrophs thereby reducing the primary productivity of the ecosystems.

Sedimentary Cycles: Phosphorous Cycle

Phosphorous cycle is a sedimentary cycle and therefore not a perfect cycle. Phosphorous does not have any atmospheric content. It has a large reservoir of deposit in the earth's crust and has an active pool in the soil of the earth. It is a nutrient of major importance to biological systems and is a constituent of nucleic acid, phospholipids and numerous phosphorous compounds.

The ratio of phosphorous to other chemical elements in constituting an organism is considerably larger than the ratio of their respective availabilities in the abiotic natural environment. Phosphorous is thus ecologically significant as the most likely productivity limiting or regulating element.

Plants take in phosphorous from soil through roots in the form of orthophosphate ions which is absorbed in their biomass. Phosphate moves on to heterotrophs and decomposers as an organic compound through food chain. The decomposers finally return the phosphate as an inorganic compound to the soil by breaking down dead organic matters and mineralizing them. In aquatic ecosystem, the bacterial degradation is too slow to account for the rapid turnover of phosphorous. Since phosphate can be dissolved in water, any human activity which would cause increased water run off, will affect the phosphorus cycle by removing it from the local ecosystem. Phosphate after being carried away by run offs would end up in ocean where it would settle down in stable form compound combined with calcium and sodium as sediment. The downhill loss of phosphorous is reversed on a geological time scale when mountain building occurs, and deep sea sediments are lifted up. Figure 4.5 outlines the phosphorous cycle.

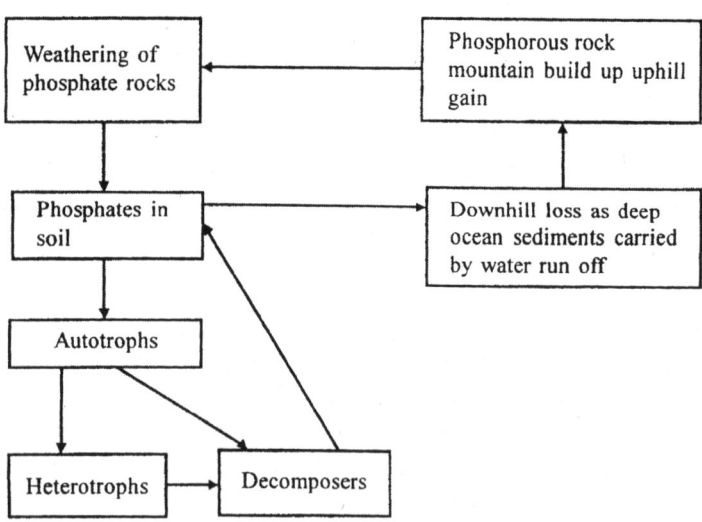

Figure 4.5 Phosphorous cycle.

The phosphorous cycle is, however, often disturbed by human actions resulting in addition of phosphorous compounds to the local environment of soil in the form of phosphate fertilizer, detergents, human and animal wastes, etc. The increased run off of water carries phosphorous from local environment and pollutes water bodies causing eutrophication. The acid rain as induced by nitric oxide emission from human activities reduced pH level of soil. Below the pH level of 5.5, phosphorous reacts with iron and aluminum and forms an insoluble compound and is lost to the cycle as autotrophs would not be able to access phosphrous. Acid rain affects the availability of phosporous in soil for its absorption by autotrophs and the subsequent flow through the food chain.

Sulphur Cycle

Sulphur is a constituent of proteins (certain amino acids) which are essential for living organisms. A large deposit of sulphur exists in the terrestrial system and there is a small reservoir in the atmosphere. Sulphur circulates mainly within the terrestrial system. Sulphur cycle is a sedimentary cycle. Autotrophs absorb sulphur in sulphate form through root system. Sulphate is absorbed into the plant biomass and is then passed on to other species through food chain. With decomposition of dead organic matter sulphur is released into the soil as hydrogen sulphide (H_2S) and is further converted either into sulphate or sulphur dioxide by bacteria. Different types of bacteria are active in the different conversion processes at different phases of the sulphur cycle. Some of these bacteria are called chemosynthetic organisms, because they produce energy from chemical oxidation of sulphide instead of from sunlight or from organic matters, The green sulphur bacteria are photosynthetic bacteria which oxidizes H_2S into elemental sulphur while the purple bacteria make their own food by oxidation of H_2S to the stage of sulphate. Organic wastes excreted by heterotrophs contain sulphate which is directly returned to soil. Similar circular movement of sulphur takes place in the aquatic system. Some uphill gain to the cycle occurs from the volcanic gases and hot springs, while down hill loss from the cycle occurs as hydrogen sulphide or sulphates are washed off from the soil by run off water. The washed off compounds finally settle down as sediments in ground water, lake or ocean. The sulphur cycle is outlined in Figure 4.6.

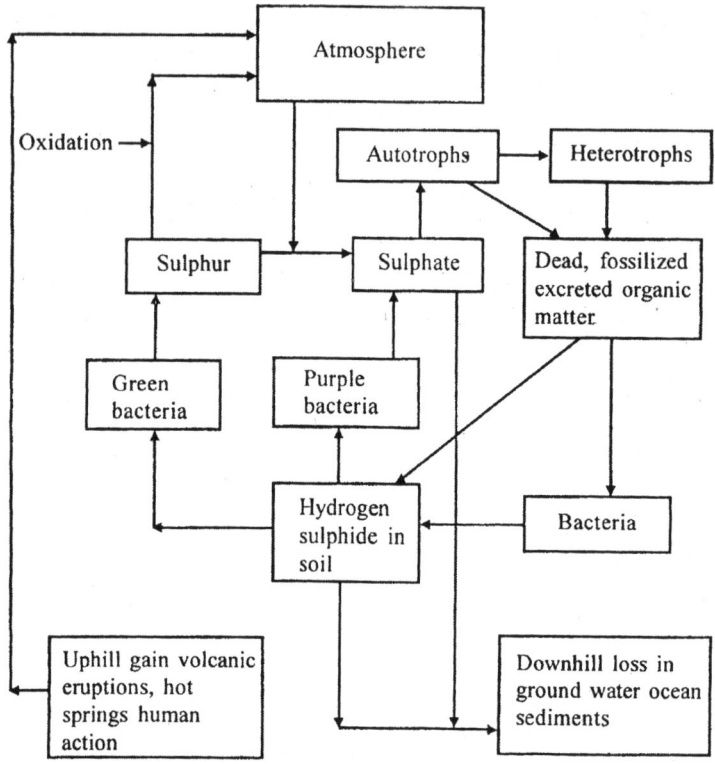

Figure 4.6 Sulphur cycle.

Some organic sulphur gains entry into atmosphere in the form of sulphur dioxide (SO_2) through incomplete combustion of fossil fuels which is a major source of air pollution today. Atmospheric sulphur, hydrogen sulphide and sulphur dioxide are oxidised into sulphur trioxide (SO_3). SO_3, when combined with water in the atmosphere, produces surphuric acid which is precipitated as acid rain. Acid rain reduces the productivity of the autotrophs by damaging their photosynthetic tissues and reduces the pH level of the terrestrial and aquatic systems causing stress to the biotic components of such system and affecting their ability to function normally. Besides, SO_2 gases in the atmosphere affect the health of the heterotrophs as these pollutants damage the lungs of the heterotrophs.

If sulphur combines with iron in any phase of its cycle, it forms into ferrous sulphide or ferric sulphide compounds under anaerobic conditions in the aquatic system and becomes insoluble in neutral or alkaline water. As a result sulphur becomes unavailable for the biotic system to the extent of presence of iron in the environment. Sulphur cycle however interacts with phosphorous cycle when iron sulphide compounds are formed facilitating the chemical conversion of phosphorous from insoluble compound to soluble compound forms and making it available to biotic system.

Nutrient Budget and Ecosystem

Different nutrient cycles of an ecosystem have different time frames to complete the full cycle operation and are often linked with each other because of the interconnections of some of the pathways of movement of nutrient elements. In such a situation the ecological balance is maintained by the interaction of the cycles over a long time frame. The budget of the nutrients in an ecosystem would together determine the growth and function of the biotic component of the ecosystem. The nutrient budget would contribute to the determination of the level of carrying capacity of an ecosystem. Nature optimizes the biotic growth subject to the nutrient budget constraint of the ecosystem which is analogous to consumer's optimizing consumption subject to income budget constraint in a market economy.

The nutrient budget which shows the balances of total flows of each nutrient for an ecosystem has two components—internal budget and external budget. Internal budget deals with the movement of nutrients within the ecosystem along the food chain of producers, consumers and decomposers and in the exchanges between reservoirs and sediments of the concerned ecosystem. External budget pertains to the intake and output of the entire ecosystem in relation to other ecosystems. Geological, meteorological and biotic actions like volcanic eruptions, rock weathering or death of animal species of one ecosystem in another system cause flows of nutrients across ecosystems. Human activities like biomass export from one ecosystem to another are responsible for influencing external nutrient budgets of the ecosystem. The internal and external nutrients budgets are interrelated. The nutrient budget and cycle for nitrogen and phosphorous for tree layers of an Indian forest is presented in Table 4.4.

Table 4.4 compares the total N and P budget for dry deciduous, moist sal, pine and oak forests and gives the storage of N and P existing in the vegetation compartment of such trees in the concerned ecosystems. Vegetation pool of sal forest accounts for half of N and two-third of of P stored in the total ecosystem. Among the flows, Table 4.4 shows both the accumulation of N and P in the net production of plant biomass in a year as well as the amount of the nutrients which go back to the soil through the fall of dead leaves, decomposition of dead roots, etc. Some re-absorption or withdrawal of nutrients by plants occurs from the aging leaves before they fall in the forests. As a result the net uptake of these nutrients from soil is the accumulation of the nutrients in the plant biomass growth in a period minus the amount of such nutrients which were obtained through the withdrawal process from the aging or dying leaves. The table shows the balance between nutrient uptake from soil and return to the soil. It shows that some portion of nitrogen and phosphorous in their circular movements is being retained in the growing vegetation stock every period as a constituent nutrient. The table shows that the sal forest ecosystem is endowed with nitrogen of 8.51 tonnes/hectare out of which 4.45 tonnes are stored in the vegetation component, 0.05 tonnes in litter and 4.01 tonnes in soil. The growth of the sal forest results in accumulation of 0.154 tonnes of nitrogen/hectare/year while an amount of 0.034 tonnes out of this growth requirement is being recovered per hectare per year of nitrogen from aging leaves. The balance net amount of 0.12 tonnes of nitrogen is thus the rate of uptake from soil per hectare per year. The decomposition process of dead leaves, woods and roots of plants of sal forest, returns 0.079 tonnes of nitrogen/ hectare/year to the soil. This results in a net transfer of nitrogen from soil to vegetation which is bound for some time amounting to 0.04 tonne per hectare per year approximately which together with 0.034 tonnes of nitrogen recovered from dying leaves contributes 0.075 tonnes of nitrogen to the growth of sal forest biomass per hectare per year. Table 4.4 shows similar details for dry deciduous, pine and oak forests of India for nitrogen and phosphorous.

Table 4.4
Nitrogen and phosphorous budgets for tree layer of certain Indian forests

	Dry deciduous		Sal		Pine		Oak	
	N	P	N	P	N	P	N	P
Compartment pool vegetation (t/ha)	0.65	0.054	4.45	0.403	1.108	0.145	3.299	0.135
Litter	0.036	0.003	0.05	0.003	0.131	0.011	0.094	0.004
Soil	2.97	0.119	4.01	0.151	3.964	0.218	5.82	0.186
Total	3.662	0.176	8.51	0.558	5.203	0.374	9.212	0.325
Accumulation in net production (t/ha/yr)	0.141	0.009	0.154	0.0126	0.1387	0.0136	0.185	0.009
Reabsorption from leaves (t/ha/yr)	0.033	0.001	0.0339	0.0024	0.0460	0.0037	0.018	0.001
Net uptake from soil (t/ha/yr)	0.108	0.008	0.120	0.0102	0.092	0.009	0.167	0.008
Return of nutrient through litter, dead roots, etc. (t/ha/yr)	0.084	0.006	0.079	0.007	0.067	0.006	0.107	0.007
Retention in vegetation (t/ha/yr)	0.057	0.003	0.075	0.005	0.071	0.0076	0.078	0.002

Source: Singh L. et al. 1992, p. 426.

Nutrient Cycles and Human Well-being

Living organisms play an important role in the circular movements of important nutrients which are either constituents of the organisms or provide crucial life support service. The sum total of processes of a large number of living species in a well ordered ecosystem ensures the supply of material and energy for life. The organisms on earth have controlled the chemical composition of sea and atmosphere over a long period of time. Human beings are dependent on other species for their survival and need to control the biosphere in their own interest. In addition to science and technology human beings need bacteria and micro-organisms, plants and animals for controlling nature for maximizing the well-being of human society. Any human activity giving rise to poisonous hazardous waste would affect bacteria, micro-organisms and other organisms and threaten the operation of the nutrient cycles. Although the bacteria and micro-organisms have high degree of adaptability they are vulnerable to poisons.

As heterotophs including man can access carbon, nitrogen, phosphorous, sulphur and all micro nutrients only through the food chain, any human activity which interferes with the nutrient cycle by removing the basic elements from local environment or converting the nutrient element into an insoluble chemical compound, would cause inaccessibility and shortage of the nutrients for the autotrophs (e.g., acid rain causing formation of insoluble phosphorous compound in the presence of iron or calcium). Any activity affecting the availability of the nutrients for the autotrophs is considered as violating the basic conditions of sustainability of the natural processes but also of human life support.

Any addition of the nutrients in a local environment as a result of human activities may also lead to environmental pollution if it disturbs the cycle (e.g., water pollution due to use of inorganic fertilizers, air pollution due to nitric oxide emission). The maintenance of the level of nutrient flows without disturbing their cycles in the ecosystems is an important consideration for ensuring the conditions of sustainability. Human activities need to be regulated to control impacts on nutrient cycles.

Chapter 5

POPULATION ECOLOGY AND HUMAN POPULATION GROWTH

Populations of Species and Human System

In Chapters 2, 3 and 4, the role of the great physical and chemical forces in determining the energy flows and the cycling and recycling of materials (nutrients) in the biosphere which provide life support to its biotic segment was outlined. Populations of various species are adapted and limited by temperature, light, nutrients and other abiotic factors. Various natural communities of various species modify, change and regulate the environment within certain limits. The states of the ecosystems of the biosphere are influenced by the size and the composition of the biotic components which are changing because of population characteristics of various species and the group attributes. The population dynamics of the natural communities would determine the allocation of natural resources and ecological space of this planet. Since human well-being depends on the direct natural resource use in production and consumption, allocation of ecological space and resources among species may raise an issue of conflict of interest between human and other species. Human population has important influence on land use and the availability of space for food and habitat for other species. The species structure and aggregate size of biotic segment of the ecosystem is an important determinant of the natural resource base for human economic system. The biological forces as represented by the population characteristics of various species play an important role determining the functioning of the biosphere and influencing the conditions of sustainability of human development.

Population Attributes

Population is defined as a collective group of members of a species inter-breeding and inhabiting in a particular area or region for example, human population of a city or of a nation–state or of a continent, fish population in a tank, bird population of a natural park. The important attributes of a population are:

(a)   density: size of population per unit of space, that is, surface area or volume,

(b)   birth rate: the rate at which new individuals are added to an existing population by the process of reproduction per unit of time,

(c)   death rate or mortality: the rate at which individuals are lost to a population by death per unit of time,

(d)   dispersal: the rate at which the individual members of a species immigrate into or emigrate out of a population per unit of time,

(e)   population growth rate: the net effect of natality, mortality and dispersal per unit of time,

(f)   spatial distribution: pattern of distributions of population over space—random, uniform or clumped. The distributions of individuals in some species approach complete randomness, for example plants with air borne seed dispersal mechanism. Uniform distributions are observed in species in an environment with severe competition for resources. (e.g., creosote bushes in desert). Most of the species are non-uniformly distributed (clumped) as the nutrients are distributed over space or the abiotic conditions of living differs (e.g. moss grows on the side of a plant that is moist). Social factors influence the dispersion of a species. For example, members of species (like bees, ants, termites) form into packs to mobilize food and protect themselves and are found to be distributed in clumps.

(g)   Age distribution: proportion of population in different age groups—pre-reproductive, reproductive and post-reproductive.

(h)   Genetic characteristics: reproductive fitness of the population as indicated by the fertility rate (i.e., number of births as a ratio of the size of female population in reproductive age group.); adaptiveness to natural environment, and the ability of persistence as reflected in the survivability given by the age specific pattern in which individuals survive or die.

While the individual members of a population are born, grow and die, the attributes like birth rate, death rate, migration rate, density, etc. are defined at a group or community level. At the group level the discussion is focussed on the role of the population attributes in population growth of a species enabling the understanding of the source of conflict between population dynamics of species and the sustainability of human well-being.

Population Growth

Growth of the size of species population is completely determined by the birth rate, the death rate and the rate of net immigration into (immigration minus emigration) population of a species. Birth rate is determined by the inherent reproductive potential of species governed by its genetic attributes. The biotic potential of a species is the maximum possible growth rate determined by the reproductive potential. The concept is based on the number of births per female per unit of time (a year or month or day or hour) in the absence of any limiting conditions, like limitedness of food availability and habitat. The biotic potential varies from species to species; for example, one female housefly and her offspring theoretically can produce 6 trillion house flies in a year, while a female elephant and her offspring will produce 19 million elephants in 750 years. The population doubling time is an indicator of biotic potential, with higher the potential, lower the time. The doubling time varies from minutes in the case of bacteria to several years in the case of elephants.

Biotic potentials are not fully realized due to environmental resistance factors like lack of food, disease, predation, lack of space, etc. The environmental resistance factors are of two basic types—density dependent factors and density independent factors. Density dependent factors are those which exert pressure on population due to its size in a particular region. Climatic conditions, seasonal changes or temperature fluctuations exercise basic influence on the reproductive ability of each individual irrespective of the size of the local population of the concerned species. The same is true of the adverse reproductive effect of chemical pollution of an area on the individuals of population of species.

The density dependent factors of environmental resistance include a wide range of factors like access to food, access to habitat, impact of parasites, predators, pathogens, epidemic disease, etc. Certain physiological control mechanisms may act as population growth regulators, especially in vertebrates, depending on the density of population. For example, increase in the density of rat population has been found to cause enlargement of their adrenal gland indicating stress with adverse effect on fertility rate. All the factors together influence population growth rate by: (a) the probability that an individual will live till maturity, and (b) the fertility rate. At the limit, density dependent factors set a bound on the population size exerting increasing pressure for suppressing population growth. The environmental carrying capacity is the largest size of a population that can be sustained by the resources of an ecosystem and describes an equilibrium situation where the forces of biotic potential and environmental resistance balance each other. The future population growth of a species is influenced not only by the biotic potential and the environmental resistance to its realization, but also by the age specific pattern of survival and the age structure of the concerned population. The relationship between the age and the number of survivors till that age is represented by the curve of survivorship. Among the species there are three types of survivorship as represented by curves A, B, and C in Figure 5.1. The pattern of survivorship following curve C indicates that most of the individual organisms survive to their maximum life span because the factors causing death among young organisms are relatively few as seen in man and mountain sheep. The survivorship pattern as exhibited by curve B indicates equiprobability of death at any age; for example, some birds and aquatic organisms like hydra. The survivorship pattern as described by curve A is illustrated by organisms like oak tree, frogs, oysters, etc. A large proportion of the offsprings die young and cannot survive the age of reproductivity. The reproductive pattern as determined by the genetic characteristics and environmental resistance factors for the concerned species,, influence the shape of its survivorship

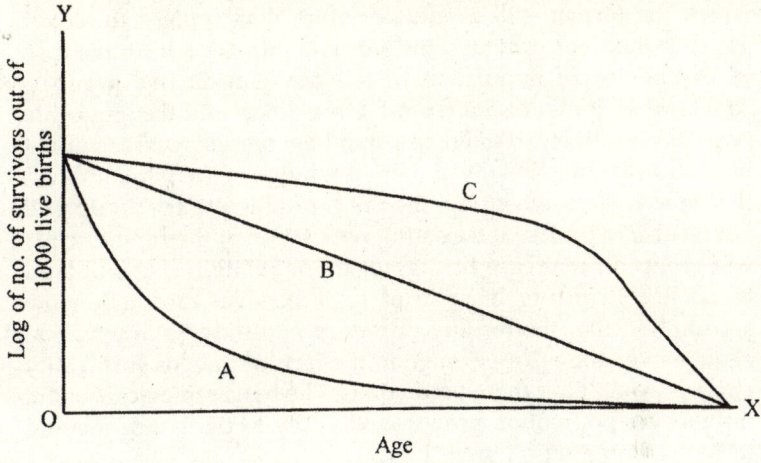

Figure 5.1   Age survivality curve.

curve. Any improvement of survival pattern for a time will have the greatest effect on population growth for the case of curve C, relatively less in the case of curve B and the least for species characterized by curve A.

The age structure of population of species at any time as represented by the agewise frequency distribution of the entire population, indicates its growth potential in future. The classification of age classes into three groups—pre-reproductive, reproductive and post-reproductive is quite useful for the purpose of examining the population growth potential of any species at any given time. The distribution of population into these three groups would indicate whether a population is growing or shrinking or remaining in steady state. Figure 5.2 shows the growth potential of population for the different distributions of population among the age classes assuming high rate of survival. The patterns A, B and C in the figure show existence of bulges in the distribution in the pre-reproductive, reproductive and post-reproductive age groups and predicts growing, stable and declining population respectively for high survival rate. In the case of age distribution of A, the population of the range $L_0 = 0$ to $L_1 = $ maximum life span, pre-reproductive group is much larger in size than that of the reproductive group as a result of which the former will eventually more than replace the latter group in number provided the survivorship is high. In the case of B, the size of population of the pre-reproductive group is comparable to that of the reproductive group and the aggregate population is likely to stabilize around the present level assuming high survival rate. Finally, if there is a bulge in the population in the reproductive age group, the pre-reproductive age group will not be able to replace the existing population of the reproductive age group. In that case the aggregate population size will tend to decline in future in spite of high survival rate, given the assumption that the fertility rate does not undergo any radical change over time. Any change in the fertility rate or survivality pattern would alter these predictions. The basic ecological factors influencing population growth will apply to the issues relating to human population growth.

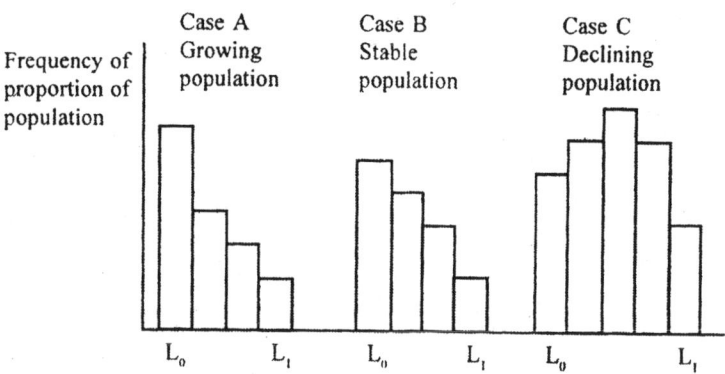

Figure 5.2   Age structure and population growth

Biotic Population Growth Pattern

If a species is introduced in a new habitat and favourable environment, the biotic potential would have a dominating influence on the actual behaviour of population growth. Let N be the size of female population in reproductive age group, r be the reproductive potentials, that is, of births per female per year. Thus rN would be the addition to population per unit of time. If the age structure of population and the sex ratio remain stable, then

N can be interpreted as the total population and r the number of births per unit of population per year. However, since any ecosystem provides only limited space and food energy resources, density dependent factors would very likely delimit this exponential growth and what is likely to follow is either a J-shaped growth curve or a sigmoid curve. The J-shaped curve (i.e., like the letter J) describes exponential growth up to a point at which the most of the population dies off because of the density dependent pressure which causes a sudden change in the conditions of existence resulting in collapse. For example, the growth of bacteria in a bottle of milk ends up with a crash that occurs due to food depletion. Figure 5.3 illustrates such growth of population, p showing population size and the stage of population growth at which sharp adverse impact of density dependent factors causes most of the members of population to die off in the immediate future. The population growth curve OAB is an illustration. The p often substantively exceeds the environmental carrying capacity size. Such species are opportunists as they literally eat and live themselves out of house and local existence. It is, however, possible that the species experiences collapse of its population size even before the carrying capacity size of the population has been reached, which occurs due to the density independent environmental resistance factor

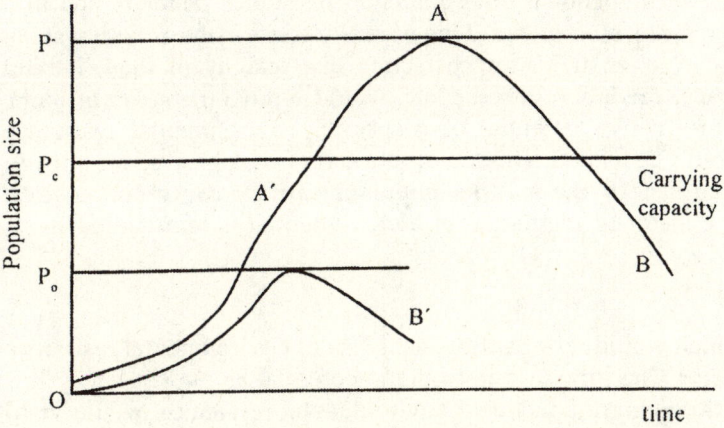

Figure 5.3   J-shaped patterns of population growth.

like cyclical or seasonal change in temperature, climate change in physical conditions of existence for organisms like annual plants and insects. The population growth curve OA' B' is an illustration. The species of this category are often called seasonal or cyclical opportunists.

The more common pattern of population growth among animals and plants is represented by Sigmoid (S-shaped) growth curve (see Figure 5.4(a)) where density dependent limiting factors gradually limit population growth. In this case population size is so regulated by such limiting factors that it gradually approaches the environmental carrying capacity of the ecosystem. Initially, growth may, push the population size above the carrying capacity. In such an event, the size of the population is expected to quickly fall back towards the carrying capacity or approach it through damped oscillations around the carrying capacity value (see Figure 5.4(b)).

The mathematical form of the Sigmoid pattern of population growth for Figure 5.4(a) can be represented and explained as follows:

$$\frac{dN}{dt} = rN\frac{A-N}{A}$$

where N = population, A = carrying capacity of the ecosystem in terms of the size of the concerned species and t = time. The density dependent environmental resistance factor builds in a regulating mechanism of the population size in the growth system. Environmental resistance factors like scarcity of food, habitat space, predation, disease, etc. would reduce the effect of biotic reproductive potential of a species. Environmental resistance would be related with the proportion of ecological space already occupied by the existing population of the concerned species. The factor of regulation of biotic potential is represented by

$$\frac{A-N}{A}$$

which would represent the net effect of environmental resistance factor. The growth due to biotic potential as multiplied by this ratio giving the factor of environmental resistance, would yield the net effect on the growth of population (addition of number of organisms in the species) as given in the above equation. While

Population size

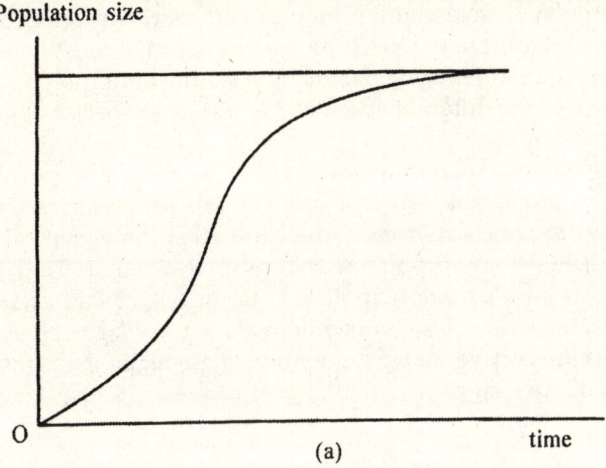

(a)   time

Population size

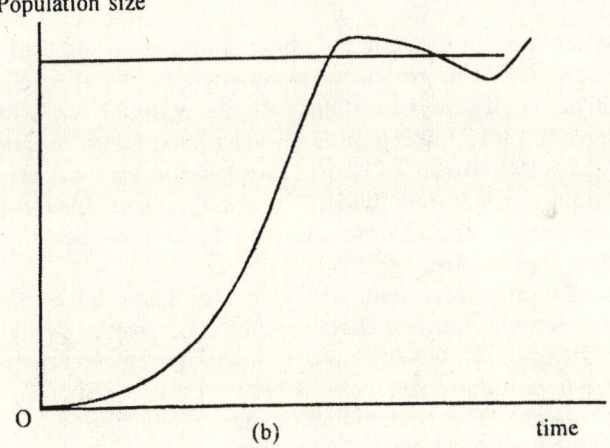

(b)   time

Figure 5.4   S-shaped pattern of population growth

the ratio of (A–N)/A is quite simple, it is, difficult to demonstrate how different individual resistance factors like habitat space, predation competition or disease etc. would have the delimiting effect on the realization of biotic potential. Although food is the ultimate regulator for many population in various ecosystems, growth of a species has collapsed or halted at times even before the food supply became scarce. The question of ultimate regulation of population size is quite complex and controversial. Ecologists point out different regulation factors which are ultimately of significance in reducing natality and setting limits on population growth of the different species or of the same species in varying circumstances.

The Sigmoid curve equation is not the only mathematical form that would characterize population growth of species and is subject to criticism. There are several other mathematical forms which might be appropriate for empirical estimation. The sigmoid curve is an illustration applicable to unicellar plant or animals which have short life span without almost any lag between birth and reproductive maturity, reproduce asexually and have high reproductive rates.

Human Population Growth

What has been the dynamics of human population and the history of its growth? The growth of population at global level is the result of natality and mortality. At the regional level, the net immigration into the region is an additional factor to consider. The growth pattern of world population has experienced enormous changes over time due to changes in the birth rate and the death rate, and their underlying factors like fertility rate, survival pattern and age distribution.

Population grew very slowly for many millennia but accelerated in the last two centuries. There have been occasional periods like the fourteenth century in Europe which experienced an absolute decline in population of about 25 per cent due to bubonic plague (black death). The first major increase in the growth rate of population took place 10,000 years ago with the successful mobilization of energy for human life support through development of agriculture. The second major acceleration in population growth occurred at the advent of industrial revolution approximately two centuries ago with the development of fuel powered ecosystem which provided stronger life support. During the same period, the developments in medicine and health care as a result of advances in science and technology contributed to substantive reductions in death rates.

In AD 1650 human population numbered around 0.5 billion and was growing at the rate 0.3 per cent per annum corresponding to a doubling time of 250 years. By AD 1900 the world population had reached 1.6 billion with a growth rate of 0.5 per cent per year. By 1970 world population became 3.6 billion and with a growth of 2.1 per cent per year with substantive acceleration of population growth due to fall in death rate. Between 1971 and 1991 world population further rose to the level of 5.4 billion accompanied by the fall of rate of growth of population from the level of 2.1 per cent in 1971 to 1.7 per cent in 1991. While global birth rate were falling since the middle of the 20th century, it was falling slower than the death rate. Since 1970, the average birth rate has fallen slightly faster than the death rate contributing to the deceleration of the global population growth rate. The time pattern of growth of human population can be seen in terms of time taken in increment of every one billion people as in Table 5.1. World population has doubled from 0.75 billion in 1750 to 1.6 billion in 1900, further doubled to 3.3 billion in 1965 and is expected to achieve the doubling level of 7.0 billion in 2010. The doubling time has been reduced from 150 years to 65 years to 45 years in the period of 250 years. The reduction in time indicates the increasing pressure that population growth and the accompanying human activities are going to cause on the limited resources of the biosphere (see Koromondy 1999).

Neither the growth rates nor the absolute size of the population are uniformly distributed over the different regions of the world (see Tables 5.2 to 5.5). The different fertility and mortality combinations as determined by the economic, historical and

Table 5.1
Historical patterns of human population growth

Increment in population	Year of reaching the billion level
From 0 to 1 billion	1800 or 2 to 5 million years
1 to 2 billion	1930 or 130 years
2 to 3 billion	1960 or 30 years
3 to 4 billion	1975 or 15 years
4 to 5 billion	1987 or 12 years
5 to 6 billion	1998 or 11 years

Source: Koromondy (1999), p. 390

Table 5.2
Distribution of the world population by per capita GNP (1998)

GNP per capita	Population (in million)	GNP per capita US$	GNP $ billion	Population density (No. of persons per km²)
Low income	3515	520	1843.7	85
Lower-middle income	908	1710	1557.4	25
Upper-middle income	588	4860	2862.1	27
High income	885	25510	22599.0	29
World	5897	4890	28862.0	45

Source: World Bank (1999), World Development Report, 1999–2000.

Table 5.3
Distribution of the population of low and middle income countries
in different regions (1998)

Regions	GNP per capita $	Population in millions	GNP billion $	Number of persons per km²
East Asia and Pacific	990	1817	1801.6	114
Europe and Central Asia	2190	473	1038.8	20
Latin America and Caribbean	3940	502	1977.6	25
Middle East and North Africa	2050	285	585.6	26
South Asia	430	1305	555.5	273
sub-Saharan Africa	480	628	304.2	27
Overall	1250	5011	6263.3	50

Source: World Bank (1999), World Development Report 1999–2000.

cultural conditions along with demographic characteristics of societies would explain these variations in the growth of population across regions. Some of the least industrialized countries of Africa (sub-Saharan Africa) have population with high mortality rate and an even higher fertility rate. Their population growth ranges between 2 and 3 per cent which would possibly go up as mortality declines with rise in income. The currently industrializing countries of the southern world like Brazil, Thailand, Egypt, etc. have low mortality rate while their fertility is still high, though declining. These countries have population growth rate in the medium to high range like 1 per cent to 4 per cent per year. Most of the industrialized countries

Table 5.4
Natural growth of population and state of development (1993)

Regions	GNP per capita US$	Crude Birth rate%	Crude Death rate%	Natural growth rate%	Total fertility rate%
Low income countries	380	28	10	1.8	3.6
Lower-middle income	1590	23	9	1.4	3.0
Upper-middle income	4370	24	7	1.7	3.0
High income	23090	13	9	0.4	1.7
World	4420	25	9	1.6	3.2
India	300	29	10	1.9	3.7

Source: World Bank (1995), World Development Report.

Table 5.5
Distribution of world population according to population growth rate and per capita GNP (1985–94)

Population growth rate (per annum) (%)	GNP per capita ($)*	Proportion of population in %
> 3	1410	5.3
2.2–3	1300	16.0
1.5–2.1	1010	33.6
1.0–1.4	5680	28.9
< 1.0	14660	15.9
No data	870	0.1

*Data pertains to 1994.
Source: Gupta and Asher (1998), p. 33.

Table 5.6
Population estimates* for the world and South Asia (1970–2150)

(million)

Major areas	1970	1980	2000	2050	2100	2150
1. World						
Rapid	3645	4387	5923	8172	8389	8382
Slow	3645	4460	6670	13025	15102	15148
2. South Asia						
Rapid	1103	1413	2079	3077	3166	3163
Slow	1103	1447	2469	5916	7170	7197

*The estimates are based on rapid and slow paths of convergence to a stationary state of population; rapid path and slow path are based on the respective time horizons 2000–5 and 2040–5 for the achievement of net reproduction rate of 1.
Source: Koromondy (1994), ch. 6.

on the other hand like North America, Japan and Europe have low mortality and low fertility rates contributing to very low population growth rate below 1 per cent. Table 5.6 gives population estimates for the world and South Asia region for the period 1970 to 2150. It shows the population sizes at different points of time with the approach to stabilized population characterized by net reproductive rate of 1. The net reproductive rate is defined as the number of female offsprings of the next generation replacing a single female of a given generation. The projections are based on rapid and slow paths of convergence to stabilized population depending on the time horizon by which net reproductive rate of unity is achieved—2000–5 for rapid and 2040–5 for slow paths. The regional variation in the future size of population will have important implications in respect of differential environmental stress that would be caused by the size of human population and their activities relative to natural and environmental resource endowments in the different parts of the world (see Meadows *et al.* 1992; Gupta *et al.* 1998; World Bank 2000; Koromondy 1994).

The basic principles of population growth and its regulation by environmental resistance factors are valid for all species. In the case of human beings, the biotic potential is similarly determined by biological conditions and is given by the natural fertility rate of women, that is, the potential maximum number of live births delivered by a woman in her reproductive life using age specific fertility rate in a favourable environment in the absence of socio-cultural restriction. However, the natural fertility rate is not realised because of socio-cultural factors induced by environmental resistance. Unlike other species, man has made almost continuous adaptation of his technology, institutions, socio-economic practices, customs and culture to changes in environment due to population growth. The population density-induced scarcity of food and resources has driven human society to innovate technology and social arrangement of production and distribution so that the environmental resistance is weakened, on the one hand, and on the other, evolve socio-cultural conditions which would restrain the realization of the natural fertility rate and reduce birth rate.

Malthus pointed out that in the fourth, food production of human society would grow at the slower rate of arithmetic progression due to the limitedness of land resource, whereas the realization of the natural fertility rate would result in faster growth of population in geometric progression. Malthus predicted that as a result of the growth process human population would exceed the carrying capacity of land, and the environmental resistance factors such as acute scarcity of food, war, disease, pestilence, etc. would control the natural fertility rate and bring down the population level. The population growth curve should then be a J-shaped curve followed by a crash as per such theory. Since, man's ability to control nature has been considerably enhanced over time, the Malthusian predictions have been falsified. In human culture the size of family in terms of number of children has evolved as a matter of choice, determined by the relative scarcity or abundance of food and other resources required for life support and well-being. Human culture adopted birth control measures and self-regulation of population growth has become a built in feature of the process. As a result, the growth curve of human population is likely to be of Sigmoid or S-shaped curve with damped oscillations in case of any overshooting, and convergence to environmental carrying capacity, instead of being a Malthusian J-shaped curve followed by crash. The adaptive capacity of human society to changing population density has, however, depended upon the stage of development of manmade capital, technology and knowledge base. According to the theory of demographic transition of human societies, at the low levels of industrialization and income, both birth and death rates are high and population growth is slow. As an economy industrializes and develops in terms of growth of income, employment and quality of life index, the death rate falls and the birth rate falls with a lag behind by one generation or two causing a gap between the fertility and the mortality rate resulting in rapid population growth. Finally, as an economy reaches the advanced stage of industrial development and people's life style evolves in full industrial mode, birth rate falls further and nearer to death rate level and population growth rate falls if not becomes zero. As an economy is better able to mobilize energy for providing more of food (energy), nutrition and health care, on the one hand, the death rate falls and, on the other hand, the environmental resistance factor is weakened. The rise in the availability of food, nutrition and health care with development causes first of all a fall in the infant mortality rate and the mortality of women of reproductive age group while delivering. All these contribute to changes in the shape of the survivorship pattern and the age structure of population of the concerned country. However, economic development also gives rise to changes in the level of education, women's status in society and cultural condition which cause a shift in the preference pattern of the people in favour of a smaller family (i.e., lower number of children per family) and use of family planning methods (like use of pill, condom, IUD, sterilization, etc.). The reduction in the infant mortality rate has a definite role in influencing the choices in favour of a lower fertility rate. Besides, the presence or absence of societal policy initiatives regarding population control and the role of female education, women's employment, and the gender related cultural condition would make difference in the nature of corresponding level of development and birth or fertility rate; for example, China and Sri Lanka have anomalously low birth rates of 19 and 20 for their respective level of incomes of US$ 490 and 600 in 1993 while several middle Eastern countries like United Arab Emirates have anomalously high birth rate (23 for United Arab Republic) for their respective high levels of income (US$ 21430 per capita). Table 5.4 shows that the relationship between the per capita GNP and total fertility rate is not a strict one although there exists a broad correlation between demographic parameters and stages of development.

The time lag between the fall in death rate and a matching fall in birth rate is the real challenge in the form of population explosion. Given the ecological resource endowments of a country it is important that the self-regulatory mechanism for population control is effective before the population surpasses the environment's carrying capacity. If a high energy consuming population exceeds the environmental carrying capacity the alternative to self-regulation would be a painful adjustment process through realization of high death rates due to pestilence, starvation, severe pollution, war and social upheavals as posited by Malthus. The choice seems to be between reduction of birth rate or rise in death rate as a fall out of exceeding the carrying capacity of the land.

The entire problem arises from the crisis of unsustainable growth of population which is realized at macro level as a result of the aggregate effect of all individual decisions regarding family size at micro level. If the delay in the shift of preference of individual households in favour of lower fertility stresses the environmental capacity limit, it would lead to a situation of conflict between the right of the parents to have the number of children they want and the right of society to have the number of children it needs. Some macro-level policy initiatives for birth control like forced sterilization which have been adopted in China to ensure fall in birth rate, violates the spirit of individual's freedom and democratic norm. It has, therefore, become important that economic development is accompanied by fast rise in female literacy, knowledge and social awareness about family planning, status of women in society, etc. so that the aggregate birth rate as a result of free individual choice falls in line with the falling death rate. To meet the problem of population growth, the policy initiatives backed by science and technology have to play a role in reducing the potential growth rate of population by influencing economic and cultural factors and raising the environmental carrying capacity of human population.

Population Density, Migration and Trade

With growth of population density, the natural resource to human population ratio goes down, straining the life support system of humans and resource supply to their economy. In order to counter the effect of such pressures, the people of a given geographic unit adapt to the new resource—population ratio by any of the following methods:

(a) Introduction of technical change which raises productivity of resources and thereby augments the carrying capacity of a given amount of resource (in terms of number of people that can be supported).

(b) Migration of population from a region of lower per capita resource endowment to one with higher per capita resource endowment.

(c) Trade of goods and services between countries, which would ensure inflow of commodities or services whose domestic availability is limited due to scarcity of natural resources. Trade would also (by way of exports) cause outflow of items which can be produced in surplus by the concerned country due to favourable resource supply situation.

All these can contribute in different ways to the expansion of the global carrying capacity of human population. The following three subsections explain further, these three ways of adaptation of a socio-economic system to population growth.

Density and Use of Manmade Capital and Technology

As per the relationship between density and rate of growth of natural population of many species in the ecosystems, the rate of population growth is expected to increase in a favourable environment and decline subsequently in the face of environmental resistance. However, population growth has not shown any strict correlation between density and demographic growth rate of population. In the cross section data of various regions it is observed that high population density has been accompanied by both high and low natural growth rate as determined by the birth and the death rates. Both Asia and Europe had density of 99 per sq. km. and 98 per sq. km. respectively with corresponding respective population growth of 1.9 per cent and 0.4 per cent as per the World Population Data Sheet 1982 of the World Bank. Africa and Latin America have had low density and high growth rate of population as against North

America and the former Soviet Union which have low density and low growth rate.

The difference between the behaviour of the human population and the natural population of other species lies in the fact that unlike other species, human beings control natural forces and utilise resources through production processes to create goods and services with utilitarian values determining their level of well-being. In the mechanics of transformation to create values and render well-being, manmade capital (i.e., machines, buildings, infrastructure, know-how, etc.) made out of the accumulated surplus of past products and values play an important role as the use of man made capital facilitates such division of labour that augments productivity of labour, per capita income. It is, therefore, the endowment of land and natural resources per capita along with the endowment of manmade capital per capita which together determine the level of per capita net social product and the level of development of an economy. The theory of demographic transition of human population points to the role of the stage of development (and thereby implicitly of manmade capital) in the dynamics of population growth. The difference between the Asian and the European population growth rates is easily explainable in terms of the relative high level of accumulation of manmade capital per capita in Europe vis-à-vis Asia. The development of technology enhances the environmental carrying capacity of a region. In developed industrialized economies, technology enables a higher carrying capacity for a unit of its area or environmental resources of its ecosystem independent of population density in a certain range. Population density has also played an important role in inducing such development and application of technology which efficiently resolve problems of housing and urban development, water adequacy, etc. Technology, however, cannot substitute critical environmental services like air purification, life support function of biodiversity, etc. thereby setting limits to the role of technology in increasing the carrying capacity of the ecosystem.

Migration

Human society in any given region has attempted to overcome the constraint of environmental resistance due to growth in the density of population in two more ways other than technology development in a closed system—(a) migration and (b) trade across regions. Most of the great intercontinental or intracontinental migrations took place because of the pressure of population on the local land and resources. While migration in the world of other animal species like birds or fishes has often been seasonal and induced by the limiting factors imposed by the climatic conditions or suitability of environment for reproduction, for example, penguin's or hilsas' seasonal migration, human migration has been of more permanent duration. Although seasonal rural-urban migration has been a phenomenon in India induced by the seasonality of agricultural operations and labour scarcity in rural economy, most of the permanent migrations have been in search of employment and economic opportunities as offered by the endowments of natural resource, manmade capital and technology. While low natural resource endowment per capita has tended to push people out of a place or a region, high natural resource endowment tended to pull or attract population. Although the natural environmental resource and the manmade capital together would define the pull or push factor, environmental and natural resource per capita like land-man ratio or fresh water-man ratio, other biotic/abiotic resource to man ratio, has in the long run played a more fundamental role in migration. The great migrations of the 19th and the 20th centuries from Europe and Asia into North America, Africa, Latin America and Oceania can be explained in terms of such variation in resource to man ratio among other factors. Manmade capital has higher marginal return where resource to man ratio is high and manmade capital base is small when compared to economies with high population density and low capital as well as resource availability per capita, for example, the history of immigration of various peoples into India since ancient times till the advent of British. The current reversal trend of people emigrating out of the Indian subcontinent for obtaining work or business opportunities and settling in North America, Middle East or other continents is substantiated by the high density of populations and increasing pressure on the nature's resources when combined with the scarcity of manmade capital in South Asia.

One may, however, argue that migration from rural to urban areas had happened significantly until the 1970s in India in spite of the low land–man ratio and scarcity of other natural resources in an urban ecosystem. The explanation is given in terms of high level of development and availability of infrastructural capital and heavy import of resources from outside into the urban centres vis-à-vis the rural areas of the economy. The highly energy intensive industrial development and technological achievements in the urban centres and the contiguous suburban areas vastly increase the number of people that can live in those areas. Hundreds of acres of land, thousands of sources of water resources and huge amounts of other natural resources are required to provide support to these 'hot spots' i.e. locations of high concentration of urban population and infrastructural construct per unit of area, by supplying food and other life supporting services and raw materials for industrial development. The high import of resources from rural ecosystem to urban ecosystem as induced by the higher level of development of infrastructural and industrial capital has turned urban centres into places of better economic opportunities by improving the supply side conditions. Such urban centres thus attract population while rural poverty as combined with lack of manmade infrastrural capital pushes people out of rural economies particularly in places where agricultural productivity is low, land is too fragmented, non-farm income opportunities are low and consequently poorer people do not have enough cash income to meet their basic needs.

Trade and Liberalization

The pressure of growing human population has been mitigated not only by the migration of population but by direct or indirect import-export of natural resources from one ecosystem to another. The natural resources flow into the urban system either in raw primary product form or as processed goods. Such flows of natural resources in primary or secondary processed form also take place across regions and countries to mitigate the impact of adverse resource to man ratio for certain product items. Development of trade pattern is complicated. Trade—internal or external, of goods as well as services—ensures the ultimate distribution of natural resources or their benefits as per the needs of the people of the different parts of the world as supported by their respective purchasing power and expressed through prices in the different markets. The relative per capita availability of resources when compared across regions or countries indicates the comparative advantages of countries in trade based on natural resource endowments and influences the terms of trade among them in the long run competitive situation. Given the development of complex human culture and multiplication of needs, trade mediates directly or indirectly between the needs of human population of different regions for various natural resources and environmental services and their availabilities. Among the various needs, food and energy are quite crucial as life support. We have states like West Bengal and Kerala which are deficit in food supply while Punjab and Haryana are surplus states. The hydrocarbon energy resources are also very unevenly distributed across the countries. The Organisation of Petroleum Exporting Countries or the OPEC of the Middle East and the South-East Asia own almost three-fourths of the balance of recoverable oil reserves of the world. Most of the industrialized nations are, therefore, deficit in energy. Europe is deficit in food while the North America or Oceania are surplus in food. Trade has mediated between domestic demand and availabilities while the global market and prices have served as institutions for trade.

The growing global pressure of population on ecological resources has over time strengthened the tendency of migration of people from poverty-stricken regions of the world to the higher income countries with favourable land–man ratio or resource–man ratio. The development of nationalism in tandem with industrialization and economic development has gradually induced many countries to resist immigration of people from other countries. The nationalist interest to protect their own economic interest, identity and culture has led to legal and political initiatives on the part of the relatively developed countries to deal with the pressure of immigration. The present global consensus is, however, in favour of encouraging movement of capital, technology and trade in goods and services instead of migration of people for settlement to correct the adverse effect of regional imbalance of ecological resource to human population ratio. This presumes market to be free from imperfections, uncertainties and any significant transaction cost of policies of such liberalization. The problem of low manmade capital to man ratio and low land resource to man ratio resulting in poverty, creates the condition of inadequate or small home market and the attendant problem of uncertainty of return to capital. If liberalization is not adequate to resolve the problem posed by unequal distribution of natural resource and income among the peoples of the world, poverty and inequality are bound to persist giving rise to socio-political tensions, conflicts, and more of security and military expenditure which would again in turn counter the basic objectives of resolving the problem of inequality. While the global community will have a responsibility of making manmade resource transfer, that is, transfer of finance and technology to alleviate poverty, the countries would be required at national level to put great emphasis on demographic management and population control through policy initiatives such as female literacy, gender status, family planning, etc. The rise in the density of population is likely to induce sooner or later such policy behaviour which would result in moderating and ultimately stabilizing the population at the level of environmental carrying capacity. Even if an over populated country like India or China is found to have exercised the limit of carrying capacity, their societal level policy behaviour is expected to delimit the extent of overshooting and dampen any oscillations, to ensure the convergence of population size to a level at carrying capacity if not lower. The policy initiatives in such countries would be in the spheres of population and technology. While the population policy's main concern would be the factors for stabilization of population, the technology policy would aim at the enhancing of nature's carrying capacity of human number.

Population and Environment

Human society creates demand on environment in two ways: first, like all other species of the ecosystem homo sapiens as one of the biotic species, depends on nature for life support that is, oxygen, water, and some natural foods. Second, unlike other species homo sapiens, transform through production process, materials and energy drawn from nature into consumable goods and services. The size of an economy whose growth would cause strain and pressure on the nature has two aspects requiring consideration: (a) size in terms of population and (b) size in terms of GDP. These two factors have interactive relationship. The stage of capital accumulation and development of an economy influences the process of demographic transition and the growth of population. On the other hand, the growth of population in an economy would have an effect on the production system and influence the scale, composition and technology of the economy depending among others on the local natural resource base. Every society and economy adapt to the population pressure so that in spite of the pressure of numbers the distribution of social product among the members of population does not go beyond the tolerance limits of inequality or gap between the rich and the poor. The institutional arrangement of an economy—legal, economic (market and non-market) and socio-cultural—determines the nature of distribution of its social product. The institutions evolve arrangements to accommodate the needs of the growing population while attempting at the same time to control the population growth through policies. However, the nature of such a structural adjustment of society and economy to growing population would depend on the endowment of manmade capital and access to technology. Even if two economies are found to have the same absolute level of GDP (measured in terms of international purchasing power parity dollar), but very different size of population, the likely difference in capital to man ratio would make the composition of the social product as aggregated into GDP and the associated technology to be quite different. The economy with higher population is likely to have: (a) a greater share of food and necessities in the basket of commodities services which the social product or GDP comprises of and (b) higher labour intensity because of the likely low ratio of capital to population. Such choices of product mix and technology are often driven by distribution considerations arising from the political economic compulsions specially of a democratic regime. To the extent the choice of technology and product-mix as guided by the initiatives of institutions are influenced by the population size the latter would have its impact on the ecosystem. The ecological and economic effects of population growth would have a feed back effect on population growth itself. The demographic, technological, economic, ecological and cultural factors of a society influence each other in a web-like manner. The mechanics of these interactions is quite complex and it is difficult, if not impossible, to strictly separate the partial effects of variation of population and that of GDP as pure scale factors on nature and environmental quality. However, it remains true that the interaction of the complex factors is likely to exert a regulating influence on population growth so that it does not violate the carrying capacity.

Ecology of the Poor

There is, no definite law of behaviour of the socio-economic systems which would guarantee that carrying capacity limits are not violated by human population growth. The success of a society in regulating population growth and not violating sustainability condition of resource use would depend on the extent of success in resolving the distribution problem which is attendant with growing population. In the countries of high population density in the Afro-Asian region the extent of success has often been far less than the sustainability mark. To the extent an economy can successfully absorb the growing labour force in effective employment, it can mitigate the problem of poverty and accompanying environmental degradation. The growing unemployment in developing countries which is a consequence of population growth, would lead to a rise in the number of people without any income and property right to well defined resource endowment. Even if in the rural economy, everybody has property right, the availability of land per capita is bound to fall with increase in population leading to fragmentation of landholdings. As agricultural productivity of small holdings is likely to decline due to increased fragmentation, agricultural income per family would decline and lead to dispossession of land due to cash need of families to meet basic necessities. Landless people would join either the landless labour class in the rural system or migrate to urban area to join the urban labour force. The other option which is often exercised by the poor in developing countries is forest burning or forcible occupation of open access common property land and its conversion into cropland, leading to ecological imbalance in land use. Deforestation and farming on hill areas causes soil erosion and flooding. However, even if the rural marginal or poor farmers are able to practise agriculture, they often over use the land for cultivation by unsustainable agricultural practices such as mono-cropping and shifting cultivation with too short fallow periods resulting in exhaustion of nutrients in soil. Overpopulation and poverty do not permit investment consideration in land and resulted in its degradation and unsustainable agricultural practices in many Afro–Asian countries. Besides, the fuel needs of the poor has been met from trees or plants from forests causing deforestation. The collection of fuel wood has also been time consuming resulting in loss of opportunity of earning income.

The rural–urban migration of the poor in overpopulated economic system has often led to the unauthorised occupation and use of land in both rural and urban areas. In rural or urban areas most of the unauthorised settlements have been in open access land, forest, pasture, community land or in private land by forcible occupation. In a metropolitan city like Calcutta in India the city footpath or roadside land area reserved for road use have become either habitat of the poor or centers of unauthorized commercial activities. Most of the city slums in developing countries like India first develop as unauthorized colonies which are later given legal recognition under political and economic pressure. The violation of property rights with their resultant dilution has become the strategy of the poor and the marginalised against the mainstream economic system.

In spite of property right violation the density of population in such unauthorized settlements of urban areas is very high with inadequate access to water and almost no access to sanitation. In rural area the same problems exist although the density of such settlement may not be too high at one place. Water collection, like that of fuel wood, has often involved long hours of travel and labour and loss of income opportunities in hilly or dry areas. Besides the inadequacy of water availability combined with the lack of access to sanitation leads to serious problem of water pollution and health problem. Given the limited access of common people to water, people are forced to use the same water for their own bathing, bathing of cattle as well as for drinking. While the local ecosystems of rural areas can absorb the household wastes (including human excreta), urban slums with high population density and paved surfaces, pose serious problems of uncollected unabsorbed wastes. It is quite natural that the settlements of the poor whch have grown in unauthorized unplanned manner in the urban system would face problems of serious pollution due to lack of adequate water supply, sanitation and waste disposal. The ill-defined nature of property rights has in fact been an impediment in the way of appropriate social intervention by way of investment in infrastructure in such unauthorized settlements.

Population growth with growing number of the unemployed, endowed with little or no natural resources in a country with low manmade capital to population ratio, leads to appropriation of natural resources of land, water and forest, which are apparently open access property irrespective of their legal status in respect of property rights. Such resources are inevitably overused leading to either depletion or degradation. The poor would operate outside the market system and consume natural resources directly for survival by either over harvesting it (for example, deforestation) or depleting useful chemical contents (for example, exhaustion of nutrients of soil). The degradation of natural resource would mean decline in its efficiency in production or in rendering direct use value and decline of availability of the concerned natural resources in efficiency unit with reference to human use and requirement. The growth of population pressure with worsening of the distribution problem thus reduces further the resource to man ratio through not only rise in the denominator but also fall in the value of the numerator. This decline in ratio reduces carrying capacity of nature and biological limits to growth and aggravates the problem of sustainable development.

Ecology of the Affluent

Does the above discussion hint at that the affluent would be environmentally friendly and cause little stress on the environment and moderate the rise in entropy in comparison with the effects of the living of the poor? The development theorists propagating the idea of Environmental Kuznet's Curve (World Bank 1992; Grossman and Krueger 1995) believe and try to empirically establish that in the initial phase of development the environmental quality of a society will deteriorate up to a threshhold level of per capita income. Beyond that level, environmental quality improves as the per capita income increases for the economy. The environmental quality is defined in terms of concentration of some pollutants or short duration pollution flows in air, water body or in the soil. While the issue is still debated, the major thrust of the argument behind such thesis is that the demand for environmental quality and services is income elastic. In other words, the rich have a stronger preference for cleaner environment which is reflected in their voting for resource conservation and stringent regulation for ensuring environmental quality. The industrialized countries, as a result, have lower energy intensity and material resource intensity per unit of their income or social product. Besides, given the higher ability to pay for technology and infrastructure, a rich society has access to latest technological developments and has a better infrastructural arrangement for waste disposal and treatment. It is argued that all these should contribute to the resolution of conflict between development and environment.

The problem, however, emerges elsewhere. Environmental stress arises not just because of the high or low per capita income or consumption or of the high or low pollution intensity of product, but also due to the absolute pressure on nature imposed by the size of the population and the aggregate level of economic activities as summarily measured by the GDP. While the rich would choose a smaller family size and not be responsible for taxing the environment with increasing population pressure, they would nevertheless create pressure by way of their appropriation of a major share of the GDP and a large absolute size of income. This is particularly true for most of the developing countries where the income and assets are very unequally distributed. The high per capita income of the rich promotes high level of per capita as well as aggregate consumption. Many of the products and infrastructural services consumed by them are highly energy and pollution intensive when compared with the product-mix of consumption of the poor. This is valid even if the rich have chosen the cleanest available technology to produce the same. Besides, high per capita income often leads to wasteful consumption and life style because of consumerism. Since the rich procure all their consumption items through market and the capitalist market system is destined to promote consumerism to ensure the prevalence of a high level of effective demand, saleability of products and returns to investment, the rich are doomed to develop values of wasteful consumption and life style. The rich in India may switch to an energy efficient car and save energy; but the benefit of such energy saving would be offset if the total number of vehicles used by the community increases due to higher income of the rich and consumerism. Use of packaging is also an example of wasteful practice which becomes imperative due to the organization of production of such societies.

The enormously high per capita energy and material consumption level in an industrialized economy as compared to a poorer one, impacts negatively the ecosystem. In spite of the higher energy or material efficiency of the production processes of the former, huge consumption would have its impact on nature by way of large scale withdrawal of virgin resources as well as large scale disposal of wastes for absorption. Besides, the product-mix of the rich involves use of chemicals and man made compounds that are non-biodegradable and hazardous which leads to the serious problem of absorption of wastes by the ecosystem. The rich in the developing countries compounds the problem further in comparison with the rich of the industrialized countries, since the former often tries to follow the model of the life style of the latter while the economic system of the former has not as yet been able to adopt the best of the technologies and infrastructure for producing the concerned pollution intensive products and disposing wastes.

Both the poor and the rich in a developing country cause environmental stress in different ways and for different reasons. The poor spoil the environment because of not having employment, income and access to market which in turn forces them to directly consume and destroy the natural environment. The rich, on the other hand, have access to employment and income and operate only through market. For their having too large a share of income in a skewed distribution, the market promotes wasteful and indefinitely increasing consumption for the rich. Both the classes thus contribute to the degradation of the environment and rise in entropy in completely two different ways underscoring the need for social and environmental policies to resolve the problem of duality in environmental stress.

India's Human Settlement

One of the major factors behind India's environmental degradation has been identified to be India's population growth and pattern of human settlement. India has approximately 18 per cent of world population and 2 per cent of the geographical area. India's population increased from 238 million in March 1901 to 361.09 million in 1951 and 846.90 million in 1991. The annual average growth rate of population increased from 0.56 per cent in the first decade of the twentieth century to 1.96 per cent in the 1950s and reached the peak of 2.22 per cent in the decade of 1970s. The 1991 census shows a decline of the rate to 2.16 per cent for the 1980s. The Technical Group of Population Projection has estimated the population to be 934.2 million as on March 1996 implying an annual average growth rate of 2.0 per cent in the period 1991–6. Table 5.7 gives the dynamics of India's population growth and shows slower pace of decline of the birth rate per 1000 population than the death rate. The almost constant decadal natural growth rate of population since 1970s has however masked the underlying demographic transition experienced by the country. The overall socio-economic development has contributed to the rise of the natural fertility rate as measured by the number of live births per life time of Indian woman in the absence of any environmental resistance and measures for restraining the number of births by deliberate socio-economic choice at micro or macro level. The natural rate has traditionally been only about 6 which is considered low. Despite the tradition of early marriage, the socio-cultural factors (which are mostly population density independent) like religious and cultural restriction on sex, prohibitions against widow re-marriage, prolonged breast feeding and the health related factors like malnutrition, effects of diseases like malaria, tuberculosis, etc. have been responsible for such low value. However, as a result of weakening of these factors since 1970s and improvement of general health condition the natural fertility of an Indian woman has risen to 8 or 9 by 1991. The decline in birth rate in India has taken place in the face of such rise in natural fertility of Indian women due to change in their choices regarding the size of family as induced by economic development, decline in poverty, rise in female literacy and status of women. The decline in death rate has been due to the favourable shift in the survivability curve of the Indian population caused by the fall in poverty from 55 per cent in

1973–4 to 36 per cent in 1993–4, fall in infant mortality rate from 137 in 1971 to 80 in 1993 per 1000 live birth and rise of life expectancy from 45.6 years in 1970–1 to 60.3 years in 1993–4. The drop in infant mortality rate which has been greater in the 1980s than in the 1970s (mainly due to decline in the rural infant mortality rate since 1980s) along with the rise in life expectancy had affected the age distribution of population by raising the share of population in pre-reproductive age group (see Table 5.8). This has been one of the important factors behind overall demographic status-quo of Indian population dynamics (see Pachauri *et al.* 1993 and Repetto 1997). These factors would run counter to the forces of socio-economic development to delay substantive reduction in birth rate which would match the death rate to stabilize population. The birth rate, the death rate and the natural growth rate of population are in fact projected to decline to 20.9 per thousand, 7.1 per thousand and 1.38 per cent respectively by 2011 (Government of India, Planning Commission 1992).

However, the achievements of demographic transition in India has been very unevenly distributed regionally. The states of UP, Bihar, Madhya Pradesh and Rajasthan account for about 40 per cent of India's population. The total fertility rate in these states

Table 5.7
Dynamics of India's population growth (1901–95)

Period	Population at the end of the period (in million)	Rates per 1000 population			Per capital availability of farm land (ha)
		Birth	Death	Natural growth	
1911	252.09	49.20	42.60	6.60	–
1921	251.32	48.10	48.60	–0.50	–
1931	278.98	46.40	36.30	10.10	–
1941	318.66	45.20	31.20	14.00	–
1951	361.09	39.90	27.40	12.50	0.91
1961	439.23	41.70	24.80	18.90	0.75
1971	548.16	41.20	19.00	22.20	0.60
1981	683.33	37.20	15.00	22.20	0.48
1991	846.30	32.50	11.40	21.10	0.39
1996	925.01	27.50	9.4	18.10	0.36

Source: Pachauri *et al.* (1998), p. 23.

is as high as 6 live births per woman during her reproductive life while the national average is 4 (World Resource Institute, UNDP and UNEP 1994). This is explained by the prevalence of poverty, high female illiteracy, low life expectancy and high infant mortality rate of this region (see Table 5.9).

Table 5.8
Percentage distribution of population by age and sex in India

(age in years)

Period	0–14		15–49		50 and above	
	male	female	male	female	male	female
1951	38.2	38.6	49.7	49.1	12.1	12.2
1961	40.9	41.1	47.2	47.1	11.8	11.7
1971	41.7	42.2	45.8	46.0	12.3	11.8
1981	39.6	39.8	47.7	47.7	12.7	12.5
1990	37.1	36.6	50.4	50.3	12.5	13.1
1993*	36.4	35.8	51.1	50.9	12.7	13.4
1994*	36.8	36.1	50.4	50.5	12.9	13.5

*These are provisional estimates.
Source: Family Welfare Programme in India (1996-7), Department of Family Welfare, Government of India.

Table 5.9
Poverty, female literacy, infant mortality rate and
life expectancy at birth in India

States	Poverty ratio (1993–4)			Female literacy (1991)	Infant mortality (1991)	Life expectancy at birth (1991–5)
	Rural	Urban	Overall			
Bihar	58.21	34.5	54.96	22.89	71	59.3
Uttar Pradesh	42.68	35.39	40.85	25.31	85	56.8
Madhya Pradesh	40.64	48.38	42.52	28.85	94	54.7
Rajasthan	26.46	30.49	27.41	20.44	85	59.1
Kerala	25.76	24.55	25.43	86.17	12	72.9
Tamil Nadu	32.48	39.77	35.03	51.33	53	63.3
Overall	37.27	32.36	35.97	39.29	71	60.3

Source: Government of India, CSO (1997); Economic Survey, 1998-9.

While poverty is a consequence of over population relative to the availability of manmade and natural capital endowments, it also reinforces the problem of high growth rate of population by adversely influencing the demographic factors. The removal of poverty in a developing country is a result partly of the process of growth and partly of the policy initiatives that shape the strategy of development and of distribution of the benefit of economic growth. Poverty being an important attribute of the quality of human life and a factor associated with the state of environment the poverty index is considered as one of the important proxies of environmental indicators of a society. In India poverty has been measured in terms of the alternative indices of Head count (H), Poverty Gap (PG) and Squared Poverty

Table 5.10
Poverty in India (1951–94)

NSS round	Survey period	Regional coverage	Head count index	Poverty gap index	Squared poverty gap index
3	Aug 1951–Nov 1992	Rural	47.37	16.05	7.53
		Urban	35.46	11.14	4.82
		National	45.31	15.20	7.06
24	June 1969–June 1970	Rural	57.61	18.24	7.73
		Urban	47.16	14.32	5.86
		National	55.56	17.47	7.32
45	July 1989–June 1990	Rural	34.30	7.80	2.58
		Urban	33.40	8.51	3.04
		National	34.07	7.98	2.69
50	July 1993–June 1994	Rural	36.66	8.39	2.79
		Urban	30.51	7.41	2.42
		National	35.04	8.13	2.69
Trend rate of growth of poverty					
1951–94 (% per year)		Rural	–0.86	–1.84	–2.65
		Urban	–0.75	–1.43	–2.05
		National	–0.88	–1.79	–2.56

Source: Gaurav Datt (1998).

Gap (SPG), indicating respectively the incidence, the depth and the severity of poverty with reference to a poverty line of Rs. 49/- per capita per month at October 1973–June 1974 all India rural prices. While H index is the proportion of population below the poverty line, PG index is the measure of average short fall of consumption level of a poor from the poverty line as a proportion of the poverty line. SPG is square of the proportion that the PG represents expressed in percentage terms. The head count poverty ratio of India fell from 45.31 per cent in 1951–2 as per NSS Round 3, to 35.04 per cent in 1993–4 as per NSS Round 50. Table 5.10 gives the rural-urban poverty indices for all the three measures showing that poverty declined also in terms of indices for depth and severity over the same period. Most of the decline in poverty has, however, taken place since 1970 and seems to have occurred by 1989–90.

Like population, poverty has been unevenly distributed across the States of India, the head count poverty ratio varying from 20.64 per cent in Punjab-Haryana to 63.20 per cent in Bihar as per the average estimates for the period 1990–1 to 1993–4 shown in Table 5.11. This table also shows similar wide variation in the depth and the severity indices of poverty across the states. Such variations in poverty measures will be able to partly explain the variations in the extent and the nature of environmental degradation in the different regions of India.

What are the environmental implications of India's growing population and their poverty? Has the population size of India hit nature's carrying capacity? Are the present pressure of population in terms of size and growth, in conflict with the sustainability of development? The demographic status quo regarding population growth rate in the last two decades leading to growth in population density has led to environmental stress in India and adaptation of the economy and society to mitigate the effects of stress. In spite of addition of 251 million people in India between 1981 and 1995 which is 95 per cent of USA's population as in 1995, Malthusian disasters have not happened, nor have the biophysical limits constrained India's development process. Although per capita availabilities of land and farm land have declined from the level of 0.91 hectare and 0.64 hectare respectively in 1951 to 0.39 hectare and 0.30 hectare respectively in 1991, the per capita availability of foodgrain improved from

Table 5.11
Interstate variation in living standard and
poverty in India (average over 1990–1 to 1993–4 covering
15 major states)

State	Mean consumption	Head count index	Poverty Poverty gap index	Squared poverty index
Punjab–Haryana	83.27	20.64	4.02	1.18
Jammu and Kashmir	70.70	31.20	7.29	2.61
West Bengal	68.13	31.51	6.51	1.93
Kerala	73.32	33.01	7.96	2.77
Orissa	66.32	34.66	7.43	2.28
Andhra Pradesh	68.34	35.89	7.70	2.43
Uttar Pradesh	62.57	41.72	10.66	3.80
Gujarat	59.27	41.77	9.64	3.40
Tamil Nadu	63.93	41.80	11.02	4.09
Rajasthan	60.02	45.79	12.54	4.80
Karnataka	57.69	46.88	12.94	4.99
Assam	52.63	49.33	10.80	3.41
Madhya Pradesh	60.56	49.79	12.74	4.50
Maharashtra	58.76	50.50	14.39	5.55
Bihar	48.60	63.20	16.40	5.95

Note: Mean consumption is measured in Rs per person per day at October 1973–June 1974 all India rural prices. All the estimates of mean consumption and poverty index are based on the data of NSS rounds available for the period of coverage.
Source: Gaurav Datt (1998).

141 kg in 1950–1 to 193 kg in 1995. Technology has played an important role in augmenting the carrying capacity of the Indian resource base. In agriculture the new technology along with extension of irrigation facilities enhanced the gross cropped area, output and yield at an annual rate of 0.5 per cent, 3 per cent and 2.4 per cent, respectively, for foodgrains between 1950–1 and 1994–5 (see Table 5.12).

In spite of the growth in the availability of foodgrain, inequality in distribution of land asset in Indian rural society and pressure of population on agricultural land have resulted in fragmentation of holdings, migration of population to urban centres and upward pressure on the poverty ratio contributing to the slow pace of

Table 5.12
Growth of gross cropped area, output and
yield of foodgrains in India

	1950-1	1994-5	Compound growth rate
Area in million ha	97.3	123.5	0.5
Production in million tonnes	50.8	191.0	3.0
Yield in kg/ha	522	1547	2.4

Source: Data derived from Government of India (1996), Economic Survey 1995-6.

alleviation of poverty in India and its persistence even after 50 years of Independence. The number of agricultural holdings under the category of small and marginal farmers have in fact increased by 65 per cent from 49 million in 1970-1 to 82 million in 1990-1. The productivity of such small and marginal holdings increasingly declined over time because of fragmentation which stood in the way of realizing technology benefits in land.

While technology has enabled the shifting of the overall carrying capacity of land upwards, the limitation of renewable fresh water resource essentially fixed for any region of the world or a country, poses a big problem in respect of carrying capacity of our ecosystem as any growth of population would mean reduced per capita availability of fresh water. Annual availability of fresh water declined in India from 5400 m^3 in 1950 to just over 2400 m^3 in 1991 characterizing India now as a water stressed country. Since water availability is again unevenly distributed across the country, the future growth of population and economic activities would make the availability of water a critical factor for both the sustainability of the life processes as well as the development processes in several parts of the country.

The growing population needs not only more food and fresh water, but also requires living space, infrastructural facilities of sanitation, drinking water supply, waste (excreta) disposal facility, and health care. The health and hygienic condition of the people—their morbidity, life expectancy, infant mortality, etc.—depend on the availability of these basic facilities. The scarcity of manmade or financial capital resources in India and the inequality in the distribution of income result in housing shortage and inadequate access for people to such infrastructural facilities. About 45 per cent of Indian population lives in one roomed housing units with 2.7 persons living per room. The number of homeless households and that of population have been 522,000 and 2.007 million respectively in 1991. Although the numbers were higher in 1981, the absolute magnitudes as in 1991 are quite staggering for India to be called a civilized equitable society. The statistics on homeless people in 1991 as given in Table 5.13 highlights the fact that population pressure and poverty in India have led to the deprivation of 827,000 women in respect of shelter and habitat as per norms of civilized society. It also reveals that majority of the homeless in India are in villages. The share of rural homeless in the total homeless population of India was 74 per cent in 1981 which later decline to 64 per cent in 1991.

Homelessness, that is, not having access to any kind of housing, is not an adequate criterion for deprivation. Households which are enumerated as not homeless may not have separate housing or dwelling unit and have to share it with others. The difference between households with home or housing units is an index of housing shortage. The inadequacy of living room space and the

Table 5.13
Rural–urban and sex-wise distribution of homeless
population in India

(millions)

Year and Item	No. of homeless households	Home less population		
		Total	Male	Female
1981*				
Total	6.30	23.43	13.77	9.66
Urban	2.10	6.19	4.06	2.13
Rural	4.20	17.24	9.70	7.54
1991@				
Total	5.22	20.07	11.80	8.27
Urban	2.17	7.25	4.71	2.55
Rural	3.05	12.82	7.09	5.73

* Excludes Assam
@ Excludes Jammu and Kashmir
Source: Government of India, CSO (1998).

condition of the housing unit with reference to dilapidation or obsolescence need also to be taken into account for any adequate housing norm. The estimate of shortage of housing would be 2.147 million in metropolitan cities only after taking account of the congestion factor and the obsolescence factor for the same date (see Table 5.14).

Table 5.14
Housing shortage in selected urban areas and
all metropolitan cities (as on 1 March 1991)

(millions)

City	Total house-holds	No. of houses	Housing shortage	Congestion factor	Obsole-scence	Total shortage
Greater Mumbai	2.683	2.651	0.078	0.128	0.111	0.318
Calcutta	2.163	2.139	0.052	0.103	0.090	0.245
Delhi	1.701	1.633	0.227	0.081	0.069	0.377
Chennai	1.085	10.071	0.127	0.052	0.045	0.224
All metro-politan cities	13.728	13.421	0.927	0.656	0.564	2.147

Source: Government of India, CSO (1997).

So far as the coverage of population with drinking water is concerned, the coverage improved over time, particularly for the rural areas. There has been substantive improvement in the coverage for the rural areas during the 1980s. However, the coverage of villages is defined in terms of availability of drinking water within a radius of 1.6 km in plain areas and within an elevation difference of 100 metres in hilly areas. As per such definition the coverage of rural and urban population by drinking water supply has reached the mark of 78.4 per cent in rural area and 84.9 per cent in urban areas in 1993 (see Table 5.15). If one considers the connectivity of housing units by piped water, the coverage has been 65.1 per cent of housing units in urban areas (with the break up 42.3 per cent inside supply and 22.8 per cent outside supply) and 20.6 per cent of housing units in rural areas (with the break up of 6.0 per cent inside supply and 14.6 per cent outside supply) (see Table 5.16).

The situation has been much more stressful for sanitation in both rural and urban areas. The coverage of population by sanitation has been as awfully low as 3.15 per cent in March 1991 (see Table 5.15) in rural areas. In urban areas the coverage has been 47.9 per cent which has also serious public health implication in view of density and congestion factor of living in the urban areas. The share of occupied housing units without any type of toilet facilities has been 36.2 per cent in urban areas and 90.5 per cent in rural areas, the overall share of no toilet facility for such occupied units being 76.3 per cent (see Table 5.16).

The inadequacy of housing units, drinking water supply and toilets is the consequence of lack of manmade capital in a country with large growing population. Lack of appropriate institutions to meet the challenge of providing adequate access to basic intrastructural facilities resulted in the suffering of the marginalised section of the population from environmental degradation.

Finally, urbanization is an important dimension of demographic process of an industrializing country like India. India's share of urban population has grown from 10.84 per cent in 1901, 23.34 per cent in 1981 to 25.72 per cent in 1991 (see Table 5.17). The increased urbanization has been due to better job opportunities in urban areas and lack of basic infrastructural services like drinking water, sanitation, transport and communications, etc. in rural areas. The rural–urban migration was quite significant till

Table 5.15
Population with access to drinking water and
sanitation facilities in India

Areas	(% covered as on 31 March of the year)		
	1985	1990	1993
Drinking water supply			
Rural	56.3	73.9	78.4
Urban	72.9	83.8	84.9
Sanitation Facilities			
Rural	0.7	2.4	3.15
Urban	28.7	45.9	47.90

Source: Government of India, CSO (1997).

Table 5.16
Occupied housing units with piped water supply and
toilets installed in India

					(% covered)
Year and Area	Total occupied housing units	Pipe water supply system			Toilet installation of any type
		Total	Inside	Outside	
1981					
Rural	100 (90.1)	10.3	2.8	7.5	NA
Urban	100 (28.5)	63.2	36.1	27.1	58.1
Overall	100 (118.6)	23.0	10.8	12.2	NA
1991					
Rural	100 (111.6)	20.6	6.0	14.6	9.5
Urban	100 (39.5)	65.1	42.3	22.8	63.9
Overall	100 (151.1)	32.3	15.5	16.8	23.7

Note: Figures in brackets give total number of houses in millions.
Source: Government of India, CSO (1997).

the 1970s because of the pressure of population in rural areas
which has been a push factor. A feature of India's urbanization
has been the increasing concentration of urban population in a
few large cities (see Table 5.18). The population of urban complexes
with population higher than 100,000 has had a decadal growth
of 46.87 per cent while the population of all other size classes had
growth less than the average urban decadal population growth
of 36.09 per cent. The urban settlements with less than 10,000
people had an absolute decline of population in the decade of the
1980s. The metropolitan cities have had again a share of half of
the population of class one cities. It has been predicted that by
the end of the twentieth century the mega cities like Calcutta and
Mumbai will be among the ten largest cities of the world with an
estimated population of 15.9 million and 15.4 million, respectively
(UNDP 1999).

Table 5.17
Urbanization trends in India

Census year	Urban population in millions	Urban population as % of total population	Growth rate	
			Decennial	Annual average
1901	25.85	10.84	–	–
1971	109.11	19.91	38.23	3.21
1981	159.46	23.24	46.14	3.83
1991	217.18	25.72	36.19	3.09

Source: Government of India, CSO (1997).

Table 5.18
Urban sizewise distribution and decennial
growth of urban population

Population size class	% Share of total population				Decennial growth rate %	
	1901	1971	1981	1991	1971–81	1981–91
< 5000	6.1	0.4	0.5	0.3	65.73	–21.70
5000–10000	20.1	4.5	3.6	2.6	17.82	–1.27
10000–20000	20.8	10.9	9.5	7.8	27.54	10.72
20000–50000	15.6	16.0	14.4	13.2	30.85	25.30
50000–100000	11.3	10.9	11.6	14.3	55.73	28.14
Over 100000	26.0	57.2	60.4	65.2	54.35	46.87
All Classes	100	100	100	100	46.23	36.09

Source: Government of India, CSO (1997).

Increased urbanization and greater concentration of urban population in large metropolis in India has created environmental stress and challenges. As the density of population per unit of area is higher for larger cities in terms of population size, environmental stress is expected to be higher for larger towns and cities. It becomes an increasingly difficult challenge to accommodate an increasing size of population in a given space of a city or metropolis with shelter, water and sanitation with the choice of appropriate technology. Cities are the main hubs of economic activities of an industrializing economy and their infrastructure is often over-stretched and becomes inadequate due to lack of adequate manmade capital and of access to appropriate high technology in a country like India. Poor reside in slums which begins as unauthorized settlements, with no direct access to sanitation or safe drinking water and poor waste disposal facility. The poor in India have carved out space for themselves in cities and constructed their own shelters to form slums by diluting the property rights defined on some apparent open access space. A slum is defined as an area unit having twenty-five or more *kutcha* structures mostly of temporary nature or fifty or more households residing mostly in *kutcha structures*, huddled together, and inhabited by persons with practically no private latrine and inadequate public latrine and water facilities. The growth of slum is a manifestation of poverty in an industrializing society like India with growing pressure of population, inadequate infrastructural capital and unresolved distribution problem. The slum population of India as on 1991 was of the order of 46.3 million, constituting nearly 21 per cent of urban population. The larger cities have greater share of total slum population. The class I cities had 68.8 per cent of total slum population in 1991. The share of slum population in the metropolitan cities has been about 26.6 per cent in the same year. In spite of efforts to control the growth of slums, the number of slum dwellers has been growing fast and is projected to increase to 61.8 million in 2001 (see Table 5.19).

Slum dwellers are the immediate sufferers of environment degradation due to the lack of safe water and sanitation which

Table 5.19
Trend of slum population in urban India
and metropolitan cities

(population in millions)

Area	1981			1991			2001	
	Total popu-lation	Slum popu-lation	%	Total popu-lation	Slum popu-lation	%	Total popu-lation	Slum popu-lation
Urban India	159.460	27.914	17.5	217.611	46.261	21.3	290.94	61.826
All metros	51.567	14.825	28.7	70.997	18.866	26.6	96.628	25.481

Source: Government of India, CSO (1997).

has adverse impact on morbidity and life expectancy of slum dwellers. If one of the consequences of growing population pressure and industrialization is urbanization along with growth of slums, the latter would be an expression of environmental resistance to population growth and also an indication of failure or neglect of the problem of income distribution and poverty and that of providing environmentally safe habitat for all. The solution of distribution of the developmental benefits depends on many factors relating to the institutional arrangements of an economic system. If distribution is left to be determined increasingly by market driven forces, then urban poverty is likely to persist and slums continue to grow in India in spite of the best of efforts to curtail them. With an unfavourable population to manmade capital ratio, market as the prime economic institution and a large existing surplus labour, the urbanization process of Indian population would very likely be environmentally unsustainable.

India faces a big challenge in respect of carrying its population along a sustainable development path without violating the democratic rights of individuals of deciding choices pertaining to family and society. There are the following three options or any of their combinations to meet the challenge:

(a) Control of population growth and stabilization of population size.

(b) Development of technology for nature to support increased number of Indians with supply of resources and absorption of wastes.

(c) Development of institutional arrangement with reference to implementation of technology and distribution of benefits of economic growth among people in order to make the economic system more ecofriendly.

While man cannot undo the forces of laws of nature or ecological principle, the socio-economic policies on population, technology and institutions can create more space for human beings to sustain as per the norms of clean and decent life. Indian developmental policies need to be shaped with conscious focus on the issues of ecological principles and socio-economic policies.

Chapter

6 HUMAN ECOLOGY: THE LIMITS OF SOURCES AND SINKS

Nature as Source and Sink

In capitalist economy human population and industrial capital have the potential for reproduction. Population grows at a rate determined by the biological and the socio-economic factors. It also supplies the labour force for economic activities. Manmade industrial capital gives rise to surplus which is appropriated as profit and results in accumulation, assuming that all wages are consumed and all profits are saved. Accumulated capital in the following period gives rise to profit and causes further addition to the existing capital stock. The inanimate manmade capital also grows like biotic species through reproduction scheme of surplus generation in labour–capital mode of production. Population and manmade capital drive the present world economic system of man which would draw material and energy from earth, produce physical goods and services with values and return wastes and heat to earth after appropriating the values. A constant flow exists of inputs from the planetary sources through the human economy to the planetary sink where the wastes and pollutants end up. Limits exist on the rates of flow of resources from the sources and that of wastes to the sink so as to prevent harm to the people, and damage to the economy and earth's process of absorption, regeneration and regulation of the biosphere. An interactive relationship exists between nature as source and as sink. If a lake is used as a sink for deposit of nitrogen or phosphorous fertilizer from the neighbouring agricultural land being carried by run off water, its use as source for aquaculture and fishery is restricted if not eliminated by the eutrophication of the lake. While Chapter 5 focussed the discussion on the interactive relations among population growth, capital accumulation and environmental process, this chapter elaborates the limits of the interactive relations between source and sink as influenced by the functioning of the human economic system and illustrates the limits and problems with Indian data.

Land, Soil and Food

Food Security

Food is the single most important item for the determination of human well-being as it is the supplier of energy for life support to the body. Homo sapiens are different from other species as they have domesticated numerous wild crops, extensively modified the natural landscape into agricultural fields to effect the domestication and subsidized energy to the agricultural field ecosystem in animate (human or other animal based) or chemical forms. Since photosynthesis provides food energy, nature could have supported a world population size 170 times of 5.7 billion figure of 1997, if the entire net primary production on land and oceans through photosynthesis (250000 petacal on ocean + 520000 petacal on land = 770000 petacal per year, where 1 petacal = 10^{12} kcal) could be appropriated for food for human consumption assuming all persons to be herbivores with an energy requirement of 2200 kcal per day per person. All photosynthesis products are not fit for the edible use of human beings and a significant number of products are inaccessible particularly in ocean and hence untapped.

The carrying capacity of land resource is determined by the capacity of the land for agricultural purpose. The agricultural usability of a plot of land is determined by soil moisture, temperature, soil quality, topography (Chapter 2). Table 6.1 gives the break up of the total land area excluding ice covered portions of Antarctica and Greenland into arable use of land.

The data thus shows that more than half of the arable land has not as yet been put to use until the late 1980s. Food production

Table 6.1
World resource of arable and grazing land

	(billion hectares)
1. Total land surface (excluding ice covered Antarctica and Greenland)	13.0
2. Unusable (deserts, mountains, tundra, sandy, lateritic soil)	6.6
3. Arable:	
a. Currently in use	1.4
b. Currently not in use	1.8
4. Grazing:	
Currently in use	1.8
Current not in use	1.4

Source: Koromondy (1999), p. 411.

of the world has increased at slightly higher rate than population since 1950. The farmers across the globe produced three times as much grain output in 1990 as they did in 1950, resulting in an increase of 50 per cent in per capita food production. The per capita food production index of the world increased by a total of 24 per cent between 1989–91 and 1997. The daily per capita calorie supply has gone up from 2336 calories in 1970 to 2751 calories in 1996 and the daily per capita protein supply has gone up to 73.5 grams showing a total rise of 26.5 per cent over 1970 level. However, the distribution of food production and land productivity has been very uneven over different regions. In most of the world the crop yield is quite low, India and Pakistan having an yield rate of 1 metric tonne/hectare. On a world wide basis 1 hectare can support 3 persons while 1 hectare of highly productive farm land in USA supports 24 persons with food. The adequacy of land is dependent on the use of water and technology. The carrying capacity of land is sensitive to land productivity. Cultivable land produces not only foodgrains, but cash crops like cotton, tobacco, rubber, etc., and food for livestock. In the calculation of land adequacy the requirements of the amount of fallow land to maintain land fertility and of pastures for pastorage need also to be taken into account.

Given the state of affairs in 1997, the amount of food production in the world in that year could have supplied a subsistence diet for 8.1 billion people, a moderate diet for 5.3 billion people and diet at the West European level to 3.97 billion people. These estimates assume 40 per cent waste factor for losses between production and consumption. In addition to the distribution of land productivity, distribution of food across the people of different regions would determine the adequacy or the inadequacy of land use for agriculture. The amount of food that is grown in the world is sufficient to feed the present world population adequately, but not lavishly. However, the phenomena of waste and unequal distribution have resulted in lavish and wasteful food consumption by a section of population of the world belonging mainly to the industrialized countries and the richer section of the population in developing countries, while 20 per cent of the population of the developing countries remains under-nourished. The inequality of distribution is indicated by the variation in the daily per capita consumption of calorie and protein across countries ranging from 2095 cal and 51.4 gm respectively for the least developed countries to 3377 cal and 104.8 gm respectively for the industrialized countries in 1996. For South Asia the estimates are marginally better at 2402 cal and 58.2 gm for daily food energy and protein intake per capita respectively, while for India it was 2415 cal and 58.6 gm respectively, in 1996. The unequal distribution of food and nutrition is reflected in the share of under weight children below the age of 5 which has been as high as 48 per cent for South Asia and 53 per cent for India. Persistence of hunger in the world today is not due to the limits of capacity of the ecosystems to produce food, but due to distribution. In a study of soil and climate for 117 countries of Africa, Asia and Latin America it was estimated that only 19 countries with 109 million population would not be able to feed their expected population in 2000 from their own land even if they could use every hectare of their useful land and get the highest technically possible yield. According to the study the total food output of the 117 counties could be multiplied by 16 times provided if there is no soil erosion; all cultivable land is used for agriculture; conditions of elastic supply of agricultural inputs; perfect weather and idealized management prevail. Idealized management involves the optimum mix and use of irrigation, organic and chemical fertilizer, pesticides and biotechnology of the right kind and in the right proportion.

Ultimately land is the limit to growth of food production. The land under cultivation globally as of today can be more than doubled to the level of 4.0 billion hectares from the level of 1.5 billion hectares of 1990. The expansion of area under cultivation along with technological and social flexibility will be able to feed the projected 12.5 billion population of the world at the end of the 21st country. However, land has other uses in forestry and urban development. The alternative uses of land between agriculture and non-agriculture and within agriculture between food and cash crop need to be planned as to strike the right balance among the different end uses and also meet the other requirements of industrial development of the developing countries, as well as those of eco-services rendered by forests in the forms of control of the climate and conservation of the biodiversity.

Land Use

Out of the total geographical area of 329 million hectares in India, 280 million hectares of land is available for biomass production. Of the balance 49 million hectares, urbanization and industrialization have taken away 22 million hectares. Of the land available for biomass production, the net sown agricultural area in 1993-4 has been 186 million hectares and fallow land 24 million hectares. The net sown area increased from 119 million hectares in 1950-1 to 140 million hectares mostly through the reclamation of old fallow lands, culturable wastelands and diversion of land with groves to agricultural use. Since 1970-1 the net sown area did not grow by any significant measure indicating that private initiatives of reclamation have reached the maximum extent as permitted by the consideration of private benefit cost ratio. However, the net irrigated area continued to increase after 1970, which contributed to the increase of gross cropped area from 132 million hectares in 1950-1 to 166 million hectares in 1970-1 and to 185 million hectares in 1992-3. The gross irrigated area also increased from 22.56 million hectares in 1950-1 to 38 million hectares in 1970-1 and to 66 million hectares in 1992-3. It is this expansion of irrigation facility as combined with that of net sown area that has contributed to the rise of foodgrain output from 50 million tonnes in 1950-1, to 129.6 million tonnes in   1980-1 and to 191.18 million tonnes in 1996–7 and to the rise of the index of agricultural output from 46 in 1950–1 to 169.2 in 1996–7 (1980–1 being 100). The expansion of irrigation has permitted the gross cropped area to grow without involving any cost in terms of the area under forest, although the area under permanent pasture and grazing initially fluctuated but now has stabilized around 11 to 12 million hectares (see Table. 6.2). However, even if India or the world produces enough food to feed the total national or the global population, food security cannot be ensured for all the individuals of the national or global population.

Even if the world production of food can cater to the entire population, distribution of production may mismatch with the distribution of population across regions within India and in the world. Regions with high population density relative to the yield of land in food production would need to import food from other regions. The terms of trade between food importers and food exporters would play a role in determining the adequacy of food supply in the regions of shortage in terms of domestic demand and indigenous supply balance. A highly indebted food importing country with adverse balance of payments situation may end up

Table 6.2
Land use in India

(billion hectares)

	1950–1	1960–1	1970–1	1980–1	1992–3
1. Geographic area	328.73	328.73	328.73	328.73	328.73
2. Not available for cultivation					
a. Non-agricultural uses (urban dev.)	9.36	14.84	16.48	19.66	21.88
b. Barren unculturable waste	38.16	35.91	28.16	19.96	19.38
3. Other uncultivated land	49.45	37.64	35.06	32.21	29.61
4. Fallow	28.12	22.82	19.88	24.75	23.56
5. Net sown area	118.75	133.20	140.27	140.00	142.51
6. Gross cropped area	131.89	152.77	165.79	172.63	185.49
7. Net irrigated area	20.85	24.66	31.10	38.72	50.01
8. Gross irrigated area	22.56	27.98	38.19	49.78	66.14

Source: Govt. of India CSO (1997).

with hunger and high death rate even if world production of food is adequate. Social and institutional flexibility becomes important for utilizing the global food output to provide adequate food for all and eliminate hunger.

Land Degradation

Though statistics show that world food production levels can meet everybody's need for food while maintaining the ecological balance of the biosphere, the current trend of loss of agricultural land across the world is an emerging concern. Since 1970, world's farmers lost an estimated 480 billion tonnes of top soil, which is roughly equivalent to India's crop land. Shortsighted economic policies due to high time preference has resulted in soil erosion in North America, acidification of soil in Europe, deforestation and desertification in Asia, Africa and Latin America. In the third world land degradation has been quite severe due to soil erosion, water logging, salinization, alkalinization damage, depletion of nutrients due to land over use, etc. In the developing world, 6 to 7 million hectares of agricultural land becomes unproductive every year due to soil erosion and another 1.5 million hectares due to other reasons. During the 20 year period since 1970 the desert area of the world expanded by some 120 million hectares which is more than the cropped land area in China in the early nineties. In India the total degraded land area has been 191.8 million hectare as on 1994 out of which 80 million hectares have been degraded between 1947 and 1994. Out of the degraded 191.8 million hectares, 162.4 million hectares of land were degraded due to soil erosion, 11.6 million hectares due to water logging, and 10.1 million hectares due to salinity. The degradation of land due to soil erosion or salinity often involves irreversible damages in the human time scale of planning. The recreation of eroded top soil would take enormous time so that for economic calculations, soil erosion is an irreversible damage. Sustainable accounting system of income and wealth should focus on the valuation of all such irreversible losses of agricultural land or productivity (Parikh 1991; Parikh et al. 1991; Parikh et al. 1992). The Net National Product of an economy should be obtained after netting out all such losses of national assets.

The problem of soil degradation can be classified into the following categories:

(a)   soil erosion
(b)   chemical degradation of soil
(c)   physical degradation of soil.

These problems are explained with reference to India's situation in the following sections.

Soil Erosion

The major factor behind soil degradation is its erosion. Soil erosion can be due to water run off washing away top soil, or surface wind erosion which blows off top soil. Soil erosion by water and wind results in the loss of top soil, terrain deformation and loss of productivity of land. Water erosion of soil has been a function of geological formation, rainfall and its time distribution which would have a determining influence on the proportion of rainfall which flows as run off, susceptibility of soil to erosion, gradient of land as determined by topography, vegetation cover, agricultural and other conservational practices, etc. Water erosion of soil will be higher in regions where heavy rainfall takes place in short span of time than in regions which receive low intensity rainfall over a longer period. The physical properties particularly permeability of soil, determine its susceptibility to erosion. In India there has been degradation of 148.9 million hectares of land due to water erosion as in 1994 out of 328.7 million hectares of land area. India has an average rainfall of 1180 mm and a total annual discharge of 164.5 hectare metres annually. On the basis of the existing data on soil erosion it has been estimated that there is an annual loss of 5.3 billion tonnes of soil for the entire country, that is, at the annual average rate of 16.4 tonnes per hectare per year in India. Of this total amount 29 per cent is permanently lost to ocean, about 10 per cent of soil is deposited in the reservoirs causing loss of storage capacity due to siltage by 1 per cent to 2 per cent every year. The remaining 61 per cent of the soil is merely displaced (see Pachauri *et al.* 1998). Table 6.3 shows the intensity distribution of soil losses in India as estimated in 1990. A large part of water erosion of soil is nature induced, although human activities may aggravate the problem, for example, deforestation, over grazing of land, and shifting cultivation on the hills and hill slopes (with a too short fallow period) have been responsible for the reduction of vegetation cover of soil and affected the physical property of soil making it more susceptible to erosion in India.

Wind erosion has been also caused mainly by the loss of vegetation cover resulting from felling of trees, over grazing and extension of agriculture to marginal and forest areas. Soil with loosely bonded structure in its material formation, low organic content and low water holding capacity is susceptible to wind erosion. Wind erosion is a serious problem in arid and semi-arid regions, coastal and cold desert regions of India where soils are sandy. The total area affected by wind erosion in India is about 13.5 million hectares with most of these affected areas in Rajasthan, Gujarat, Haryana and Punjab. The loss of top soil accounts for almost half of soil degradation, while terrain deformation has a share of 30 per cent in the total degradation due to wind erosion of soil.

Total soil erosion in India is distributed over regions in varying intensities. In dense forest area the rate of erosion is as low a rate as 5 tonnes/hectare/annum while the intensity goes up to 80 tonnes/hectare/annum for arid regions of Rajasthan like Shivalik hills. Out of the total geographic area, about 104 million hectares have been classified as high to very severely eroded land accounting for 64 per cent of total annual soil loss in India as estimated in 1990 (see Table 6.3).

Table 6.3
Area under different degrees of soil erosion in India

Degree of erosion	Annual loss of soil in tonnes/ha	Area affected as a % of total	Area million ha	Annual loss of soil in million tonnes	Loss of reserve nutrients from top 15 layer cm in %
Slight	5 or less	24	80	401	0.23
Moderate	5–10	43	140	1406	0.45
High	11–20	24	80	1610	0.91
Very High	21–40	5	16	640	1.82
Severe	41–80	3	8	666	3.64
Very Severe	81 and more	1	3	255	3.64
Overall			327	4978	0.76

Source: Pachauri et al. (1998), p. 67.

Chemical Degradation

Chemical degradation of soil comes next in order of importance after soil erosion. Chemical degradation may happen for either of the following reasons:

(a) *Nutrient depletion:* Overuse of land due to increased population pressure and poverty has caused nutrient depletion of soil. The amount of uptake of nutrients by plants has not been replenished by allowing fallow for sufficient length of time and/or applying organic or inorganic fertilizer composting and other protection measures. Wrong choices of agricultural practice and cropping pattern or sequence may aggravate the problem of nutrient depletion. In India nearly 3.7 million hectares have been degraded due to such nutrient loss which are mostly located in the north eastern states.

(b) *Salinity and Alkalization:* Salt affected soils are often widespread in arid, semi-arid and coastal areas, while alkaline soils are found in areas of subhumid dry zones. While part of salinity or alkaline problem is natural, human activities like canal irrigation has caused salinization and/or alkalization due to inadequate facility of drainage of water, and inefficient use of irrigation water causing flooding and water logging. The physical degradation of water logging due to rise of ground water table aggravates this problem. In seasons of high temperature, the water rapidly evaporates. As the ground water of dry areas often contains high concentration of saline and alkaline material, such salts are deposited on the soil surface leading to salinization of land. In India, the total land area affected by salinity and alkalinity has been estimated to be 10.1 million hectares out of which the share of salt affected area has been estimated to be 7.765 million hectares. The canal command area accounts for a share of 45 per cent of such affected area.

(c) *Pollution:* Soil is polluted by industrial effluents, municipal and domestic sewage sludge and agricultural chemical inputs like pesticides and fertilizers. Pesticide application in India rose by more than 13 times in 25 years since 1960 which is comparable with the experience of other developing countries. It is often difficult to get precise estimate of soil degradation due to pollution resulting from use of industrial and agricultural chemicals. It is, however, believed that the dimension of the problem is extensive and its impact quite significant.

Physical Degradation

(a) *Water logging:* Soil suffers from certain kinds of physical degradation of which water logging is a major one and occurs either due to surface flooding or due to rise in water table. Surface flooding is routine in tropical areas every year which is aggravated by soil erosion resulting in silting of river beds as well as reservoirs. Besides, the rise in water table due to inadequate drainage of irrigation or rain water has been an important factor for water logging. In India, water logging has affected 4.527 million hectares as estimated in 1994, of which canal command area has been 2.189 million hectares. Although part of water logging may be imputed to surface flooding in monsoon season due to heavy rainfall in short duration, water logging is by and large a reflection of lack of management of water evacuation by rivers, canals and drainage. Water logging induced by canal irrigation or silting reservoirs is an example of degradation resulting from human activities without the required environmental and ecological protection measures.

(b) *Mining and Quarrying:* Mining and quarrying degrade land by disturbing the physical, chemical and biological features of soil. Mine overburdens and wastes are usually dumped around the mining area and are quite prone to slumps and slides and susceptible to erosion. This tends to choke surface drainage and often produce large quantities of acid drainage water, adversely affecting fertility of soil around the mine and water system along the gradient in the mining area. The total environmental impact of mining activities would depend on the volume of water arising from mining activities and its characteristics. While the estimate of total volume of soil is difficult to obtain, the total area of 0.8 million hectares under mining is an indication of soil degradation. The irreversible change of land use for mining and quarrying precludes any future possibility of its use for agriculture, and would be reflected in the economic valuation of the degraded land and in the accounting for depreciation of natural capital.

Unsustainable Agricultural Practice and Land Degradation

While rainfall and wind flow generate forces which degrade land by displacing top soil and spatially redistributing it, resulting in soil erosion, water logging and salinization or alkalization depending on the physiography and vegetation of the concerned region, human activities have aggravated these problems and added to the dimension of degradation, for example, nutrient depletion, soil pollution, etc. While mining and quarrying activities as well as disposal of industrial and municipal sludge in land fill have caused physical and chemical degradation respectively, the major human induced degradation factor has been unsustainable agricultural and related irrigation practices. The pressure of over population, poverty and maximisation of the return from land, either food or cash crop, has led to short-sighted resource management. The over use of land has led to depletion of nutrients which are not often replenished by chemical fertilizers, for example, in spite of the intensive use of chemical fertilizers land may suffer from carbon deficiency and many other micro nutrients. Nutrient depletion in soil may affect both the survivability of micro-organisms of the soil and plant growth. Besides, poverty and over population have often driven people to use marginal land. The potential for land degradation increases significantly when farming is extended to marginal lands like: (a) steep slopes on hills (as in north-eastern Himalayas), (b) moisture deficit areas where agriculture is possible with irrigation, and (c) dry lands in seasons with some rainfall and humidity. All these marginal areas of agriculture represent fragile ecosystems. While agriculture on steep slopes would always have the potential hazard of accelerated soil erosion and sediment transfer to lower region by way of slope wash, gulleying and mass movement, agriculture with irrigation in moisture deficit area involves the threat of salinization of soil as irrigation water may stagnate in fields in the absence of adequate drainage. The salinized share of irrigated land has been 15 per cent for China, 16.6 per cent India, 26.2 per cent for Pakistan, 33 per cent for Egypt and Iran, and 44.7 per cent for Argentina. Agriculture in dry land based on meagre rainfall is also unsustainable if land is over used or is used for experimentation with cash crops like cotton, soyabean or groundnut which may require less water than traditional food crops, but have much less resilience in respect of productivity in the event of changes in the climatic condition.

Impact of Soil Degradation

Soil degradation has its obvious adverse effects on the environment and the economy. First of all, it affects the primary productive capacity of the concerned terrestrial ecosystems and, therefore, its vegetation cover. Any alteration of vegetation cover would result in interference with carbon cycle as well as hydrological cycle which would in turn affect the global climate. Depletion of top soil along with nutrients will affect the biological sustenance of the micro-organisms of soil and cause disruption of the cycles of carbon, nitrogen, sulphur and other elements which have reservoir pools in soil.

As far as economy is concerned, the feed back effect of land degradation has been mainly the loss of agricultural production. As per the estimate of Food and Agricultural Organisation (Brandon, Homman, and Kishore 1995), the loss of production of major crops imputable to soil erosion only is about 7.23 million tonnes of major crops, that is, 1.5 per cent of total output of such agricultural crops in 1993. The total annual loss of 5.3 billion tonnes of top soil in India has led to a nutrient depletion of 73.93 million tonnes, that is, 1.4 per cent of the total soil loss which has been responsible for such loss of agricultural crops. It may further be noted that 91 per cent of the nutrient loss has been the loss of phosphorous in Indian situation (see Pachauri *et al.* 1998; Brandon *et al.* 1995).

The offsite effect of soil erosion is important for eco-systems' functioning and stability. The main offsite effect of soil erosion has been the silting of rivers and reservoirs which cause floods and destruction resulting in the loss of human and cattle lives, natural capital and manmade capital. In a bad year like 1978, 70.4 million people were affected in India due to floods, 10 million hectares of land suffered from crop damage, and the total value of damage to crops, homes and people was assessed to be Rs. 40.5 billion.

India's food production grew from 50 million tonnes in 1950–1 to 193.6 million tonnes in 1996. This has been possible because of the increased use of inputs of nutrients in the forms of fertilizers and water. In spite of such increased use which had been of the order of 11.56 million tonne of chemical fertilizers and 2.97 million tonnes of organic fertilizer, the efficiency of use of these fertilizers has been as low as 40 per cent and the remaining fertilizers are either leached out or lost by volatization. As a consequence the fertilizers whether inorganic or organic can meet only 28 per cent of the plant uptake. The balance of requirement has to be derived by the plants from the soil's natural sources. However, bio-geo-chemical cycles have a time rate of regenerating the nutrients Nitrogen, Phosphorous and Potassium which tends to be exceeded by the plants' requirement depending on cropping intensity, cropping cycle and fallow period for land. Deficiency of other micro-nutrients in the soil may arise because of the over use of soil for maximizing the short run yield of land. The nutrient content along with the base saturation level of soil as determined by the humus content which is crucial for accessibility of nutrients in dissolved forms by the plants, determines the overall productivity condition of land. Brandon, Homman and Kishore estimated the losses of crops to be of the order of 0.5 to 1.3 million tonnes in India due to nutrient deficiency combined with low base saturation levels for alternative soil types such as alluvial or black. These estimates exclude the effects of nutrient loss due to soil erosion.

The sodium or saline content of soil adversely affects its productivity by damaging the nutrient regeneration process by affecting the growth of soil, its micro-flora and other soil micro-organisms which play crucial role in the nutrient cycles. The estimate for loss of output of major crops due to salinity has been estimated to be of the order of 6.2 million tonnes in India.

Industrial and municipal solid waste and sludge, pollute soil with their heavy metal contents. Chemical fertilizers and pesticides with their heavy metal content pose threat to living organisms. The heavy metals present in soil—arsenic, cadmium, chromium, copper, mercury, nickel, lead and zinc—enter the food chain and get concentrated in living tissues and reach toxic level by the time they enter human body or animals of higher trophic levels in the food chain due to biological magnification. Some of these heavy metals interfere with the microbiological processes and can affect the population of soil organism, which play a crucial role in nutrient recycling. Heavy metal toxicity in soil can also affect plant's metabolism and growth. As sewage sludge is being increasingly used as organic manure for crops like rice and wheat in India, it is important to monitor the heavy metal contents of sludge and fertilizers in soil and their effects on crop productivity due to heavy metal toxicity.

Pesticides used in India are chemical compounds—mostly organo-chloride compounds which are resistant to biodegradation and have a half life of 80 to 110 days in cultivated soil and are potential sources of toxins. The studies of soil samples in India have shown the inevitable contamination with DDT or HCH. Pesticides in soil enter food chain and cause toxicity problem due to biological magnification at higher trophic levels. They cause high mortality and damage reproductive ability of many organisms including organisms crucial for the bio-geo-chemical cycles. Indiscriminate use of pesticides causes loss of biodiversity and productive potential of natural resources in the ecosystem, and leads to the development of resistance to pesticides in many of the target and nontarget species due to their adaptation through necessary genetic mutation process to the changed environmental condition created by pesticides. Agricultural practices like monoculture, that is, producing the same crop year after year, sometimes lead to increasing incidence of plant diseases and alarming pest problem; for example, the mono-cropping of potato in Nilgiris has led to the proliferation of the pest golden nematode which may threaten entire potato cultivation of the country. Use of pesticides in containing such menacing growth of pests would pose the problem of impacting the microbial activities crucial for soil fertility and biodiversity of the ecosystem.

Finally, the physical impact of degradation of land on the long run productivity of the agrarian system needs to be translated into economic terms. Such valuation should not only measure the capitalized value of stream of loss of agricultural income, but also the valuation of loss of any ecological services. The cost of monoculture, for example, in terms of risk of alarming pest problem, should be taken into account in the valuation process in terms of expected loss of income. The loss of microbial activities affecting soil fertility should lead to the estimate of asset depreciation either in terms of extra cost to be incurred to offset its adverse impact on physical agricultural productivity or in terms of loss of income if no such defensive measures are taken. The simulation of values for services lost due to degradation (as in the case of eco-services) for which no market exists for giving price and/or value signal is important in the valuation of natural asset and depreciation accounting.

Water

Water Resource Balance

One of the major constraining factors on the growth of human economic activities is the fresh water resources. The renewable flow of fresh water resource which can be potentially utilized by the human economy is estimated to be a huge amount of 41.02 thousand km^3 per year, i.e., 69118 $meter^3$ per capita per year. The current water use is of the order of 3.240 thousand km^3 per year, implying a per capita use of 645 $meter^3$ per annum. However, the total renewable resource is not harvestable because much of the fresh water flow, as much as 33000 km^3, goes to the sea as seasonal run off and flood and there is no way of storing such an amount of water which is unevenly distributed over the months. This estimate also includes the share of the inaccessible water in the tropics and poles. The balance 9000 km^3 of water is the limit for human use. Human technology and capital formation are being directed to augment the accessible supply by building storage dams by as much as 3500 km^3 by 2000, making the total availability to be 12500 km^3 per year. Desalinization of sea water and long distance transportation of water by pipeline may also be considered as costly options of augmenting supply. The estimate of accessible water could thus be a function of benefit cost ratios of dams and long distance pipeline transportations or disalinization. Besides, in a situation of water stress the ability to pay for augmentation of water availability is dependent on the manmade capital stock and the stage of development of a society. As a result the poor society suffers more of water stress in a situation of water scarcity.

One of the major problems of water availability is its uneven global distribution across regions. At one extreme there exist deserts receiving little or no rainfall, while on the other extreme there are humid regions which receive several meters of rainfall annually. Most of the surface water flow is restricted to a number of major rivers, for example, the Amazon river carries 16 per cent of global run off and Congo-Zaire river carries one-third of river flow of fresh water of entire Africa. The arid and the semi-arid regions of the world which constitute 40 per cent of global land mass receive only 2 per cent of global run off. 71 districts of India in different states are drought prone. The relative availability of water vis-à-vis population distribution can be observed in Table 6.4 which gives the data on per capita availability for the different regions of the world. Water availability in an over-populated country like India has been decreasing. Population grows over time while the hydrological cycle would yield a given stable level of supply of fresh water. India receives a rainfall of 4 million km^3 per annum out of which 30 per cent flows as surface water, 17 per cent evaporates immediately from soil and the balance 53 per cent percolates into soil. Taking water flows as received from other neighbouring countries through rivers, which is estimated to be 235 km^3 per year for India, the estimate of per capita overall availability of fresh water in India has declined from 5277 m^3 in 1955 to 1896 m^3 per annum in 1997, which is still above the 1700 m^3 mark of water stress. The interregional distribution of such fresh water resource is quite uneven across the states of India because of the wide variations in rainfall, river flows within the respective state boundaries and population density. While the per capita availability of water is as high as 18417 m^3 in the Brahmaputra Valley, it comes down to as low as 411 m^3 in the East flowing rivers between Pennar and Kanyakumari, which is below the 500 m^3 mark of severe water stress. Within the Ganges

Table 6.4
Per capita renewable water resource and fresh water

Continents	Per capita annual internal renewable water resource (1998) $10^3 m^3$	Year	Per capita annual withdrawal in m^3
Africa	5.133	1995	202
Asia	3.68	1987	542
North America	17.458	1991	1798
Central America	8.084	1987	916
South America	28.702	1995	335
Europe	8.547	1995	625
Oceania	54.795	1995	591
India	1.896	1975	612
China	2.231	1980	460
World	6.918	1987	645

Source: World Resource Institute (1998), World Resources, 1998–9.

basin, too, we find a variation between a per capita availability of 740 m^3 in the Yamuna to 3379 m^3 in the Gandak sub-basin (see Pachauri *et al.* 1998). The Ganges sub-basin, the Tapi and Krishna basins are affected by water scarcity problem if not water stress. Thus, it is not surprising that this ecological factor of fresh water flow and its regional distribution becomes an important driving force of the political economic developments in matters of national as well as international cooperation areas.

In the use of water the global sectoral shares of household, industry and agriculture have been 8 per cent, 23 per cent and 69 per cent respectively approximately. In India, 93 per cent of fresh water use is for agriculture and livestock and out of the balance 7 per cent, the domestic consumption accounts for 3 per cent and industrial use and power generation the remaining 4 per cent. The total fresh water used for human activity is drawn partly from surface water and partly from ground water sources. The ground water which is rechargeable, supplies the water requirement of one-third of the world's population and is the main source of supply in rural areas in many parts of the world. In India, the aggregate replenishable ground water potential has been estimated to be 431 km^3 per year. A river-basinwise break up of the ground water resource potential for India is given in Table 6.5. Out of the total ground water potential, 71 km^3 of water is used for industrial and domestic use and most of it leaves the local ecosystem after use and flows through the streams and rivers and moves towards sea. The net draft of ground water for irrigation has been of the order of 115 km^3 as per the state of development of ground water till 1993. The balance of ground water resource potential usable in future on sustainable basis is 245 km^3 of water per annum. India has reached a stage of development of 32 per cent approximately of its replenishable ground water potential. The total utilizable potential of irrigation on the basis of such ground water resources works out to be 64 million hectares.

One of the major problems with ground water resource has been its over use in certain regions with water being pumped out at a rate higher than its replenishing rates, resulting in the lowering of water table by several meters at places making it increasingly difficult for the people to access ground water. The over use of ground water can have serious effect on the base flow of rivers

Table 6.5

Ground water resource potential for various basins in India

(calculated on pro-rata basis in million cubic metres)

Sl. No.	Basin	Total replenishable ground water resource	Provision for domestic, industrial and other uses	Available for irrigation	New draft	Balance for future use	% level of of ground water development
1.	Brahmaputra	26545.69	3981.35	22564.34	760.06	21804.29	3.37
2.	Brahmani with bait	4054.23	608.13	3446.09	291.22	3154.88	8.45
3.	Cambai composite	7187.25	1078.09	6109.16	2449.06	3660.10	40.09
4.	Caveri	12295.71	1844.35	10451.35	5782.85	4668.50	55.33
5.	Ganga	170994.74	26030.47	144964.26	48593.67	96370.56	33.52
6.	Godavari	40649.82	9657.69	30992.12	6054.23	24937.90	19.53
7.	Indus	26485.42	3053.95	23431.47	18209.30	5222.17	77.71
8.	Krishna	26406.97	5578.34	20828.63	6330.45	14498.19	30.39
9.	Kutch and Saurashtra	11225.09	1738.10	9486.99	4851.87	4791.02	51.14
10.	Madras and Southern	18219.72	2738.95	15486.77	8933.25	6553.52	57.68
11.	Mahanadi	16460.55	2471.10	13989.45	972.63	13016.81	6.95
12.	Meghna	8516.69	1277.48	7239.21	285.34	6953.87	3.94
13.	Narmada	10826.54	1653.75	9172.79	1994.16	7178.61	21.74
14.	Northeast comos	18842.61	2826.39	16016.22	2754.93	13261.29	17.20
15.	Pennar	4929.29	739.39	4189.89	1533.38	2656.51	36.60
16.	Subarnarekha	1819.41	272.91	1546.50	148.06	1398.43	9.57
17.	Tapi	8269.50	2335.79	5933.70	1961.33	3972.38	33.05
18.	Western Ghat	17693.72	3194.78	14499.18	3318.12	11181.06	22.88
	Total	431422.95	71075.01	360348.12	115223.91	245280.09	31.92

Source: Government of India (1997), p. 146.

particularly in dry season, affecting badly the riverine aquatic ecosystem. The overutilization of aquifer may further cause subsidence of land above the aquifer. Water table level is dropping by 4 to 10 meters per year in Tamil Nadu in South India. The depletion of ground water near coastal region may result in the intrusion of salty sea water into the aquifer which would result in salt contamination. Small islands suffer from such problem because of the fragile character of their ecological resources.

Water Pollution

Another important reason of water deficiency in water balance has been water pollution. Human beings have been using water bodies as sink for dumping wastes over millenia. Major water pollution problems arise from the following sources:

(a) Micro-organisms found in human and animal wastes include a wide range of bacteria, viruses, protozoa and other organisms which are major causes of human illness. The sewage waste containing such waste is often discharged into rivers contaminating water with such water, necessitating treatment for drinking purposes to prevent diseases.

(b) Accelerated growth of algae due to fertilization by phosphorous and nitrogen present in the discharges and run offs of fertilizers from agricultural fields is another situation of water pollution. Nitrogen and phosphorous being nutrients cause algal growth in water bodies and speed up the eutrophication process. The growth of algae contributes to the decomposition of increased quantum of dead algae collected at the bottom of the water bodies and growth of the decomposer bacteria population. The growing bacteria population uses up more of oxygen than the amount of possible oxidation in the water body through natural processes in a given environment. The decline in the dissolved oxygen content suffocates the aquatic life and kills the water body beyond a threshold. The draining of nutrients in oceans can lead to increase in toxic alagal booms described as red tides, which can affect sea food making it unsafe for consumption. The decline of dissolved oxygen in water due to such nutrient contamination imparts a foul taste to drinking water.

(c) Nitrates from fertilizers and human wastes may contaminate ground water. High nitrate level in drinking water decreases oxygen carrying capacity of haemoglobin which can threaten health of infants.

(d)   Disposal of organic industrial waste or use of water body for organic industrial raw material processing may be a source of water pollution. For example, retting of coconut husk for the coir industry in the estuaries in Kerala has caused extensive pollution of this water body and mass destruction of the benthic flora and fauna. A sizable section of these estuaries in Kerala supporting a rich and diverse fauna of finfish and shelfishes making the state the biggest producer and exporter of marine products, have been converted into virtual cesspools of foul smelling water. Retting zones of the estuaries have developed the characteristic acidic water and sediments with total depletion of dissolved oxygen leading to a toxic condition coupled with the production of large amount of hydrogen sulphide and rise in BOD values. Comparative analysis of these estimates with the data for the non-retting zones of estuaries, suggests that such condition of the water-bodies has resulted in the loss of regenerative power of this ecosystem and significant loss of benthic faunal biodiversity (Nandan et al. 1995).

(e)   Most of the commercial 100,000 chemical compounds and chemical wastes as by-products of our industrial system are considered to be harmful for human, plant and animal life. Since all matter has to flow back to the nature's sink the wastes and by-products of these chemical wastes flow into nature's sink. These are carried into the water bodies through industrial and other effluent discharge or dumped into the land fills. The contamination of soil in the latter mode of disposal can lead to the contamination of water because of the soil water interaction. One class of organic compounds including substances like polychlorinated biphenyls (PCBS) and dichloro-diphenyltrichlororethane (DDT), are highly resistant to degradation and persist in the environment and build up in the food chain through biological magnification. These two classes and other chlorinated organic compounds are so widely distributed by air and ocean currents that they are found today in the tissues of human beings and animals almost everywhere.

(f)   Heavy metals are another source of toxicity found both in soil and water and are produced in large scale by industry, agriculture and mining activities resulting in their contamination of soil and water. The metals of greatest concern for human health are lead, mercury, arsenic and cadmium. Many other useful metals like copper, zinc, silver, selenium, chromium are also toxic to aquatic life. Over use of groundwater often causes higher concentration level of these metals in the balance of aquifer water. The incidence of arsenic poisoning as experienced in certain parts of West Bengal in recent times is an example of such a phenomenon.

Most of the water pollution in India is from domestic sewage, industrial effluent and agricultural run off. Major industrial sources of pollution in India are fertilizer plants, refineries, pulp and paper mills, leather tanneries, metal plating and other chemical industry. Water pollution problem varies in severity across the countries of the world depending on population density, the nature and composition of industrial or agricultural development, and the extent and efficiency of the waste treatment system. In principle all wastes can be treated to control the contents of coliform organisms, dissolved oxygen, biochemical oxygen demand, pH level, sodium absorption ratio, electrical conductivity, etc. to meet the qualitative requirement of the end use. However, any treatment involves costs. Whether country would treat the wastes before its disposal into the water stream or not, and if so, to what extent it would be treated, would depend on the ability of the economy to bear the cost. As a result we find that in developing countries which often lack resources to build and maintain sewage treatment plants, almost 90 per cent of waste water is discharged without treatment as in the case of the Ganga. In many areas of poor Afro-Asian regions, there are evidences of seepage of domestic and human wastes into the shallow aquifer and its contamination while people use the same source for drinking water. The problem of salinity in West Asia and the problem of high sediment loads in rivers due to soil erosion in addition to the domestic and industrial waste loads, add to the dimensions of the problem of water pollution.

Development and Water Management

As the economy needs water of specific qualities to different end use purposes, the availability of usable fresh water is impaired by the extent of water pollution. The amount of water polluted is almost as large as the amount of water used by the global economic system. As a result, the balance of usable water potential declines in supporting future growth of human population and economy. The treatment of wastes for protecting water quality is dependent on the stage of economic development and the level of manmade capital to population ratio of a society. In a situation of increased water pollution the well-being index of a society goes down either because of the lower availability of the target quality of water or due to the use of the polluted water. In a poor society the scarcity leads to higher use of polluted water. Apart from the immediate human economic gain, very important indirect gain of life support function of water in the ecosystem is also affected by such degradation. The bivariate distribution of population over gross national income per capita and water stress as a ratio of withdrawal to availability shows that over one-half of the world population falls in the low income category and more than one-third of these people face medium to high water stress. An additional 39 per cent of the poor people are in medium water stress (Table 6.6).

The socio-economic developmental consideration thus needs management of water resources with efficiency and equity. Water resource management advocates a two-way solution to the

Table 6.6
Distribution of world population according to income and
water stress categories

(population in millions)

Income class (per capita per annum income in US $)	Withdrawal/Availability of water (1995)				
	1 (< 10%)	2 (10-20%)	3 (20-40%)	4 (> 40%)	Total
Low income ≤ 795	806.18	1265.89	957.70	238.07	3267.84
Lower-middle income 796-2895	542.40	285.95	165.33	137.91	1131.59
Upper-middle income 2896–8955	258.95	13.10	137.30	63.44	472.79
High income ≥ 8956	108.44	514.41	181.25	19.74	823.84
Total:	1721.97	2079.35	1441.58	459.16	5696.06

Source: Stockholm Environmental Institute (1997).

problem of reduction of water stress: (a) by augmenting supply, and (b) by treating effluent waste to control pollution. Augmentation of supply not only has the problem of mobilization of capital, but also that of ecosystem degradation. While the dam reservoirs augment water supply, they also affect the environmental quality by altering the sedimentation rates, adversely affecting the aquatic life in the down stream, and causing permanent loss of vegetation, forest and wildlife due to submergence, floods in rainy season because of heavy rainfall exceeding the storage limits, indirect effect on salinity of soil around the storage area and in the irrigated area if drainage provision is not adequate, etc. The qualities of soil, water and forests are interactive. The management of these resources therefore warrants an integrated approach of resource management. Besides, proper protection of soil and water involves the requirement of manmade capital and technology. Manmade capital has a complementary role with natural capital in resource management and has not always a competing role as neoclassical resource allocation theory tends to highlight in the context of sustainable development. As the scope of interaction between the manmade capital and the natural capital is dependent on the stage of economic development, a global cooperation in the form of transfer of appropriate technology and capital is required for combining resource management with equity and development (see Stockholm Environment Institute 1997).

Forest

Forest as a Resource

Earth was covered with diverse natural vegetation prior to human domestication of plant species and invention of agriculture when 6 billion hectares of forest covered earth. The development of agriculture and later on of industry and urbanization, have led to the loss of about 2 billion hectares of forests. Of the balance 4 billion hectares about 1.5 billion hectares are still in pristine condition.

Forests provide two kinds of products and services which benefit the human system:

(a)   Forest supplies harvestible products which have direct use value—timber, fuel-wood, industrial raw materials, fodder and fibre grasses, and a wide spectrum of non-timber forest products derived from plants and animals. It provides the services of amenity and ecotourism which have direct use value. These use values are converted into exchange values depending on the definition of property rights on forest resources and the institutional arrangement of these supplies reaching the individual consumers.

(b)   Forest provides the non-market ecological services—local and global, which are crucial in giving life support to the biosphere; for example, soil conservation by protecting it against erosion, watershed protection and regulation of local water regime, protection of local ecosystems against floods, carbon sequestration and provision of habitat for biodiversity which is a repository of genetic wealth. All these eco-services provide indirect use value, or some option value, but not readily transformable into exchange value as these are public good type services with actual or potential future use. The possible discovery of new medicinal use of an existing plant or animal species of a forest in future gives an example of a case of option value of that plant or animal species as the absence of the concerned species would have caused the loss of opportunity of such discovery.

Forest conserves soil by holding soil materials together by the roots of its trees. Soil is thus protected against erosion by wind or water flow. Secondly, it also breaks the wind blast and reduces the impact on the environment. Thirdly, the wastes and decomposition of forest biomass of plants and animals species provide the very organic component of soil, that is, humus which performs the capillary function of holding water and contributes to the water retention capacity of soil. Thus forest interacts with soil and water and creates the basic condition of primary production for land and the ecosystem of a region. As forests retain rain water in the plant bodies and soil, the moisture of forest area has a cooling effect on the local atmosphere. Finally, the photosynthesis function fixes carbon dioxide of the atmosphere and contributes to the reduction of stock of green house gas in the atmosphere and to the stabilization of the climate and precipitation.

Forest, land quality and water resource interact with each other. One of the major threats from the loss of forest is the desertification of land. The existence of forest along with its biomass density, plant species composition and biodiversity depends on the moisture availability which is in turn determined by the temperature and the precipitation. Broadly speaking, the vegetation cover can be classified into the following:

(a) Forest cover with crown density 40 per cent or more
(b) Open forest with crown density between 10 per cent and 40 per cent
(c) Grass lands
(d) Scrubs with crown density less than 10 per cent
(e) Deserts

It is only the vegetation cover of the type (a) and (b) which can be considered to describe forests. Forests can be classified as natural forests and managed plantation. In the latter category farm forestry, community wood lots and forestry department wood lots are included. In these forestry modes farmers are provided with seedlings to grow more trees for community use as fuel or timber. Any managed plantation with crown density more than 10 per cent is included into the category of forests.

The vegetation of earth varies with the climatic condition which is correlated to latitude and altitude of a place. The vegetations of the arctic zone, temperate zone and tropical zones are therefore different. The forests of temperate zone like those of North America, Europe, Russia are different in their composition of plant species and associated animal species from those of tropical zone, because the tropical soils, climates and ecosystems are quite different from the temperate zone. Tropical forests are faster growing and richer in biodiversity, but more vulnerable than temperate forests. There is no guarantee that they can survive an extensive clear-cut felling without severely degrading the soil and ecosystem. The selective harvesting of certain types of trees or harvesting in strips as currently being practised, allow better regeneration.

Destruction and degradation of forest is one of the major environmental crisis of the world. Deforestation occurred in the developed countries due to industrialization, warranting land use change and also consumption of wood for construction and industrial purposes. In the developing countries the stress on forest is occurring due to the following factors:

(a)   diversion of land use from forest use to agriculture, pasture, urban development, development of infrastructural projects like river valley, transport (inter city road and rail development), transmission lines, mining and quarrying activities, etc.;

(b)   degradation of forests due to unsustainable harvesting of forest products or its overuse for livestock grazing, pests and diseases, fire, industrial pollution like acid rain, or climate change due to global warming;

(c)   loss of natural forests due to conversion of natural forests into modified or planted forests driven by economic necessities, that is, removal of natural vegetation by selective felling and promoting the introduction of commercially remunerative species only; for example, plantation forestry or monoculture.

Deforestation, degradation and human intervention for controlling species have some interactive effects and have resulted in the following consequences:

(a)   loss of natural regeneration or growth;

(b)   change in species composition having adverse effect on energy flow through food chain, biodiversity as well as pests and diseases;

(c)   forest fragmentation due to loss of habitats for bio-diversity;

(d)   degrading impact on the quality of soil, water and climate.

All these, contribute to the lowering of the productivity of organic matter in an ecosystem and affect ultimately the forest base resource support to human economy.

Extent of Deforestation and Degradation

What has been the extent or dimensions of deforestation or degradation globally or in India? India has recorded forest area of 76.52 million hectares while the actual forest area as per satellite imagery data have been found to be 63.96 million hectares that is, 83.6 per cent of total recorded area. The land use of 16.5 per cent of recorded forest area has changed due to the following reasons:

(a)   degradation of forests to scrub land with less than 10 per cent crown density having a 7.9 per cent of total recorded area;

(b)   shifting cultivation by people particularly of hilly regions accounting for 1.4 per cent of the recorded area;

(c)   encroachment on government owned forest land for cultivation and habitation by way of unauthorised settlement due to the pressure of population, accounting for 1 per cent of recorded forest land;

(d)   diversion of forest land to other uses accounting for 4.696 million hectares between 1951 and 1995 accounting for 6.1 per cent of recorded area. This balance of diversion of land use includes the respective shares of agriculture, river valley projects and industries and infrastructure which have been 2.764, 0.518 and 0.141 million hectares respectively.

Table 6.7 shows the changes in the actual cover of forest in India from 1981 to 1995, the period for which reliable satellite imagery data was available.

In the global scenario as per FAO (1993) estimates tropical forests at the end of 1990 covered an area of 17.56 million hectares. South America and the Caribbean had 52 per cent share, Africa 30 per cent and Asia and Pacific 18 per cent. Four countries—Brazil, Zaire, Indonesia and Peru—had about half of the tropical

Table 6.7
Change in forest cover in the period 1981–95 in India

		(million hectares)
	1981	*1995*
Recorded forest area	75.13	76.52
Actual forest area	64.20	63.96
Desert forest	36.14	38.57
Open forest	27.65	24.93
Mangroves	0.40	0.45
Scrubland	7.67	6.05
Uninterpreted	1.15	–
Non-forest area	255.74	258.7
Total land	328.78	328.7

Source: Pachauri *et al.* (1998), p. 107.

forests of the world. However, in the 10-year period between 1980 and 1990, tropical forests have been lost at the rate of 154000 km^2 per year. The total decadal loss in terms of area constitutes almost 80 per cent of Indonesia's land area. The rate of annual deforestation has been highest in South-east Asia, and Central America and Mexico. Table 6.8 gives an ecosystem-wise loss of forests and its broad regional break up. FAO (1993) estimated that for each year the total loss of standing biomass above ground had been 2500 million tonnes in the tropical countries. This would mean 4100 million tonnes of CO_2 which is 75 per cent of USA's CO_2 emission (see Gupta *et al.* 1998).

The annual deforestation rates of the world has been 0.8 per cent of the total forested area during the 1980s. Large areas of surviving forests have been fragmented due to degradation for various reasons and have resulted in biodiversity loss. During 1980–90 the area under plantation agriculture increased from 180,000 km^2 to 400,000 km^2 and there has been very marginal increase of forest area in the industrialized countries. The round wood annual production, globally, increased by 8 per cent between 1983–5 to 1993–5, the total amount being 3374.1 million m^3 in 1993–5, the share of fuel and charcoal being 56 per cent and that of industrial round wood for paper, furniture construction, etc. 44 per cent.

In India one of the basic reasons for the degradation of forests has been unsustainable harvesting or overuse of its resources for livestock maintenance. The ratio of requirement to sustainable supply has been 5.8:1 for fuel-wood and 2.4:1 for industrial timber. The pressure of population and poverty has made rural households increasingly dependent on forest for their needs. The total fuel wood consumption in India has been 260 million m^3 in 1997 while the sustainable production for the same year was estimated to be 52.6 million m^3. As per the survey of NCAER (1985) rural households of most of the populous states had more than 90 per cent dependence of non-commercial energy including fuel wood. The household sector accounts for 40–50 per cent of the total energy consumed in India. In 1992–3 the share of non-commercial energy in rural households was 91.95 per cent while those of fuel logs, fuel twigs, dung-cake, agricultural wastes have been 32.49 per cent, 29.11 per cent, 17.0 per cent and 13.35 per

Table 6.8

Extent of global forest loss by forest ecosystems (1990)

(area in million hectares)

	World		Africa		Asia		Oceania		Americas	
	Area	Annual loss %	Area	Annual loss %	Area	Annual loss %	Area	Annual loss %	Area	Annual loss %
Total forest	1756.3	0.8	527.6	0.7	274.6	1.2	36.0	0.3	918.1	0.7
Rain	713.7	0.6	86.4	0.5	148.0	1.2	29.3	0.3	450.1	0.4
Moist deciduous	591.8	0.9	251.3	0.8	41.8	1.4	0.7	0.3	297.9	1.0
Hill and montane	201.4	1.1	35.3	0.8	41.1	1.2	5.4	0.3	119.7	1.2
Dry deciduous	178.6	0.9	92.5	0.8	40.7	1.0	0.4	0.4	44.9	1.2
Very dry	59.7	0.5	59.7	0.5	0.037	2.9	-	-	1.0	1.8
Desert	8.1	0.9	3.4	0.4	2.9	0.9	-	-	1.6	2.0

Source: World Resource Institute (1994), *World Resources 1994–5*, pp. 308–9.

cent respectively. Since animal dung and agricultural crop wastes have important opportunity use as compost and manure in agriculture, any shortage of such fuel resource creates more demand for fuel wood. Over harvesting of fuel wood relative to rate of regeneration causes depletion of forest leading to degradation of soil through erosion and loss of moisture. On the other hand, shortage of fuel wood may force increased diversion of cow dung and agro-waste from agricultural use to fuel use which would lead to the depletion of organic and nutrient content of soil in agricultural land. Energy use of biomass in a particularly over populated society would create a stress either on land or forest resources which interact with one another.

As far as the industrial wood requirement is concerned, it increased from 2.5 million m^3 in 1947 to 34 million m^3 in 1997, while the production increased from 2.5 million m^3 in 1947 (with zero gap between demand and supply) to 14 million m^3 in 1997 meeting only 41 per cent of the requirement. As per the sectoral break up as available, the latest for 1987, the shares of pulp and packaging and that of pulp and paper were dominant with 24.7 per cent and 23.8 per cent respectively (see Pachauri *et al.* 1998). The shortage of industrial wood has led to the growth of import of round woods and to the structural change in the capacities of the paper industry in terms of raw material base of its technology. The shares of crop waste and waste paper (recycling) in the total capacity of paper mills have increased from 10 per cent and nil in 1970 to 35 per cent and 26 per cent in 1995 and that of wood declined from 84 per cent in 1970 to 38 per cent in 1995.

In India, cattle grazing has been an important stress factor for forests. Although India accounts for 13 per cent of the live-stock population of the world, there are virtually no identified and managed pastures in India. All common property resources including long term fallow, cultivable wastes, pastures and other grazing lands and protected and unclassed forest land have been considered as being available as grazing land. Table 6.9 shows the growth of livestock and availability of grazing land in India, and points to the growing pressure on forest land. While there has been a growth of livestock population at 1 per cent rate per annum, the common property land availability declined substantively at the annual average rate of 0.3 per cent. The forest land availability for grazing also has showed a downward trend. The current availability of green fodder has been estimated to be 434 million tonnes of which 250 million tonnes can be sustainably extracted. Since the current requirement has been estimated to be 932 million tonnes, the wide gap between requirement and supply has been met by unlimited grazing in forest land. While the use of crop waste for fodder has met some part of the gap in terms of green fodder, the opportunity cost of such use of waste with alternative compost use has driven the rural community to fall back upon forest resource for support to the livestocks, resulting in over grazing of forest land. Over grazing carries both physical and chemical degradation of soil. The removal of green foliage interferes with the process of nutrient cycling and affects the chemical composition and fertility of soil. As the productivity of grass lands and their nutrition values deteriorate because of such degradation, fodder supply is reduced and the livestock gets under nourished. For the same target supply of livestock products and services, society tends to maintain a larger stock of cattle population leading to further scarcity of green fodder and problem of resource balance for maintaining the livestock. Over grazing would occur in the absence of careful and consistent livestock, forest and fodder management policy.

Table 6.9
Livestock population and land use for grazing in India

(land area in million hectares)

Year	Common property resource land	Protected and unclassed forest land	Total land used for grazing as open access	Live stock population (million)	Grazing area
1950-1	66.89	38.96	105.85	292	0.36
1970-1	43.82	32.79	76.61	353	0.22
1997	38.00	34.80	72.80	467	0.15

Source: Pachauri et al. (1998), p. 124.

The industrial pollution of sulphuric oxides and nitric oxides emission are a source of great risk for forest. When combined with rain water they form weak acid lowering the pH level. Acid rain stresses the biotic components of terrestrial and aquatic system destroying the photosynthetic tissues of plant and stunting their autotrophic activities. Ultraviolet radiation too produces photochemical smog out of nitric oxides and unburnt hydrocarbons. Smog affects the productivity of vegetation of the ecosystem since air pollutants can travel over long distances. These pollutants may often create transnational problems of externality and affect forests or water bodies or agricultural fields located at a long distance from the source of pollution.

The impact of deforestation and degradation is visible in soil erosion and depletion of organic component of soil making the soil sandy and causing desertification. Deforestation reduces moisture level of the atmosphere of the surrounding ecosystem as soil loses its water holding capability. Deforestation also reduces the rate of carbon recycling and contributes a higher rate of accumulation of green house gases in the atmosphere. The land use change due to deforestation in India has caused 21 million tonnes of carbon dioxide emission by way of reduced carbon sequestration. Besides, marshes, and forest wet lands have tremendous capacity to absorb pollutants. The reduction of such areas of non-forest water bodies with more of unabsorbed urban, industrial and chemical wastes would have higher damage effect due to pollution.

Forests provide habitats to diverse living species. Destruction of habitats due to deforestation or forest degradation causes loss of biodiversity. As biodiversity is an immensely valuable repository of genetic information, such a loss would mean a huge opportunity loss for shaping a better future of human kind and the planet.

Finally, it would be important to see the implication of forest degradation in terms of loss of economic values. Such valuation accounting should not only take account of loss of flow of timber and non-timber marketable economic products, but also of those ecoservices rendered by soil conservation, watershed, carbon sequestration and biodiversity. While soil erosion can be evaluated in terms of irreversible loss of stream of agricultural income, loss of watershed service can be evaluated in terms of the value of loss of rechargeable ground water every year caused by deforestation. The value of water can be taken as per the marginal value productivity of irrigation water in agriculture or in terms of the cost of supply of equivalent water from alternative sources like canal irrigation. The loss of the service of carbon fixation through photosynthesis process may be valued in terms of the cost of abatement of the associated amount of CO_2 which would not be absorbed by the plants because of the degradation of forests. The cost of abatement may be based on the cheapest way of abating CO_2 emission from power plant or steel plant. Similarly the loss of biodiversity due to degradation of forest may be valued in terms of the major loss of option values of possible future economic uses of flora and fauna contained in the forest. In short, economic implication of any environmental degradation needs the adjustment of the accounting system to internalize the valuation of natural capital and account for its depreciation in such context. Such an adjustment should take care not only of its loss of contribution to marketable product flows, but also to that of non-market ecological services by appropriate method of indirect imputation of values or other simulation method. The accounting for such ecological services would make such a model of valuation an interdisciplinary model of ecological economics.

Biodiversity

Extent of Biodiversity

Biodiversity represents the wealth of life of the earth—the millions of plants, animals and micro-organisms, the genes they contain and the intricate ecosystem they build into living ecosystem. There may exist anywhere between 10 million to 100 million species of life on earth out of which only 1.4 million have been identified, classified and named. Of these 1.4 million living and described species, 750,000 are insects, 41000 are vertebrates and 250,000 are plants. The remainder consists of a complex variety of invertebrates, fungi, algae and micro-organisms (see Table 6.10 for the details) (see Wilson 1988). This is, of course, a highly incomplete enumeration except for a few well studied groups like vertebrates and flowering plants. Some of the studies of local diversity like the one of Peruvian Amazon rain forest (see Erwin 1983) after extrapolation have raised the plausible number of

Table 6.10
Number of described species of living organisms

Kingdom/major subdivision	Common name	No. of described species	Sub totals
1. Virus	Viruses	1000	1000
2. Minera	Bacteria	3000	
	Bacteria (Myxoplasma)	60	
	Blue-green algae	1700	4760
3. Fungi	Zygomycete fungi	665	
	Cup fungi	28650	
	Basidomycete fungi	16000	
	Water moulds	580	
	Chytrids	575	
	Cellular slime moulds	13	
	Plasmodial slime moulds	500	46983
4. Algae	Green algae	7000	
	Brown algae	1500	
	Red algae	4000	
	Chrysophyte algae	12500	
	Dinoflagellates	1100	
	Euglenoids	800	26900
5. Plantae	Mosses, Liverworts, hornworts	16600	
	Psilopsids	9	
	Lycophytes	1275	
	Horsetails	15	
	Ferus	10000	
	Gymnosperms	529	
	Dicots	170000	
	Monocots	50000	248428
6. Protozoa	Protozoans	30800	30800
7. Animalia	Sponges	5000	
	Jellyfish, corals, combjellies	9000	
	Flatworms	12200	
	Nematodes (round worms)	12000	
	Annelids (earth worms and relatives)	12000	

Table 6.10 contd.

Table 6.10 contd.

Kingdom/major subdivision	Common name	No. of described species	Sub totals
	Molluscs	50000	
	Echinoderms (starfish and relatives)	6100	
	Anthropods	6100	
	Insects	751000	
	Other anthropods	123161	
	Minor invertebrate phyla	9300	989761
8. Chordata	Tunicates	1250	
	Acorn worms	23	
	Vertebrates		
	Lampreys and other jawless fishes	63	
	Sharks and other cartilaginous fishes	843	
	Bony fishes	18150	
	Amphibians	4184	
	Reptiles	6300	
	Birds	9040	
	Mammals	4000	43853
Total:			1392485

Source: Wilson (ed.), Biodiversity, pp. 4–5.

species globally to be anywhere between 5 million and 30 million.
The maintenance of species diversity depends on the longevity
of species and the process of creation of new species. Diversity
of species as a result of the factors of longevity and new creation
has been maintained approximately at an even level over long
time except for brief periods of accelerated extinction at a more
or less regular interval of 26 million years in the last 250 million
years of the history of our planet. The scenario, however, has
been vastly changing fast over the last 200 years because of
excessive human interference into the natural processes.

Some of the ecosystems of the world have, drawn special
attention of the evolutionary biologists and conservationists. The
most important of them has been the tropical rain forest. Although

rain forests cover 7 per cent of earth's land surface, they contain half of the species of the entire world biota by providing habitats. While these forests have relatively tight upper canopy of mostly broad evergreen trees which are sustained by an annual rainfall of 100 centimeters or more, two or more of undergrowth of trees and shrubs occur beneath the upper canopy and the ground level undergrowth is quite sparse. The species diversity in such forests is fantastic. One leguminous tree in the rainforest (Tambopata Reserve) of Peru has been found to contain 43 species of ants (Wilson 1987). A sample of 10 selected plots of 1 hectare each in Borneo was found to contain 700 species of trees—the same as the diversity of similar plant species of the entire North America. The rainforests of the Central and South America provide shelter to several hundred species of birds and many thousands of butterflies, beetles and other insects. However, such tropical rain forests are ecologically very fragile as they have mostly grown on a wet desert which describes an unpromising soil base which can be washed by heavy rains and have poor nutrient content. As a result, the destruction of rain forests and consequent soil erosion would cause an irreversible loss because of the difficulty of regenerating the top soil and the forest along with its biodiversity. About 40 per cent of the land that can support tropical closed forest is now denuded of such forests because of human action. According to the estimates of the United Nations Environmental Programme, by the end of 1970s the annual rate of destruction of such forests rose to the level of 7.6 million hectares or 1 per cent of the total such forest cover which was being permanently cleared or converted into agricultural land of shifting type cultivation. Most of such land is being permanently cleared and reduced to a state in which natural reforestation would be almost impossible in future and the loss of biodiversity would be irreversible. Since no one knows how many species there are, it is difficult to say how many species are being lost currently.

In respect of biodiversity, India which is a tropical country has a share of 6 per cent of the world species and has a rich heritage of species and genetic forms. India is the tenth plant rich country of the world, eleventh in terms of endemic species of higher vertebrates and sixth in terms of centres of biodiversity and origin of agrodiversity. The total number of living species identified in India till so far is 150,000. Out of the 12 hot spots of biodiversity, two are located in India—one in the north-eastern region and the other in the western Ghats of southern India (see Government of India, CSO 1997; Khoshoo 1995) (see also Table 6.11).

The ecological balance of flora, fauna and forest has been seriously disturbed by the rapid growth of population, urbanization and industrialization in the present century all over the world. Growth of human population and industrialization have resulted in loss of habitats due to deforestation. Besides, disappearance of prey in the food chain of an ecosystem and the relentless hunting of certain animals by human beings, have also caused extinction of species. A threshold level of population size exists below which a species

Table 6.11
Biodiversity in India

Taxon	Number of species	Percentage
Bacteria	850	0.67
Algae	2500	2.00
Fungi	23000	18.23
Lichens	1600	1.30
Pryophyta	2700	2.14
Pteridophyta	1022	0.80
Gymnosperms	64	0.05
Angiosperms	17000	13.50
Protozoa	2577	2.04
Mollusca	5042	4.00
Crustacea	2970	2.35
Insecta	50717	40.00
Other invertebrates incl. hernichordata	11252	9.00
Protochordata	116	0.10
Pisces	2546	2.02
Amphibia	204	0.16
Reptilia	428	0.34
Aves	1228	1.00
Mammalia	372	0.30
Total	126188	100.00

Source: Khoshoo 1995, p. 14.

would be threatened with extinction because of the proneness of genetic and reproductive disorder which interbreeding within too small a population causes for most of the species. Besides, the biodiversity loss is irreversible and as a result the issue of loss of significant option value becomes quite serious.

One of the most important loss due to such irreversibility is the loss of genetic information. Each species is the repository of immense amount of genetic information. The number of genes range from 1000 in bacteria or 10,000 in some fungi to 400,000 or more in many flowering plants, while a mammal like house mouse has about 100,000 genes. The genetic information is an important resource for research activities in biotechnology. The number of species and the amount of genetic information in a representative organism constitutes only part of the biological diversity of the planet. Each species consists of innumerable organisms and no two individual members of the same species are genetically identical. Even if an endangered species is saved from extinction it will probably be found to have lost most of its internal variety. It is thus obvious that large range of option of future research and possible discovery would be closed and option value lost due to the loss of diversity of planet's genetic wealth.

Loss of Biodiversity

It is difficult to estimate the extent and rate of biodiversity loss for the simple reason that no one knows how many species there are exactly at any given time. There is, however, no doubt that the rate of extinction of species has been much faster than it was before 1800. Extinction rate is generally estimated from the principle of bio-geography regarding habitat loss, for example, in an island system the number of species of a particular group increases approximately as the fourth root of the land area. This is relevant for biodiversity in habitat islands, for example, lake in a land-locked area, mountain tops surrounded by evergreen forest. Using such area–species relationship, it has been predicted that the destruction of habitats of rain forest is likely to cause inevitable loss of 12 per cent of 704 birds species of Amazon basin and 15 per cent of 92000 plant species in South and Central America within a century.

The situation is worse for the biodiversity loss for less extensive habitats than the ones of rain forests of Amazon or Onnoco. If the habitats and the species are very localized, the extinction rate would be higher for the destruction of such habitats. For example, Madagascar is a biotic treasure house. Its eastern forest is a habitat of 12000 known plant species and 190,000 known animal species; at least 60 per cent of these species being never found anywhere else. It is estimated that at least half of the original species have been lost because of destruction of 90 per cent of the forests of the country. Similarly, Western Ecuador once housed about 8000 to 10000 plant species, half of which were endemic. Each species of plant supports between 10 and 30 animal species. A large part of Ecuador forests have experienced land use change giving space to banana plantations, oil wells and human settlements. Total number of species lost in the last 25 years have been estimated to be 50,000 illustrating the extent of bio-diversity loss being experienced in the developing countries. If we assume that there are 10 million species of flora and fauna in all the habitats of the world, the loss is roughly at the rate of one out of every thousand species per year. This is one thousand to ten thousand times more than the rate of loss before the period of human interference of industrial revolution since 1800. It is estimated that worldwide slightly over 1000 animal species and subspecies are threatened with extinction at the rate of one such endangered species per year. There are 20,000 flowering plants which are also exposed to the risk of facing extinction. Of the vascular plant species that India possesses, 237 of them are rare, 117 vulnerable, 170 endangered, 38 possibly exinct and 21 extinct.

The dependence of organism on appropriate environment gives the understanding to the ecologists on the position of the relation between habitat destruction and modifications with species loss. Most of the cases of extinction of species take place due to habitat loss in areas of intense biological activities and food energy concentration like tropical forests, coral reefs and wet lands. Wet lands are possibly more endangered than tropical forests. The share of wet lands on earth surface is 6 per cent. World's wet lands are being lost due to dredging, draining and filling for developmental purposes. It is possible to estimate fairly reliably the number of habitat loss in an ecosystem. The number of species dependent on such a habitat is a factor 10 times the number of habitat losses. A rule of thumb is used which assumes that 50 per cent of species will be lost if 90 per cent of the habitats are gone.

One can also get an idea of the stress on biodiversity by looking at the human appropriation of net primary production of the world. Ecologists of the Stanford University estimated that of the global net primary production (NPP) of 225 billion metric tonne, nearly 60 per cent of it being on land which is available as a food resource for all animal organisms, humanity is now directly using a share of 3 per cent, about 4 per cent of that on land (see Vitousek *et al.* 1986 and Ehrlich 1988). Such estimates consider all the energy that has flown up to the concerned trophic level which supports the incremental biomass (that is, the NPP fixed in its living tissues) which is directly consumed by human being as food, fodder, energy or industrial raw materials. People indirectly uses NPP as the biomass consumed in fire used in forest clearing, crop wastes, NPP of pasture land wasted (or fodder not consumed by livestock), etc. With the inclusion of such indirect uses the share of human appropriation rises to 30 per cent, a staggeringly high share. If we consider the NPP that is annually foregone due to conversion of land from more productive use in the natural system to less productive ones, for example, forest converted into agricultural farm land, or pasture, or grass land converted into desert due to human interference, marsh into urban settlements, the potential NPP on land in a year is reduced by about 13 per cent and the human share in unreduced potential NPP of a year goes up to 40 per cent. This estimate does not take account of reduction of the potential NPP due to pollution arisings from human activities. If, however, human beings command over 40 per cent of net photosynthetic products on land for their direct and indirect uses, a doubling of human population and economic activity would mean appropriation of 80 per cent of similar net primary production. How would other species on land survive in such a situation of doubling the scale of human kind's size and operation? It is beyond doubt that in such an eventuality there will be retention of only selected species and serious loss of biodiversity. The world would look like Sahel or China where nature has low primary productivity due to over use by people.

People are often under a wrong impression that indefinite expansion of human population can be supported by the unmeasureable riches of the sea. The riches of the sea have been found to be scarce. Although human being uses only 2 per cent of the NPP of sea, it is very difficult to even double this share. The reason behind it is the difficulty of harvesting much of the NPP that lies in the form of phytoplankton or zooplankton. Exploitation of pool of oceanic resources is occurring intensively for fishes and larger invertebrates as can be harvested on a sustainable basis. The discrepancy in the human ability to harvest terrestrial and oceanic NPP is reflected in the general lack of extinction crisis in sea.

The extinction of species and organisms would have its primary impact on human society through the impairment of ecosystem services. All plants, animals and micro-organisms exchange gases with atmosphere and the biotic composition thus contributes to the maintenance of a mix of gases in the atmosphere. Destruction of biodiversity may result in such change in the gas mix in the long run which may end up with rapid climate change and agricultural crop failures. As already noted, destruction of forests would deprive humanity not only of timber, but also of lots of medicinal options for future. Destruction of insect species may cause decline of pollination and affect the pest control services by ecosystem resulting in sudden devastating pest outbreaks. Finally, with the loss of species humanity loses irreversibly part of the genetic library of the planet which has actual and potential of immense benefits towards human well-being. Besides, the abundance of genetic variation across and within species enables the species successfully evolve in response to long-term environmental changes. Loss of biodiversity may, therefore, destabilize the ecosystem by robbing its power of resilience. As ecosystem services falter, human mortality from various respiratory and epidemic diseases, natural disaster and famine may lower life expectancy to a point which would possibly be as fatal as nuclear winter. As human civilization is a construct of superstructure over the base of natural order, the loss of biodiversity in terms of destructive potential seems to be the most serious threat to it in the long run and next only to a nuclear holocaust.

In view of the interdependence among the various species including the human being as explained above, the bio-physical limit of human appropriation of NPP needs to be ascertained and taken seriously into account for the sustainability of our development process, and economic well-being of humanity. The problem of biodiversity conservation and economic development have their certain important complementarities. The problems of people in the tropics have mostly been biological in origin—overpopulation, habitat destruction, soil deterioration, malnutrition, disease and insecurity of food and shelter. To resolve these problems biodiversity can be used as a resource and not as an obstacle. For food supply, humanity has come to depend only on 7000 kinds of plants for food, while there are 75000 edible plants in existence, but most of them are lying untested and unused. It is important to conserve different plant and animal species, convert most of their option values into actual use value in human economic system, and harvest carefully at an optimum rate so that they are not threatened of extinction due to overuse. Economic motivation can play a positive role in conserving and using a species rather than destroying it. This would require certain restraints on consumeristic lifestyle which is destructive from the ecological point of view and therefore changes in human preferences and values. Like environmental quality, biodiversity needs to be recognized as a service rendering good which though not marketed, should enter the preference function of individuals as consumers. The economic policy modelling needs to recognize such structural change in preference function based on deep ecological consideration. While such analysis would yield useful results ranging from optimal level of species diversity and optimum share of humanity in the net photosynthetic output of the planet, new initiatives in technology and institutions will need to be taken to translate the potentials and lessons of science and human values into actual reality.

Energy

Development and Energy Security

Non-food energy is an essential requirement of human economy and is a crucial input for all kinds of transformations which the processes of production of goods and services perform. Such energy consumption per capita in an economy is one of the determinants of the level of well-being of human society. While a part of this energy requirement is met by fuel wood, traditional crop waste or dung-cakes, etc., commercial energy has the dominant share in energy supply today in an industrialized and urbanized society. Due to the higher efficiency of use the operation of manmade capital and infrastructure requires the use of commercial energy and replacement of traditional fuel. In an over-populated poor country the use of non-commercial fuel may create stress either on land or forest resources. About 88 per cent of the commercial energy is based on fossil fuels of coal, oil and natural gas. The balance 12 per cent is commercial energy uses, the hydel, nuclear or some of the non-conventional renewable resources; for example, the cases of wind power, solar power, micro-hydel, geothermals, etc. Fossil fuels being exhaustible resources raise the problem of sustainability of development process. The total global consumption of commercial energy has grown from 3.771 billion oil equivalent tonnes in 1980 to 4.665 billion tonnes of oil equivalent in 1996 at an annual average rate of 1.33 per cent. However, the per capita energy use varies very widely across the different countries and is related with the stages of development, industrialization, infrastructural development, fuel composition and fuel efficiency. The per capita commercial energy use has been as low as 486 of oil equivalent kg for low income countries excluding India and China (902 kg for China, 476 kg for India), 1801 kg for middle income countries, 5346 kg for high income countries, and 8051 kg for USA. The per capita electricity consumption has increased from 1568 kwh (Kilowatt-hour) in 1980 to 2370 kwh in 1996 for the world. The per capita electricity consumption has been 9491 kwh for industrialized countries, 845 kwh for all the developing countries together and 81 for the least developed countries in the same year 1996. The share of the traditional fuel in the total energy consumption has been as high as 91 per cent in poorer countries like Nepal or Congo, Duke republic, Tanzania and Ethiopia, and as low as 1 per cent in Canada or U.K. and 4 per cent for USA in 1995. The shares of traditional fuel have been 23 per cent for India and 6 per cent for China. The relative share of commercial energy depends on both the endowment of manmade capital to population ratio (or alternatively per capita GDP) and the endowment of biomass in the natural environment of the country.

The commercial energy production and use are both capital intensive. Hence, it is expected that with industrialization and capital formation, there will be increasing penetration of the use of electricity and use of oil and natural gas in a developing economy. Besides the capital deepening and associated energy penetration, the income elasticity of final use of electricity, LPG gas, motor spirit and diesel will raise the demand of fossil fuel based energy and over all per capita commercial energy consumption of the country with rise in income (see Sengupta 1997).

In view of the very likely rise in the per capita energy consumption of developing countries, there will be inevitable rise in the aggregate commercial energy consumption in future given any positive population growth scenario. This tendency of rise in aggregate commercial energy would, however, be moderated by the rise in the efficiency of energy use with economic development. It may be noted that the productivity of energy in terms of GDP per kg of oil equivalent energy is low for developing countries and rises with the rise in the per capita income level. Cross-country data on efficiency of energy shows the average of GDP per kg oil equivalent of energy to be $5 for high income countries, $1.7 for middle income countries and $0.8 for low income countries, excluding China and India, $0.7 for China and $0.8 for India in 1996. The corresponding GDP per capita in 1998 has been $25510 for high income countries, $2950 for middle income country, $580 for low income country excluding China and India ($750 for China and $430 for India). In the initial phase of development, the process of industrialization leads to increased penetration of commercial energy into the economy and raises the energy intensity of GDP. However, beyond a threshold level of development as indicated by the per capita income, the sectoral composition of national income would change in favour of services at the cost of share of manufacture. Besides, the ability to pay for efficient energy using technology also goes up and preference of the people switches in favour of the environmentally cleaner and less energy and emission intensive technologies. As a result, the energy intensity of GDP as a function of per capita GDP is represented by a reversed U-shaped curve. Some of the industrialized countries of Europe have in fact been able to experience growth occasionally involving only little or no rise in their aggregate commercial energy consumption. The GDP elasticity of commercial energy thus starts from a high value in the early stage of industrialization and thus declines with its progress and comes down below 1. Thus, the development process has got both the tendencies of raising total commercial energy use through increased penetration effect and that of lowering it by way of efficiency effect. Given the expected distribution of future growth of global income among the countries at the different stages of development, the aggregate global demand for commercial energy is likely to go up for a considerable time in future although with a continuously declining global GDP elasticity of energy consumption.

How would such growing requirement of commercial energy over time be met from the fossil fuels which are exhaustible? Between 1970 and 1989, the world economy burnt 450 billion barrels of oil, 90 billion tonnes of coal and 1100 billion m^3 of natural gas. With such depletion the balance of reserve is supposed to come down. The reserve to production ratio of an individual fuel indicates the balance of reserve as measured in terms of number of years of production. This ratio however increased between 1970 and 1989 as shown in Table 6.12, although the annual production has gone up over time. The discovery of new reserves contributed to the upward movement of the ratio. The accretion of reserves through exploration for which capital and finance have to be employed, does not make this non-renewable resource, renewable. As the total quantity of discovered and undiscovered reserve is a constant, any amount of production would mean that there remains that much fewer resources to

Table 6.12
World production and R/P ratio for fossil fuels

	Annual production		R/P ratio	
	1970	1989	1970	1989
Oil (billion barrels)	16.7	21.4	31	41
Coal (billion tonnes)	2.2	5.2	230	326 (hard coal)
				434 (soft coal)
Natural gas (trillion cubic feet)	30	68	38	60

Source: Meadows et al. 1992, p. 68.

meet the human need in future. Every discovery of resource comes from the ultimate stock of undiscovered reserve which is non-replenishable and declining. All the fossil fuels will be sooner or later exhausted and raise the problem of sustainability of development process. The actual phasing out of an exhaustible resource would depend not just on when the stock would get physically exhausted, but also on when the competing backstop or newly emerging technology (like solar-powered thermal or photovoltaic) would become competitive with the cost of the existing technology. With increasing depletion, the economy has to go into the increasingly difficult area for discovery and exploit increasingly difficult reserves from among the discovered ones. The marginal cost of supply of hydrocarbons or coal should increase over time. On the other hand, the scarcity value of any such resource should ideally go up and be reflected in the optimal rental value to be built into the price for an optimal rate of depletion of the stock. All these would make the use of such a resource costlier over time. The research and development capital, on the other hand, is expected to bring down the cost of the competing technology over time. The cost of solar photovoltaic power was $150 per watt in 1970 and it came down to $4.5 per watt in 1990. If the cost declines at the same trend rate it should be competitive in the next decade. As a result of such developments a new technology would take over an existing one as soon as it becomes cost competitive. The employment of exploration, development and operational capital would then depend on the development in respect of its potential substitutes. The actual amount of a discovered reserve is thus determined by not only what the biosphere can provide in a region, but also by the economic factors that determine the dynamics of competitiveness of one resource vis-à-vis another and associated technology. Besides, at the macro level, a country's ability to discover and develop a resource depends also on the availability of capital for employment for such purpose and, therefore, at the stage of development of the economy. The magnitude of the known reserves of fuel or non-fuel exhaustible resource, their pattern of use and the time horizon of their switching to other resources and technology (like from coal-based to solar power) are all determined by the interaction of the economy and the ecosystems containing the deposits of the known or unknown amounts of reserves of the economy (see Meadows *et al.* 1992).

Are we going to face an energy crisis because of our dependence on fossil fuel? The answer would depend on the rate of growth of demand for fossil fuel vis-à-vis the rate of discovery of new deposits of reserves or new technologies, possibly based on renewable resources. Other things remaining the same a higher economic growth rate would reduce the life of balance of reserves on the earth. The life of reserves is quite sensitive with respect to the rate of economic growth. However, the reserves of the dominant fuel, that is, oil, is very unevenly distributed across regions. The Middle East countries of Asia and Russia produced near about 45 per cent of world's oil production in 1988 while between the two regions they had 72 per cent of known oil reserves. This is reflected in the share of energy import in the total commercial energy use of the different countries. This share has been 24 per cent for high income industrialized countries, (–) 577 per cent for middle eastern and north African countries and 26 per cent for India (see World Bank 2000). If one calculates the share of oil import in the total oil use, the ratio is about 66 per cent for India which imposes a requirement of 20 to 25 per cent of India's export earning to be spent to meet the oil import bill. As oil is by and large non-substitutable in a wide area of the transportation sector, the unequal distribution of oil reserves makes a country vulnerable to oil price fluctuation. An oil importing developing country with external debt problem may face an energy crisis even if the world reserves are enough to meet the requirement of the world for a century at a moderate growth rate. The industrialised north would also find a problem of instability due to any sharp oil price hike in an oligopolistic market situation of such resource. The sustainability issue therefore often turns out to be a globally political economic one because of the skewed regional distribution of fossil fuel resources in the biosphere in the given context of technology and resource options as of present.

Energy and Environmental Pollution

The problem of environmental sustainability arises for commercial energy use not merely from the scarcity of resource availability, but also from the pollution arising which may assume a threatening proportion in our environment at the present business as usual growth of energy use. Among the commercial energy resources, fossil fuel extraction, conversion into refined form of energy, transportation and its use would generate pollution of various kinds affecting air, water and soil. Different fuels have different extents of environmental impacts. Coal is the most abundant fossil fuel and commercial energy resource that is available on the earth in terms of oil equivalent measure. It is the most polluting fuel having disruptive effect on the environment and giving rise to adverse wastes from the stage of extraction of coal from the mine to the stage in which it is burnt. The extraction of coal often gives rise to acid mine drainage and toxic effluents which pollute water streams and rivers. The combustion of coal produces particulates, CO_2, SO_x NO_x and hydrocarbons as air pollutants and fly ash, sludge, toxic heavy metals and insoluble inorganic materials as solid wastes. Of these CO_2 and NO_x are greenhouse gases, while emissions of SO_x and NO_x or acid drainage would cause acid rain, photochemical smog and acid deposition on soil. These would affect fertility of soil, damage foliage of trees and affect the primary productivity of ecosystem. Besides, the air pollutants have adverse health effect, particularly in the form of higher incidence of respiratory, cardiovascular and other diseases, while the toxic metal deposition will raise cancer mortality.

The air pollution problems of oil cycles are also virtually the same as that of coal, the difference lies only in the amount of pollutants emitted, which are generally lower for oil. In the extraction process of crude oil, water pollution problem arises from oil slick in ocean, ground water, particularly in offshore operation, or oil seepage into ground water in onshore operation. Brine and drilling mud may also contaminate water flow in exploration and oil or gas field development drilling activities. The refining of oil generates waste water carrying toxic heavy metal contents. Finally, the combustion of oil gives rise to the arising of CO_2, SO_x, NO_x, hydrocarbons and suspended particulate matters. The solid waste arising in oil cycle is, however, minimal as compared to the coal cycle. Natural gas has mainly an air pollution effect due to the arisings of SO_x, hydrocarbons like methane, and CO_2. There is virtually negligible impact of natural gas cycle on water, land and soil.

Coal combustion accounts for 24 per cent of all NO_x and 33 per cent of all particulates produced by human beings. It generates

11 per cent more CO_2 than oil and 67 per cent more CO_2 than natural gas. While NO_x and CO_2 are principal green house gases, we have already seen that SO_x and NO_x when combined with water vapour cause acid rain with adverse effect on the productivity of the ecosystem. The extent of such adverse effect for a fuel depends on its emission coefficient for the different types of fossil fuel. Natural gas is, however, the cleanest of all the three fossil fuel resources.

Among the non-fossil fuel resources, nuclear power is a quite clean energy option in terms of routine measures of air pollution, although it generates radioactive pollutants. From mining and processing of uranium to the operation of nuclear reactor, significant amount of radioactive and solid wastes arise. A 1000 mwe (megawatt electric power) nuclear plant running at 80 per cent capacity will generate about 12000 cubic ft of radioactive wastes per year, and 17000 cubic ft of ashes and limestone per year. The advantage of negligible air pollution is offset by the risk of catastrophic accidents and the problem of storage and disposal of radioactive wastes.

Of the commercial non-fossil fuel resources hydel resource is a clean fuel in respect of impact on air quality. The hydroelectric dam and river valley projects have multiple objectives of supplying water for irrigation and domestic use, generating electricity and controlling food, etc. But the construction of dam disturbs the environmental equilibrium of the project region and even beyond. The submergence of large areas of land will have dislocating and adverse effect on human settlements, wild life habitats, biodiversity and agricultural land. The deforestation in the energy catchment area by submergence for storing water resource may lead to soil erosion and silting of reservoir and also downstream rivers and channels, and growth of vegetation at channel bed with shallow streams in substantive part of the time. All these would raise the risk of floods during monsoon in tropical regions when heavy rainfall often takes place in short duration. Besides, the stagnation of water in large storage would also contribute to the charging of ground water in the surrounding areas depending on the rock structure. The storage water and downstream water flow along rivers and irrigation canals. Irrigation being mostly by flooding, may contribute to the rise of the ground water table if there is no appropriate drainage for the flow of water to the agricultural fields. This may downgrade land by causing water logging and rise in salinity of soil which would affect its fertility. The environmental problems of a hydel project is site specific. The planning, design and management of the dam or reservoir and the entire downstream constitute a big challenge and task. Any failure in meeting the challenge is likely to end up with an environmental mess and disequilibrium of the ecosystem of the reservoir region and the river valley. Finally, the stakeholders in the context of a multipurpose dam or reservoir project—people facing dislocation of the habitat, agriculturists, user of electric power, beneficiaries of wild life conservation and forests, fishermen, government and others concerned, may have serious conflict of interests, the resolution of which becomes also a necessity to minimise the impact of socio-economic externality of hydel electric project.

India's Energy Scene and Sustainability

In India solid fossil fuels, coal and lignite constituted 33 per cent of primary commercial energy resource supply in 1998-9. The share of import in solid fuel supply has been only 5.3 per cent in oil equivalent units. The share of oil in the total primary energy supply in 1998-9 has been 35.0 per cent, import dependence in oil being about 63 per cent in that year. The cleanest of fossil fuel, natural gas had a share of 8.0 per cent, hydropower 1.8 per cent and nuclear power 1.2 per cent only. India's pattern of commercial energy use is thus heavily weighted in favour of the most air polluting fuel, coal. In power generation, the share of hydel in gross electricity generation of the utility system declined from 49 per cent in 1950-1 to 17.7 per cent in 1997-8. The share of hydel in total utility electric capacity in India also declined from 41 per cent in 1960-1 to 24 per cent in 1997-8. The long gestation lag in hydel project, interstate dispute in the sharing of scarce river water resource, and the environmental consideration in any addition to reservoir capacity of the country have among other reasons caused the decline of use of water resources for commercial energy use. The imbalance in favour of too much thermal electricity capacity is going to create serious stress on the atmosphere in India by way of air pollution unless pollution can be abated by clean coal technologies, or coal can be substituted by natural gas in power generation. The bias in favour of coal in India's primary energy supply (see Table 6.13) is to a large extent due to the relatively much larger availability of coal resource vis-à-vis others. India has coal reserves of 72.7 billion tonnes of proved reserves and 204.6 billion tonne as total reserves including the indicated and the inferred categories as in 1997, implying an R/P ratio of about 200 years for proved category assuming, of course, 100 per cent recoverability. Oil and natural gas reserves of India, on the other hand stood, at 726.5 billion tonnes and 640.1 billion m³, respectively, implying R/P ratios of 22 for oil and 28 for natural gas approximately as of 1996. While such a configuration of reserves clearly point to the inevitable dependence on coal for India in the long run, it is nevertheless important to strike a balance between the hydel energy and the thermal energy, substitute coal by natural gas in the medium term as long as possible and finally use clean technology for coal-based energy supply like integrated gassification combined cycle or fluidized bed boiler, washed coal use for power, etc.

The flow of fossil fuels to the economic system is going to be limited globally by both the sources and the sink. However, the severity of source limit and sink limit is going to vary from fuel to fuel both for India and the world. The use of coal is likely to

Table 6.13
India's primary commercial energy supply

(million tonnes of oil equivalent)

Indigenous production	Amounts in 1998–9
Coal	125.61
Lignite	4.88
Crude oil	33.80
Natural gas	20.99
Hydro power	7.12
Nuclear power	3.13
Total	195.53
Net imports	66.06
Stock changes (–)	6.54
Internaitonal bankers (–)	0.10
Total commercial energy supply	254.95

Source: Data obtained by enquiry with the Energy Division of the Planning Commission, Government of India, 1999.

be limited by the capacity of the sink in view of the enormous amount of coal availability. The use of oil, on the other hand, is going to be limited more by the source limitation than sink, although the concern of sink's limited capacity is going to influence the rate of its use and the energy and macroeconomic policies. The heavy dependence of the transport sector on oil due to limited substitutability and the serious problem of urban automobile pollution due to the growth of vehicular population with rise in income and industrialization are going to stress the ecosystem to the threshold of severe marginal damage cost. Of the 33.5 million registered vehicles in India, 9.7 million vehicles are in 23 metropolitan cities which represent more than 100 times growth of vehicular population over 1950-1 in India. The growth factor of urban metropolitan transport vehicles would obviously be even of a higher value. The overflowing of the sink of urban air shed relative to its capacity would either affect the well-being of the urban population of the developing countries or would warrant drastic restructuring of urban transport facilities and infrastructure to reduce pollution load.

Of the fossil fuel the natural gas is the cleanest. Coal and oil may be substituted by natural gas if the severity of the limitation of the sink becomes the dominating factor in setting limits to growth. In view of its non-renewability, neither the extent of substitution nor the duration of sustenance as a fuel source can be indefinite. The time horizon over which such clean fuel can sustain will depend on the growth rate of annual supply of natural gas or the rate of depletion of its stock of indigenous resource. Besides, natural gas has storage problem compared to other fossil fuels and needs development of capital intensive pipeline and storage tank infrastructure for their economy wide use in a large country with a limited number of sources.

Among non-fossil fuels, the nuclear fuel use has already been delimited because of the severity of the limitation of the terrestrial system to absorb the radioactive wastes. Although there is enough of reserves of uranium and thorium generated by this process which can be utilized for power generation for considerable time, the radiation from the radioactive materials generated can enter the bio-geo-chemical pathways and can affect the health of both the ecosystem as well as the human being. Such radiation can induce cancer, infertility, and growth deficiencies among various health effects. On the other hand, the hydro resources is alleged to unfavourably alter the surroundings of our existence through deforestation, soil erosion, floods, water logging, etc. as a result of which the sink's ability to provide life support in the concerned region may be greatly affected. This change of surroundings would in fact interfere with the functioning of the ecosystem by influencing the movement of the basic chemical elements or compounds along the pathways of the geo-chemical cycles.

One great advantage of the hydro power is, however, its renewability. The other renewable energy resources like solar radiation, wind flow, tidal wave, micro hydel and biomass can also be used for generating thermal as well as electrical energy. All these renewables including storage based hydroelectricity are in fact solar powered. The hydrological cycle and the solar energy flow produce all these resources. Wind flow or ocean tides are the direct or indirect consequences of a solar radiation reaching the earth. However, the solar radiation reaching the earth is a finite, non-storable and dilute form of energy. Wind, tide or micro-hydel water resource flow types have limited potential of electric power generation and the time distribution of their availabilities somewhat determined exogenously by nature. The divergence between the demand for electric power which is essentially non-storable and the time distribution of availability of such non-storable basic resource creates the problem of full utilization of opportunities as well as meeting the demand unless there is a grid connection with such renewable resource based power supply. In the latter case, the surplus wind power can be sold to and the deficit of an area can be drawn from the grid. In the calculus of relative competitiveness, it is pointed out that the decentralized energy system in remote areas based on such locally available resources becomes competitive as there is no need to invest in transmission and the distribution cost would also be quite low. However, the mismatch between the time distribution of demand and supply of the basic resource would require either grid connection or alternative storable energy resource based supply, for example, oil or hydro storage if such potential is available for meeting at least the consumers' satisfaction.

Just as renewable energy resources are not unlimited, they are also not entirely environmentally harmless. Windmills require land and access roads. Biomass energy has the same set of environmental problems as with agricultural and forestry practices. Some solar sources are of higher dilution depending on the location and climatic condition. Harvesting and effective use of the radiation may involve large collection areas and complex hi-tech storage mechanism. Besides, photovoltaic solar cells have some toxic material content and involve huge material yield loss from raw material. If any renewable energy resource use becomes again manmade capital intensive or construction intensive, the machinery and construction will generate substantive amount of environmental pollution.

The cost of renewable newly emerging resources is quite high. The research and development (R&D) investments and activities will bring the costs down over time. The date of non-conventional back stop technologies overtaking the conventional fossil fuel based ones would depend on the price movements of fossil fuel based energy supplies which should reflect its scarcity premium. However, economy can have cheaper energy supply along conventional route over a longer horizon if the efficiency of use of energy is upgraded. In an era of renewable energy supply, too, the efficiency of energy use will determine the carrying capacity of renewable resources in terms of providing support to growing population and economic activities.

In developing countries like India there exists enormous scope of energy conservation by upgrading technology, equipment and appliances in a wide range of areas of application—furnace, motors, insulation system, automobile engine, cooking burner, power generating system, and innumerable others. Energy is used to power equipments for doing work. If the design of the device can be changed to make it more energy efficient, it will lead to both conservation of energy resource for the future as well as reduce the pollution externality. The efficiency considerations are also important in the supply of energy for final end use, that is, in its use in the process of energy resource extraction, conversion or refinement and transportation of energy. If the recoverability of coal for an underground mine be 40 per cent, handling and transportation loss is 5 per cent, conversion efficiency of coal be 30 per cent, transmission and distribution loss be 25 per cent, auxiliary loss or power plants' own requirement be 8 per cent, 100 unit of inplace geological thermal energy as congealed in coal will yield only 7.8 units of energy for final use. Very high transmission loss and low efficiency of conversion of energy resources into electric power causes substantive loss of energy resources and substantive pollution. Lack of adequate application of efficient technology both on demand and supply sides of energy market have been due to possible inadequacy of finance capital, absence of appropriate penalty-cum-incentive scheme to induce conservation and highly irrational energy prices in India. Low and subsidized price of energy has led to wasteful use of scarce resources and unsustainable pattern of energy use in India. With increase in energy efficiency, the same resources will last for longer period for the same pace of growth because of the virtual rise in the stock of resources in efficiency unit. Similarly, higher energy efficiency would also raise the level of flow of renewable energy in efficiency unit over time and support a higher level of economic activities. It is the employment of surplus financial resources of a society obtained from the use of capital that can be invested in R&D activities to develop energy efficient devices which would have a favourable impact on the long run marginal cost of supply of the end product produced out of energy. The rise in energy efficiency would often imply a substitution of energy by capital or other inputs. Such substitutions have to be efficient in the sense of reducing the total cost of production in terms of factor prices, the factor prices being inclusive of the due share of scarcity rental for the existing fuel resources. The efficient energy conservation along with substitution of non-renewable resources by renewables would relax the severity of the limitation of nature both as source and sink, thereby permitting sustainable development.

Non-Energy Materials

Human economy uses a large variety of abiotic materials for non-energy use. These materials constitute the physical basis of the produced items of goods and services of the economy. These are categorized as non-renewable resources. In an industrial society a large number of such material resources belonging to metals, plastics and non-mineral resources are brought together to produce one single product. However, unlike energy which is degraded finally in heat form after the work has been done, due to rise in entropy, the materials produced and used, do not always get so degraded as to make them non-reusable or non-recyclable in the production system. The material products like metal products, plastics, glass materials, concrete, etc. may either be thrown into the sink and allowed to disperse in soil, water or air or reused in the production system by appropriate treatment to be usable again as a substitute material input. Steel scrap or any metal scrap (obtained by crushing steel or metal products) can be used as a substitute for iron ore which is reducible by coke being combined with fluxes like limestone. Repair and renovation are also a variant of recycling without throwing off the basic materials as waste. All these measures increase the life of the product or that of the constituent raw materials in the economic system. Although the virgin raw material and recyclable waste (or a repaired or renovated product) are not perfect substitute of each other, the extent of substitution will be determined by their mutual marginal rate of substitution and the relative prices reflecting the relative scarcity and efficiency of virgin material (or cost of new products) vis-à-vis recyclable waste (or cost of repair or renovation). When the use of materials is considered from such a life cycle perspective, it is clear that efficient recovery, repair, renovation, remanufacturing, etc. will depend on how the raw material resource as drawn from nature has been utilized in the first place. The materials or products which are dissipated in use cannot be recovered, for example, solvents, pigments, detergents, etc. and the products that cannot be disassembled cannot also be repaired or remanufactured. The end of life time use of a product needs to be considered in the beginning at the stage of product design. The emerging concept of design for environment requires that the products be designed not only for good performance and low manufacturing cost, but also for long life, efficient disassembly, and recycling.

In spite of recycling or reuse of waste material, there is a net flow of requirement of virgin material from the nature into a growing or even a stationary economy as the recoverability of recyclable waste for recycling purpose is not 100 per cent nor is the substitutability between virgin and recyclable material is one to one because of the degradation involved with the latter. The flow of non-renewable materials from nature to economy make unavailable the tackling of the problem of sustainability of growth and development process. However, the conservation of material resources as induced by technical progress can increase the life of the raw material reserve deposits. The oil shocks of 1973 and 1979 had generated tremendous drive for energy conservation. However, the amount of energy required to produce a commodity is dependent among others, on the amount of material to be treated for obtaining the output. Any improvement in material yield would require lower amount of raw materials to be processed per unit of output and would, therefore, require lower amount of energy as well. The conservation of matter is often a co-benefit of energy conservation and of lower volume of waste flow to the sink.

Recycling of used products is the reuse only of one part of the material stream—the end one whereas waste is generated at the stage of raw materials extraction and processing and at the stage of manufacturing process. A thumb rule relation often assumed for waste generating calculation is as follows. For every 5 tonnes of output, 5 tonnes of waste generated is in the manufacturing process and another 20 tonnes at the stage of raw materials giving the material balance for 30 tonnes. If the scope of recycling raw materials waste or process waste is limited, their sustainability would emphasize on lengthening the life time of the product, thereby warranting in the lowering of the obsolescence rate of the product by discouraging too frequent change of fashion, adopting better design of products to make it more durable and using repair services to handle damage. All these, however, go against the driving forces of capitalism which require fashions to change and products to become obsolete quickly as these developments would boost the effective demand of the market. The macro-economic factors for the survival of capitalism, run, in fact, counter to the objective of material conservation for sustainability.

Apart from the quantum of waste handling and disposal, the abiotic non-energy material resource use also gives rise to a problem of qualitative degradation of environment. The nature of degradability of the waste generated at the different stages of the life cycle of material flow is quite important in deciding the qualitative impacts. The metals and plastics, phenolic chemicals, etc. are, for example, non biodegradable. The change in physical or chemical composition of discarded metal products, for example, will take place over very long period if they are left to the natural weathering process for degradation. Hence, maximization of recycling of such non-biodegradable materials is the best way to reduce stress on nature and avoid negative externalities. It is thus not only the constraints of the source but also that of the sink which induce recycle or reuse of materials. The dissipated use of materials for example, detergents causes problem of recycling.

There exist some materials which are transformed by man and are poisons for the living organism, for example, heavy metals, pesticides, etc. A large number of industrial chemicals which are manmade out of the basic resources drawn from nature, affect the metabolic function of living organism, their reproductive ability and also expose them to the threat of deadly (cancerous) diseases. If such material elements enter the food chain, the biological magnification process may cause such serious threat for animals at higher trophic level. The entry of such chemical elements into the pathways of bio-geo-chemical cycles can disrupt the regenerative function of nature affecting its primary productivity. Any disruption of natural function would directly or indirectly affect human beings until and unless man can invent methods of adaptation to the new situation.

Even if technology is restructured and material used to minimize adverse externalities from wastes of material use, the production system would face constraint due to the limits of the source. How long or to what extent the source of nature is to sustain the development process with various minerals? As resources are depleted one moves from higher to lower grade until the cut off grade is reached. The cut off grade is the marginal grade for which the cost of extraction of the mineral content would equal the price of the mineral content in the market. If the economy exhausts such mineral deposits without substitute resources being found the price of the mineral would go up, resulting in the lowering of the cut off grade. Alternatively, new technology may reduce the cost of extraction and lower the cut off grade. One environmental hazard in lowering the cut off grade is the fast rise in the generation of wastes at the raw material stage. The relative value or ratio of mineable cut off grade to the average content of mineral in earth's crust is an indicator of the proportion of the mineral contained in the earth which is economically exploitable. Higher the value of the ratio, the lower is this proportion. Table 6.14 gives these ratios for some of the minerals which are of major use in the human economy. If the technical change or price movement of a mineral relaxes the cut off grade, the severity of source would be relaxed, but the waste arising in the form of non-recyclable raw materials wastes may go up substantively causing strain on the sink. The cost of extraction of minerals from rock deposits should include the environmental damage cost to determine the cut off. In the case of any relaxation of severity of limitation of source for such materials by reducing cut off grade is likely to raise the severity of limitation of the sink and set the limit to exploitation. Table 6.14 provides the amount of reserves and the Reserve to Production ratio for some of the major metals indicating the respective extents of severity of their source limitation (see Meadows *et al.* 1992; World Resource Institute 1994 and 1998).

Materials are the underpinning of technology. The sustainability of technology depends on the availability of virgin material resources in future as well as the life cycle of material in economic system. A sustained growth of GDP will essentially require rise in material productivity. One important strategy for raising such productivity is dematerialization of production which means less use of material for a given function than previously used, for example, computer-aided design together with quality control now permits significant reductions in material thickness and

Table 6.14
World availability of mineral resources for major items

Items	Average crustal abundance in earth's surface (%)	Mineable cut off grade (%)	Ratio	Amount of reserve 1992 (million tonne)	World reserves life index (R/P ratio for 1992 in years)
Aluminium and Bauxite	8.3	18.3	2.2	23000	222
Copper	0.0063	0.35	56	310	33
Lead	0.0012	4.0	3300	63	18
Mercury	0.000089	0.1	11200	0.130	43
Nickel	0.0089	0.9	100	47.0	51
Tin	0.00017	0.35	2000	8.0	45
Zinc	0.0094	3.5	370	140.0	20
Iron ore	5.820	20	3.4	150,000	161

Source: Based on data derived from World Resource Institute (1994), *World Resources 1994–5*, pp. 338–9 and Meadows *et al.* (1992), ch. 3.

weight for many structural purposes from engines to aircraft wings without any sacrifice of safety concern. Secondly, scarce or hazardous materials need to be substituted by other exotic materials or new material technology. High temperature material, strong and new synthetics and electronic materials, when combined with the use of knowledge-based technological processes will substantially economize use of materials since information intensive processes will render some of the equipment and devices redundant. This would of course make new material objects to be less recyclable. The scope of reuse and re-engineering gets limited in scope in the context of such sophisticated materials which are difficult to reproduce. The extent of introduction of such new materials would again be dependent on the cost effectiveness of their development.

Recyclability or re-engineering of used products or wastes are also important ways of raising life cycle efficiency of materials and may include waste mining too, like salvaging steel plant slag for construction materials for making roads or blast furnace slag for making cement or coal ash for making concrete, or phosphate rock processing waste being used as a source of flurine chemicals used in aluminium industry. In these cases, the waste is not being used in the same industry, but used in a different industry. The dematerialization of production, innovation of new materials, re-engineering of old products, waste recovery and its recycling or use in the same or a different industry would all contribute to the raising of the reserve life of the non-renewable materials. But in any given technology regime such reserve life however high or low would be finite implying a limit to growth. The R&D activities in material science and technology would be required to continuously strive for change in the technology regime so that the limits to growth may be shifted to a higher level implying postponement of the non-renewable material resource crisis.

Sink and Wastes

Wastes

The waste problem has been described as one of pollution and defined as an undesirable change in the physical, chemical or biological characteristics of air, water and land that is deemed to be harmful for human being or other living organism and/or for the productivity of natural resources in delivering services for human well being. Pollution is thus a by-product of energy conversion and use of resources. It is a 'bad' that sets in fact potentially a limit on the use of resources. We have also seen that the entire problem of the so called 'bad' arises from the limitation of the sink in transforming the wastes into resources for human use or in at least rendering them harmless through transformation. The degree of difficulty in such absorption of waste by the nature or the severity of limitation of nature as a sink varies from waste to waste. Wastes are classified into three broad categories depending on the nature of degradability:

(a)   bio-degradable wastes
(b)   non-biodegradable wastes
(c)   poisonous or radioactive wastes.

The biodegradable wastes can be decomposed and absorbed by nature by its own processes. However, if the input of such wastes flows at a rate faster than the time rate of nature's recycling capacity, it may be difficult for the ecosystem to maintain the environmental quality. It may be necessary to supplement the natural process by adding a waste treatment plant (like municipal sewage waste treatment plant) where electrical energy and machines are used to speed up the decomposition of micro-organisms for the purpose of environmental protection.

There are three stages of treatment of such degradable wastes: (a) primary treatment—mechanical screening and sedimentation procedure, (b) secondary treatment—a biological reduction of organic matter, and (c) tertiary or advanced treatment—chemical removal of harmful solvents, nitrates, phosphates and other materials. After the tertiary treatment, additional special treatment is required to make water drinkable. From the tertiary stage onwards substantive amount of fuel and capital equipments are required for treatment rendering the process of waste treatment quite costly. While the entire biodegradable wastes should be treated up to the secondary stage, further treatment can be confined to the extent it is necessary to meet water balance for the different end uses for the urban complexes. Apart from the households, the major sources of biodegradable wastes in India have been fruit processing, paper mills, sugar mills and textile factories.

The non-bio-degradable wastes mostly emerge from industries or from the use of industrial products. This class includes, aluminum products, steel plant wastes, gypsum as arising from fertilizer and allied industries, long chain detergents, glass, phenolic chemicals, plastics and hundreds of other industrial chemicals. As there is no natural decay within the human time scale nor any cost effective treatment procedure which can render them harmless for the health of the environment, recycling such material is the best way of waste management. As most of such materials go into the landfill, proper separation of bio-degradable and non-bio-degradable wastes and further separation of the different types of industrial non-bio-degradable wastes at the stage of collection as per end use in recycling would be important to ensure cost effective recycling. Tables 6.15 and 6.16 give the broad estimates of annual generation of a few major non-bio-degradable solid wastes in India and provide the data on the method of solid waste disposal in India.

The third group of pollutants consists of non-bio-degradable hazardous waste. These are poisons from the production processes including items like heavy metals (for example, mercury, lead, cadmium, etc.), radioactive substances like nuclear wastes, pesticides (such as DDT), and an ever increasing array of agricultural and industrial chemicals many of which have not as yet been tested for toxicity for human or other living organisms. Nuclear wastes are hazardous to all forms of life by the criterion of toxicity as well as mutagenicity. Nature has no way of rendering these wastes harmless and radioactive substances have their own disintegration time table.

The effect of heavy metals on the ecosystem depends on the dosage condition of released heavy metal wastes into nature. In large dosage condition these can cause highly adverse health related effects in individuals and population. The effect of presence of heavy metals in soil has been varying with reference to plant productivity. In a certain situation, it may stunt the plant growth, in certain others it may not. Human intake of heavy metals is through plants, water and air. Adverse metabolic changes including neurological dysfunction and psychomotor abnormalities are found often in children in lead contaminated areas.

Table 6.15

Annual genera. ⁿⁿ of non-biodegradable industrial
. a. ·s in India

(million tonnes)

Solid wastes	Quantity
Fly ash	45.0
Slag	8.5
Phosphogypsum	5.0
Lime sludge	4.0
Red mud	3.5

Source: Pachauri et al. (1998), p. 252.

Table 6.16
Methods of waste disposal in India (23 cities)

Methods	1991
Land dumping	89.8%
Composting	8.6%
Others (pelletizing, vermicomposting)	1.6%
Recycling	plastic, metal, glass and paper

Source: Pachauri et al. (1998), p. 252.

The human synthesized chemicals constitute an intractable set of hazardous wastes. Since they did not exist in the planet in the past, no organism has evolved to break them down and render them harmless. In the economic system, 65,000 industrial chemicals exist which are in commercial use, with toxicological data not being available for more than 1 per cent of them. Every day 4 to 5 new chemicals enter the markets. The toxicity status is not known for eighty per cent of the newly introduced chemicals. Every day about 1 million tonnes of hazardous wastes are generated in the world, 90 per cent of which are generated in the industrialized world. As the soil and ground water are affected by the hazardous wastes, the governmental regulation on the use of many of these chemicals in the industrialized countries is inducing the latter to put increasing pressure on the developing countries to accept the concerned polluting technologies. While chemicals with strong poisonous effect and wide externalities are banned, problem remains in dealing with low level numerous poisons which would have little effect while acting singly, but would be having synergistic super-additive deleterious effect while many of them are working together. Table 6.17 gives the rate of various hazardous waste arisings in India.

Case of Pesticides

This section focuses on the use of chemicals for pest control which is related with the vital issue of human food security. The history of pesticides shows the evolution from the use of low grade poisons to stronger poisons with wider external effect. The first generation of pesticides mainly consisted of botanical and inorganic salts (for example, arsenicals, etc.) and was adequate to prevent any massive build up of pest population and their use did not involve any accumulation of the poisons beyond the crop field.

With the growth of density of population the drive for procuring more food from the same land resulted in the second generation pesticides DDT, generation of organic broad spectrum poisons (organochlorines or organo-phosphates). These pesticides came along with large farms, mechanized agriculture, use of chemical fertilizers and irrigation, increase of monoculture and genetic selections of crops with high yields and adapted to such conditions

Table 6.17
Hazardous wastes in India

| | (tonnes per tonne of product) |
Industry	Solid waste
Caustic soda	0.03
Drugs and pharmaceuticals	0.04
Dye and dye intermediates	1.36
Fertilizer	0.085
Inorganic chemicals	0.4
Organic chemicals	0.15
Pesticides	0.07
Petrochemical	1.38
Refinery	0.015
Textile processing	0.02/1000 m (or 2 gms/metre)

Source: Pachauri et al. (1998), p. 254.

of production. The growth and prevalence of pesticides in an agrarian ecosystem depends on these conditions of production and selection of crop as well. Besides, many insects developed immunity against these pesticides while the broad spectrum effect of the poisons killed many useful parasites. The damage effects of these developments of immunity and broad spectrum killing of organisms were underestimated. The development of immunity by the insects caused spraying of the poisons at an escalated scale because the dosage required to save a given crop became increasingly large. As spraying was not targeted to any particular pest, it involved lot of wasteful use of pesticides. As a result the pesticides contamination effect spread far beyond the crop field. As the soil and run off water got contaminated by these pesticides, the contamination effect spread to almost all corners of the globe.

One of the major harmful effects of use of such pesticides is on the regenerative function of the ecosystem. The concentration of such toxic pollutant accumulates in fresh water bodies through the run off waters to produce harmful effects on the aquatic organisms. Experimental data on the toxic effect of a number of pesticides on gross primary productivity (GPP) of a fresh water pond at Khuda Ali Sher (Chandigarh) in India (see Jindal *et al.* 1989) showed that for the use of a pesticide like Baytex of organophosphate group the percentage reduction of the GPP would be anywhere in the range 14.54 per cent to 96.8 per cent, depending on the level of concentration used. Table 6.18 gives the results of the experiment for a range of pesticides and the order of toxicity of the different pesticides with reference to GPP. The biological magnification of these non-biodegradable persistent poisonous element through food chain causes a serious threat to human health resulting in the banning of some of the persistent varieties of poisons by many countries.

A third generation of pesticides is now emerging with the objective of integrated control involving judicious mixing of the use of degradable chemical, biological control, and genetic selection for resistance. These biotechnology based narrow spectrum pesticides will be species specific target oriented and will either prevent maturation and breeding of the members of the concerned species or lure them into traps or poisons. Pests and human beings have been competing for food and will compete

Table 6.18
Effect of toxicity of pesticides on gross primary productivity
of a fresh water pond in Chandigarh
(experimental data based)

Pesticide	Concentrations (ppm)	% retardation in GPP	EC^*_{50} (ppm)
Organochlorines			
Aldrin	5–150	11.78–84.76	83.228
Endosulfan	1–50	17.62–71.62	32.628
Ekalux	5–50	17.18–92.36	19.406
Organophosphates			
Bytex	1–50	14.54–96.8	8.500
Roger	1–75	13.80–85.53	36.003
Malathion	5–50	6.34–70.52	37.704
Carbamates			
Carbayl	1–50	17.86–78.68	18.897

*EC means emulsifiable concentrate; it gives the level of concentration
in ppm which would result in 50 per cent reduction in gross primary
productivity (GPP). The lower the value of EC_{50}, the more toxic the
effect of the pesticide on the GPP.
Source: Jindal R. et al. (1989), pp. 257–61.

in future. Complete elimination of pests is a counter-productive
strategy, nor desirable. The sustainable development consideration
would require controlled use of species specific bio-degradable
pesticides, based on bio-technology methods. The agrarian
ecosystem management needs to be restructured with the help
of bio-technology without disturbing the ecological balance.

Global Pollution: Acid Rain

Reference to the flow of wastes as exceeding the absorption
capacity of nature, primarily means the violation of capacity
constraint of some local or regional ecosystem. However, there
are quite a number of pollutants which affect the global flow of
matter and energy or at least large part of a region outside the
national boundary. Such pollution problems can be classified as:
(a) pollutions with transnational external effect, and (b) those
which are truly global pollution problems. In the former case the

adverse external effect may or may not be reciprocal in nature (i.e., the polluter may or may not be affected by pollution), while in the second case the externality is necessarily reciprocal in nature (i.e., the polluter is also affected along with others by the pollution). Acid rain is an example of the former while ozone depletion or global warming is an example of the latter class of problems.

Human activities like fossil fuel burning give rise to the emissions of gases like sulphuric oxides or nitric oxides resulting in acid rain. Acid rain is any kind of precipitation—rain, snow, sleet, fog that contains high levels of acid. These are dilute solutions of two strong acids—sulphuric and nitric, with respective shares of 70 per cent and 30 per cent approximately. The rise in sulphur and nitrogen oxides in the atmosphere over the last 150 years has been causing stress on the atmosphere and depressing the pH level of water in lakes and rivers of several areas of Europe or North America below 5. The acidity beyond a level is damaging for biotic growth. Acid rain ruins forests if it falls on trees and plants as the photosynthesis tissues are destroyed by the acids. Fertility of the soil is destroyed if the precipitation falls on the ground making it acidic. Fishes are killed if the precipitation falls on water bodies or if the run off water carries acid elements from land. These acidic compounds may also be leached into underground water through soil. All these would be damaging the biotic regeneration ability of the ecosystem and deeply affect the life support system and thereby economic well-being of man. The abatement of the sulphuric oxides and the nitric oxides at sources then becomes an important policy consideration for the sustainability of the economic system. Since sulphur and nitric oxides share some of the properties of aerosols, they are often transported over considerable distances by wind flows before they are precipitated in the form of acid rain. Acid rain, in fact, occurred in North America and Europe far outside the national boundaries of the casual sources of emissions, the location of precipitation depending on the directions of wind flow and the pattern of air circulation. The emissions at the source of Ontario, Ohio river valley, or east of Missisipi river caused acid precipitation by wind flow southwards and westwards. The emissions of similar gases in England have similarly affected the Scandinavian countries.

Ozone Depletion

Of the truly global pollution problems seriously damaging the global commons, the ozone depletion in the stratosphere by chlorofluorocarbons (CFCs) has been an important one. The CFCs are some of the most useful compounds invented by human being. They are nontoxic and stable. They do not burn, nor do they corrode materials. As they have low thermal conductivity, they make excellent insulators. As some of the CFCs evaporate and recondense at room temperature, they perform as perfect coolant for refrigerators and air conditioners. Some of the CFCs are also good solvents for cleaning materials and metals in the intricate micro-spaces of joining in the sophisticated equipments. It was earlier also thought that they could be disposed of safely by simply releasing them into atmosphere.

The production of this chemical with global industrial growth increased at 7 per cent to 10 per cent rate annually. By 1980s global outputs of all the CFCs reached the level of almost 1 million tonnes. An average North American or European was using 2 pounds (0.85 kg) of CFCs per year and an average Indian or Chinese was using less than an ounce (0.03 kg) per annum.

However, the scientific research of the 1970s and the 1980s established two things: first, the ozone layer of the stratosphere was depleting over time. High up in the stratosphere exists a gossamer veil made up of the gaseous compound called ozone which is an unstable compound and quite reactive at that. It oxides almost anything it comes into contact with. Thus in the lower atmosphere (i.e. troposphere) which is dense with the presence of many materials. Ozone reacts among others with plant tissues and human lungs to cause damage, but is very short lived in troposphere. In the stratophere, on the other hand, there are not many materials to react with the ozone molecules. The ozone layer is rich in ozone, in the sense of its relative density vis-à-vis the other parts of the atmosphere. However, that order of density in stratosphere is enough to absorb the ultraviolet ray (UV-B) which itself is a part of short wave solar radiation with high energy and right frequency to break organic molecules including the DNA molecules which carry the code of life's reproduction. One possible consequence of its rays hitting the living organisms on earth's surface is skin cancer. The depletion of ozone layer is, therefore, harmful for life on the earth. In mid-1980s the scientists made surveys to show a 40 per cent decrease of ozone over Halley Bay in Antarctica which was at variance with the then scientific belief and assumption, and could also find explanation of such variance.

Secondly, scientists also established the industrial manmade chemical CFCs do not dissolve in rain nor react with other gases in the atmosphere. The CFC family gas molecules therefore rise very high up in the atmosphere until they hit ultra-violet rays. The uv-rays breaks up the CFC molecules to release chlorine atoms (Cl). Free Chlorine (Cl) can react with ozone to make Oxygen (O_2) and Chlorine Oxide (ClO). The ClO can further react with an oxygen atom to yield free Cl and Oxygen molecule. The chlorine can have another round of reaction with ozone to degrade it. In such indefinite number of chain reactions a given amount of CFC emission can cause substantive damage to deplete the ozone layer (see Koromondy 1999).

The CFCs were thus found to be a serious threat to the life support system on earth. The disposal of the CFC gases after their performing industrial function was not considered to be any longer costless. The flow of such gaseous substance was overflowing sink's absorptive capacity. Every one per cent decrease in ozone layer was to cause, as estimated by the National Academy of Sciences of USA, an increase of 2 to 5 per cent incidence of skin cancer. It is, however, gratifying to note that the United Nations Environment Program (UNEP) initiatives for international cooperation for abating the production and use of ozone depleting materials through the Montreal Protocol and subsequent negotiations in London Agreement have ended up with 92 countries agreeing to phase out all harmful CFC production by 1992 and innovate and use substitutes without such damaging environmental implications. The solution would obviously lie with technology and pattern of demand (see Meadows *et al.* 1992).

Global Warming

The most important limitation of the sink has been demonstrated by the phenomenon of global warming. The process of economic growth and development through industrialisation and urbanization have led to the emission of green house gases into the atmosphere leading to rise in global temperature. The major green house gases have been carbondioxide, methane (CH_4), nitricoxide (N_2O), CFCs, etc. These gases when accumulated in the atmosphere create obstacle in re-radiation of sun's rays when they are reflected back into space. The incoming sunlight into the earth's atmosphere comes in as short wave energy and can penetrate through the green house gas molecules. The sunlight travels back as long wave energy and part of such energy gets trapped within the atmosphere because of the absorption of some energy by the molecules of the greenhouse gases. The green house gases cause the warming of the atmosphere due to the radiative forcings of the gas molecules. The radiative forcings are the measurement of heat radiating or trapping ability of the greenhouse gas molecules. This measure differs for the molecules of the different green house gases. Relative to the major green house gas CO_2, a methane molecule has 21 times high radiative forcing while a molecule of CFC-12 has nearly 16,000 times higher forcings. By weight, CH_4 and CFC-12 would have 58 times and 5700 times high radiative forcing. It is the stock of the green house gases and not the flow of emissions, that matter so far as the warming up effect is concerned. The equivalence relation of an emission of CO_2 and another gas in respect of global warming potential would depend on both relative radiative forcings value as well as the life or residence period of the molecules of the two gases in the atmosphere. All compounds degrade and get compounded with some other atoms and form new compounds over time. The dynamics of atmospheric chemistry driving the life of such gas molecules, would, of course, depend on the atmospheric composition of gases among others in the concerned region or zone of the atmospheric space. An equivalence of the different gas molecules is given in Table 6.19. The table further gives the state of green house gas concentration in 1992 (see Hayes *et al.* 1993; Govt. of India, CSO 1998).

The rise of atmospheric temperature is the effect of accumulation of green house gases in the atmosphere. The rise in temperature warms up the upper ocean and other water bodies and then gradually the deep ocean or deeper level of other water bodies. The warming will, in fact, be very unevenly distributed; there will be more of rise in temperature near poles than near the equator. As earth's climate depends on the temperature differences between the poles and the equator among others, winds, rain and ocean currents will shift in strength and direction. The rise in temperature of atmosphere and oceans accompanied by the changes in ocean currents and pattern of wind circulation are likely to cause increase in precipitation, melting of permanent ice at the poles and in the mountain ranges, receding of the glaciers and rise in sea level. In the hydrological cycle more water of the reservoir pool would be in active circulation. This process would cause change in climate in the different parts of the world.

In terms of such equivalence relation as discussed above, it is found that CO_2 is the dominant greenhouse gas accounting for (49 per cent in the 1980s) about half of the total warming contribution by all the greenhouse gases together. The share of CH_4 comes

Table 6.19
Summary of key greenhouse gases

Items	CO_2	CH_4	N_2O	CFC_{12}
Pre-industrial concentration	280 ppmv	700 ppbv	275 ppbv	Zero
Concentration in 1992	355 ppmv	17.14 ppbv	311 ppbv	503 ppbv
Recent rate of concentration changes per year (over 1980s)	1.5 ppmv/yr 0.5 %/yr	13 ppbv/yr 0.8 %/yr	0.75 ppbv/yr 0.25 %/yr	18–20 ppbv/yr 4 %/yr
Atmospheric life time	50–200	12–17	120	102
Radiative forcing	1	58	210	5700
Equivalence Factor* in terms of global warming potential considering direct effect over 100 yr horizon	1	11	270	7100

*Numbers refer to ratio of weights.
Source: GOI, CSO (1998), p. 86; and Smith (1993), p. 24.

next with about one-fifth share (19 per cent in 1980s), CFC's have also green house effect and has had made about 17 per cent contribution in 1980s, nitric oxides about 5 per cent and remaining gases about 10 per cent. CO_2 has been released mainly from the burning of the fossil fuels and land use changes. To the extent fuel wood burning, commercial exploitation of forests, urbanization or expansion of agriculture have not been offset by equivalent biotic growth in the vegetation of the earth, there will be a reduction in photosynthesis and less of sequestration of the carbon in the atmosphere. This would mean a rise in CO_2 concentration in the atmosphere. Some of the industrial processes like those in cement industry give rise to industrial CO_2 emission due to the release of carbon from limestone. Methane emission occurs in paddy cultivation because of the growth of anaerobic organisms in stagnant water. Such emission also arises from enteric fermentation of the livestock. The global estimates had shown that energy, agriculture, including livestock, forestry and industry (including CFCs) had their respective shares in the total CO_2 emissions, equivalent emissions during the eighties to be 57 per cent, 15 per cent, 8 per cent and 20 per cent. In the countrywise distribution of the green house gas emissions, the industrialized countries are found to be contributing the major share of the annual CO_2 emission as well as green house emission. USA, European Union and former USSR had 21 per cent, 11 per cent and 12 per cent as their respective shares in the total greenhouse gas emissions during the 1980s. The per capita global CO_2 emission was 1.1 tonnes in 1990, while estimates for the developed countries (including transitional) and the developing countries were 2.8 tonnes and 0.5 tonnes respectively in the same year. The emissions per unit of GDP was 0.26 tonnes and 0.16 tonnes per unit of 1990 purchasing power parity dollar income as defined by the World Bank for the developed and the developing countries. However, there has been a rise in the total CO_2 emission from a level of 4083 million tonnes of Carbon in 1970 to 6189 million tonnes of Carbon in 1991. For a developing country like India, the total CO_2 emission has grown from 53.3 million tonne of carbon to 192.0 million tonnes of carbon during the same period. The per capita emission of CO_2 has in fact been almost doubled over the same period.

So far as the carbondioxide emissions are concerned from anthropogenic sources, this may be viewed as an uphill gain in the bio-geo-chemicals cycle of carbon. The interference in the cycle has a consequence in terms of rise in atmospheric temperature. Apart from the photosynthesis process, the oceans absorb carbondioxide by removing certain amount of it from the atmosphere. The ocean drives the climate through the movement of ocean currents around the globe. An ocean current, the Great Conveyor, circulates in a pathway from the Pacific to the Atlantic to the Pacific Oceans. The water stream while moving westward through the Indian Ocean in the tropic region contains warmer water that flows till reaching the coast of South America. The stream then moves up the eastern cost of South America to Central America, crosses to North Africa and Europe. When the current reaches North Atlantic the Atlantic Engine causes the water of the stream to sink. In the North Atlantic the winds from Iceland evaporate water which makes water saltier and heavier and causes the water of the stream to sink at the rate of 5 billion gallons per second. When the water sinks in the North Atlantic, it carries dissolved CO_2 with it removing them from the atmosphere. After the water sinks to the bottom the water stream moves down south and then towards the east through the Indian Ocean and reaches the south of Australia and moves around that continent and then turns north and comes up to the surface in the North Pacific. After reaching the North Pacific the current of water again turns South and moves towards South America. The current becomes warmer when it moves through the tropics. The warmer water being higher remains on the top of the water column. If rise in temperature melts the ice caps and dilutes the saltiness and reduces the heaviness ocean water in the North Atlantic the rate of water's sinking in North Atlantic is supposed to be reduced. This would also affect the CO_2 absorption rate by the oceans. As a result more of CO_2 would be left in the atmosphere, and the warming up process would be reinforced. There may also be other such destabilizing feed back loops which will make atmosphere further warmer with rise in temperature; for example, as the warming process causes decrease in the snow cover, earth will reflect back less of sunlight and thereby would get warmed up further. The melting down process of the tundra soils are also expected to release huge amount of frozen methane in the atmosphere which would induce further rise in temperature and further melting of ice and further methane release in gaseous form, and so on.

A number of uncertainties are there regarding the changes in the global temperature. One problem is to find out what the global temperature would have been in the absence of human interference. If the long term climatological factors unrelated to anthropogenic emissions would have cooled the planet, the green house gas would be countering that trend. But the net effect of the two trends of natural process and human activity induced green house gas emissions may not end up in the long run in net warming. Secondly, even if there is net warming of the planet there are large uncertainties regarding the spatial distribution of temperature and precipitation and what it would mean in terms of wind currents and ecosystems in any specific place or location in the latitude–longitude grid of the earth. Besides, there are also uncertainties regarding the feed backs of the entire process of green house gas emissions and warming up and the biospheric adjustments. The flows of carbon and energy on earth are immensely complex and it becomes very difficult to predict the precise impact of the concerned major climatic variables as illustrated by the range of variation in values as indicated in some of the data of the following Table 6.20 (see Nordhaus 1992).

These projections are based on the results of the different General Circulation Models which attempted to find the

Table 6.20
Range of estimates from climate models about
equilibrium impact on major variables for doubling CO_2

Variable	Probable range of global average change	Distribution of regional change	Confidence in projection	
			Global average	Regional average
Temperature	+2° to +5°C	–3° to +10°C	high	medium
Sea level	+10 to 100 cm		high	
Precipitation	+7 to 15%	–20 to +20%	high	low
Soil moisture		–50 to 50%		medium
Run off	increase	–50 to 50%	medium	low
Severe storms				

Source: Nordhaus (1992), pp. 38.

equilibrium impact of the major climate variables for a doubling of CO_2 concentration. The differences arise because of the different approaches of the different models to deal with the uncertainties of behaviour of some of the concerned variables. The medium to low level of confidence of prediction of regional changes make things difficult while defining policy initiative and approach at the country level.

The economic effects of global warming is quite difficult to estimate in view of the vast uncertainties regarding the spatial distribution of the climatic variation. However, agriculture, coastal activities, aquaculture, and forestry sectors would have some direct effect due to the links of these economic activities with the climate and ecosystem's functioning. The rise in sea level would also involve substantive economic loss due to submergence and destruction of life, land and other natural and manmade assets. The ecosystems of wet lands or fisheries would in fact be affected by such climate changes. There would be a variation in energy demand because of the climate change. The demand or supply side of various other products would also be influenced by change in the weather condition directly or indirectly through linkage effects. There are non-market effects of climate change on human health, biodiversity, air pollution, climate disaster, and extreme weather events. The latter effects need to be evaluated by indirect valuation method. With all the market and non-market effects of climate change, the global population will become more vulnerable to the problems of health and homes causing disruption in human settlement and migrations.

Different parts of the world would be impacted differently from climate changes. The rise in CO_2 concentration is likely to boost the rate of primary production of the ecosystem. However, it is the combination of effects of higher CO_2 fertilization, changes in soil moisture and temperature, etc. which will benefit the agricultural activity in certain regions and may harm the same sector elsewhere. In respect of impact on energy and other product markets, the impact may be felt on the supply or demand or both resulting in the changes in the concerned sectoral activity levels and the associated income generation process in either direction. The studies of such impact assessments, however, stress that severe impacts of climate change may be expected in the tropical region of Asia and Africa as compared to the higher latitude countries which are mostly the industrialized ones. As per the Inter-governmental Panel on Climate Change (IPCC) estimates the developing countries will have a net effect of damage amounting to 2 to 9 per cent of GDP, or 0.7 per cent of real GDP, as a result of doubling of CO_2 level, the real GDP being the GDP corrected for the differences of purchasing power of currencies. Table 6.21 provides the consequence of doubling of CO_2 or rise in temperature by 2–5°C for the different countries and regions (see IPCC 1996).

India has a coastline of about 6000 kms. Sea level rises (SLR) would submerge sections of all the coastal states. Table 6.22 shows the percentage share of state area that would be inundated and the percentage share of population of the states which would be affected by the SLR. According to a study carried out by the Jawaharlal Nehru University (as reported in GOI, CSO 1997, p. 85) a total of 5763 sq. km. is expected to be directly affected by the sea level rise in India. The frequency of tropical cyclone blowing over the coastal regions of India is expected to go up. For a doubling of CO_2 there would be increase of the number of tropical disturbance days from 17 to 29 in the north Indian Ocean. The agriculture and other associated primary activities would also be suffering loss due to the loss of land use and/or loss of yield in India for the climate change even after adaptation of agricultural practices to such changes. The losses in farm level net revenue have been estimated to be in the range between 9 per cent and 25 per cent for a temperature rise from 2 to 3.5°C in a study by the Indira Gandhi Institute of Development Research (Kumar *et al.* 1998).

The economy–nature interaction process thus points to a circular causal chain connection as follows:

Economic activities leading to greenhouse gas emissions leading to rise in global temperature leading to change in climate leading to loss of economic activities.

If the feed back effect of climate change on economic system is taken into account the problem of choice of pace of growth of economic activities can be formulated so that the inter-temporal utility from the consumption stream supported by the growth path of economic activities is optimized. The problem can be formulated as a capital theory problem involving the solution for

Table 6.21

Impact of doubling of carbon dioxide in

different regions of the world (2.5°C rise in temperature)

Type of damage	Damage indicator	Non-OECD	China	OECD	World
Agriculture	Welfare loss (%)	0.3	2.1	0.2	0.2
Forestry	Forest area lost (sq. km)	334.0	121.0	901.0	1235.0
Fishery	Reduced catch ('000 tonnes)	4326.0	464.0	2503.0	6829.0
Energy	Rise in electricity demand (TWh)	142.7	17.1	211.2	353.9
Water	Reduced water availability (sq. km)	168.5	32.2	62.2	230.7
Coastal protection	Annual capital costs (m$/year)	51.4	24.0	493.0	1007.0
Dryland loss	Area lost ('000 sq. km)	99.5	–	40.4	139.9
Wetland loss	Area lost ('000 sq. km)	219.1	11.9	33.9	253.0
Ecosystems loss	Number of protected habitats lost assuming 2% loss	53.0	4.0	53.0	106.0
Health/mortality	Number of deaths (1000)	114.8	29.4	22.9	137.7
Air pollution	Equivalent increase in emissions	2602.0	227.0	1943.0	4545.0
Troposphere	('000 tonnes NO2)	1864.0	258.0	873.0	2737.0
Migration	Additional immigrants (1000)	2279.0	583.0	455.0	2734.0
Hurricanes					
Casualties	Number of deaths	7687.0	779.0	313.0	8000.0
Damages	Million $	124.0	13.0	506.0	630.0

Source: TERI (1998), p. 305.

the optimal paths of growth of manmade capital stock and that of concentration of green house gases which would optimize inter-temporal welfare of society. Such a problem which can be meaningfully defined for a global economy, has often accommodated scope for the abatement of green house gas emission duly debiting the abatement costs from the value of output while defining the value added or income. Such global model results as attempted by say Nordhaus has shown that the variation of the optimal path from the business-as-usual path is not a big one and that the optimal growth path does not require the stabilization of climate or constancy of temperature. This is, however, based on the cost of damage or that of abatement as respective functions of temperature rise or reduction of green house gas. These functions are often assumed to be smooth ones not pointing to any nonlinear behaviour with threshold, where the marginal cost of further rise in temperature (or abatement) becomes infinitely large. The problem of global level models is that the damage costs are aggregated over all economies and societies while being related with the causal variables. As the extreme values of damage as faced by the individual countries get averaged out in aggregation, the global optimum may have little operational significance unless the regional distributive

Table 6.22
Land area and population affected by one metre sea level rise

State	% area inundated	% population affected
Goa	4.84	7.25
Tamil Nadu	0.52	2.91
Orissa	0.81	1.76
West Bengal	1.88	2.35
Andhra Pradesh	0.19	0.93
Gujarat	0.92	1.07
Maharashtra	0.18	1.75
Andaman and Nicobar Islands	0.72	N.A.
Karnataka	0.15	0.56
Total	0.41	1.68

Source: Government of India, Ministry of Environment and Forests (1995), *The State of Environment 1995.*

implications of climate change are addressed to separately. What is, nevertheless, important is to emphasize the necessity of controlling climate so that no weather variables for a region crosses the threshold value which may cause substantive loss of life, assets and income in the event of existence of any such threshold for any region. The optimal policy for abating the green house gas emissions for the control of climate would require comprehensive country level analysis of both the direct and the indirect impacts of climate change on the macro-economy as well as the scope and options of abatement of green house gas emissions and the associated costs.

Degradation of Sink: Desertification

The problem of waste overflowing the sink of nature and constraining human activity, raises a related problem of the over exploitation or misuse of natural capital like land which affects the ability of the sink to absorb waste. Deforestation and desertification are examples of such degradation of ecosystem which delimit the ability of cleaning pollution and providing life support. Among such limitations desertification due to the loss of vegetation is the most serious one from the carrying capacity point of view of nature. In the global land use one finds one-third of earth's land mass is covered by deserts which support one-sixth of human population. These deserts range from hyper arid (e.g. Sahara in Africa) to arid (e.g. Gobi in China) to semi-arid (e.g. great plains of the USA). Deserts are deficient in rainfall. The deficiency of rainfall may be due to the fact that such deserts are either situated near the centres of continents far from oceans; or they are cut off from rain bearing winds by high mountains. There are also tropical deserts in zones from 5 to 30° north or south of the equator, the deserts resulting from the global wind pattern. The moisture and temperature condition of wind sometimes in such tropic zones make them unsuitable for cloud formation with rain potential, for example, Arabian and Indian subcontinent deserts.

Deserts have also been formed in vulnerable areas by the human misuse of land. The past 150 years or so have witnessed an alarming rate of expansion of deserts or shift of land to desert-like conditions. According to the UN (Koromondy 1999, pp. 453–5), the rate of expansion of desert area each year is about 80,000 km^2. The total area of the world threatened by future desertification is some 39 million km^2, equal to the land areas of USA, USSR and Australia combined. The major reasons for such threats are overuse of grazing land and deforestation which make land vulnerable to both wind and water erosion of soil as explained earlier. The loss of topsoil and particularly humus content of soil cause the loss of its moisture content ending up in a desert like situation. Wrong cultivation and irrigation practices can lead to salinization of soil and desertification. Besides, urbanization, open cast minings and processing of wastes create unproductive areas resulting in localized desert-like condition (see Koromondy 1999).

The halting of desertification is one of the most important consideration of enhancing the sustainability potential of development. This needs intelligent management of ecosystems' resources so that the vegetation cover may be expanded, soil erosion may be contained, water or moisture retention capacity of soil may be enhanced. These may in turn imply putting certain brake on the pace of conventional development process, particularly of the kind which affects climate and contributes to desertification. The strategy, technology and management of the development process of an economy needs not only to control the flow of wastes to the nature, but also regulate the extent and pattern of use and management of the resources of nature so that its waste absorption power and regeneration ability are not impaired, if not improved.

The sustainability of a development process would depend on the intensity of resource use and that of waste flow, the latter being dependent on the former. While the resource use and the waste flows are inevitabilities, the severity of resource or environmental pollution crisis is to a large extent the expression of inefficiency, carelessness and lack of access to appropriate technology, manmade capital resources and managerial ability due to distributive problems. Human perception of situation of human being in the nature's ecosystem and the shaping of human values are also quite important in explaining part of these inefficiencies.

Chapter 7

SUSTAINABILITY OF ECONOMIC DEVELOPMENT

Concept of Sustainable Development

The first chapter traced the origin of natural resource and environmental crisis of the modern world to the violation of certain limiting conditions which are derived from the interactive relationship between the economic and ecological systems (Common and Perrings 1992). The two-way relationship of nature and economy gave the concept of environmental sustainability of the development process by pointing out the biophysical limits of use of nature as a source of resources and sink for waste disposal. Chapters 2 to 4 explained the basic ecological concepts and laws which enable the understanding the inherent entropic nature of the economic processes, the scope of sustainability of economic processes based on solar energy flow. Chapter 5 delineate how the interaction of ecological and socio-economic factors influenced human population ecology at a global level and in the Indian context. Chapter 6 characterizes human ecology by pointing to the limits of the sources and the sink and the problems of overshoot faced in the context of real life of our global and national economic system. In this chapter the definition and conditions of sustainable development are considered to operationalize the concept. A capital theoretic framework of optimal growth is used, taking an interdisciplinary integrative approach while defining the structure of the problem.

Sustainable development as defined by the World Commission on Environment and Development (World Commission on Environment and Development 1987) requires a boundary condition to be satisfied so as to take care of the considerations of intergenerational equity in resource use. Emphasis has been laid on such use of natural resources that would enable the future generations to experience at least the present generation's level of well-being. This would have obvious implications in respect of terminal stock condition of any time horizon. The terminal stocks of natural resources are determined by the rate of its use relative to the rate of regeneration during the relevant time horizon. For example, ground water stock as measured in a standardized efficiency unit in a given region would decline if the rate of extraction of ground water exceeds the recharging rate in that region. Intergenerational equity would require sustainable harvesting of ground water.

Sustainability condition has emphasized conservation which requires that stock of all the individual resources should not be declining over time. For exhaustible resources, the sustainability condition is to be interpreted as the discovery of new sources of the resource or that of an alternative resource. Economist argue that such condition of sustainability is unnecessarily strong. The ultimate objective of development with intergenerational equity would require that the development process does not end up with the decline of the human well-being index of the society after some period of growth. Natural resources are only the means to the end with strong possibilities of substitution existing between one natural capital resource and another, also between natural capital and manmade capital resources. Resource substitution would correspond to technology substitution and would result in change in waste composition with their attendant differential impact on the ecosystem. In some cases the implied nature of waste substitution would question the choice of the basic resource substitution itself. For example, uranium wastes are infinitely more harmful than the waste products of coal. This often influences the choice between coal and otherwise clean nuclear fuel in favour of the former. The problem becomes particularly acute if the wastes flow into sink and affect nature's life support function and biodiversity (see Solow 1974; Pearce *et al.* 1989).

The main issue of contention has been whether the well-being index or the stocks of natural resources would be required to be non-declining over time for characterizing sustainability. While economics would choose the former, ecology would emphasize the latter as the criterion of sustainability. This has led to the development of two approaches in modelling sustainable development. Capital theory approach focuses on the present equivalent of the utility stream as the maximand (Hartwick 1994), while the steady state economy (Daly 1991) models focus on the notion of preserving the resource and the regenerating power of nature for life support. The rationale for the emphasis on life support in economic models has been that the non-market ecoservices of life support is fundamental for long-term sustenance of well-being of human society; otherwise, famine or disease or natural disasters would wipe out civilization from certain parts of the world. However, the capital theory approach can take account of the role of regeneration of resources and life support in the formulation of the problem while retaining the utility maximization as the objective. (Dasgupta, *et al.* 1997, 1999) Ecological laws would underlie some of the parametric and structural characteristics of the model. The construction of the model should take into account of both: (a) the regeneration of resources and their availability influencing the level of well-being via production system and (b) the feed back effect of the flow of wastes into nature, on the economic system impacting the human well-being.

In any such model on sustainable development, there is often too much of emphasis on intergenerational equity which is one aspect of altruism. The issue of altruism should require the social welfare function to incorporate concern for intra-generational equity along with that for intergenerational equity. The poorer sections of the population without adequate initial endowment of assets or job opportunities, will degrade the environment by directly consuming or overusing the nature (for example, unsustainable agricultural practices in marginal lands, pavement dwelling in urban centers, deforestation for fuel wood need, etc.). If the rate of unemployment (or the absolute level of unemployment) is assumed as a proxy variable for the poverty measure (or the size of the poor), the macro-economic social welfare optimization problem for the use of ecosystem as source and sink can be conceptually defined as follows.

(p) maximise $U = \int\limits_{o}^{\infty} u(\frac{C(t)}{L_s(t)}, \frac{SL_s(t)}{L_s(t)}, P(t), N(t))_e{}^{-\rho t} dt$

$\overset{o}{K}(t) = \varphi(K(t), Ld(t), R(t), P(t)) - C(t)) - \delta K(t)$

$\overset{o}{N}(t) = F(N(t), P(t)) - R(t) - RNM(SL_s(t))$

$\overset{o}{P}(t) = E(K(t), Ld(t), R(t), P(t)) + ENM(SL_s(t)) - A(P(t))$

$\overset{o}{L}(t) = G(L_s(t))$

$L_s(t) = L_d(t) + SL_s(t)$

Nonnegativity of variables $K(0)$, $N(0)$, $L_S(0)$ and $P(0)$ are given.

Notional Explanation

u	= utility of a representative individual of the society.
$C(t)$	= aggregate consumption at time t.
$P(t)$	= stock of pollutant at time t.
$L_s(t)$	= labour force at time t.
$SL_s(t)$	= unemployed or surplus labour at time t.
$K(t)$	= stock of manmade capital at time t.
$N(t)$	= stock of natural resources at time t
ρ	= discount rate of time
$L_d(t)$	= labour demanded and employed at time t
δ	= depreciation rate of capital
$R(t)$	= amount of natural resources harvested and used in production system
φ	= production function yielding GDP
F	= regeneration or biotic growth function of resources
RNM	= non-market resource use by the poor
E	= waste arising function
ENM	= waste flow arising from non-market use of natural resources
A	= absorption function of stock of pollutants giving the amount of its degradation at time t
G	= demographic growth function giving net increase in human population of the economy at time t

The model can generalize to cover a number of varieties of manmade capital and labour. The objective of the economy is to maximize the inter-temporal well-being of a representative individual over infinite horizon which depends on the timepaths of the per capita consumption, the rate of unemployment and the pollution stock, per capita being defined with reference to the size of the labour force. It is assumed here that the average family size and average dependency ratio remains constant over time. Both the absolute pollutant level and the absolute size of national resources enter into well-being function, as people have a preference for environmental quality and for nature which is perceived as a source of amenity. Accordingly, an ordering of choices is made among the combinations of the non-environmental goods and services and the environmental goods and services. The control variables of the dynamic problem are consumption, employment of labour and harvest (use) of natural resources for use in production. The stocks of manmade capital, natural capital, the size of the labour force and the stock of pollutant are state variables of the dynamic inter-temporal problem of choice. In the closed economy for which the inter-temporal problem of choice for development has been defined, the GDP is yielded by the production function for any given configuration of labour use, capital stock, natural resource use and stock of pollutant in the ecosystem, the stock of pollutant thus influencing productivity of the economic system; for example, eutrophication of lake due to nitrogen pollution may affect productivity of fishing or aquacultural activities. The surplus of GDP over consumption, or savings, contributes to the accumulation of the manmade capital stock, the net accumulation being savings minus the depreciation of capital stock. All manmade capital is fully employed while labour may not be fully employed. The net growth of natural capital stock would be given by the ecological laws and both market and non-market use of natural resources. The laws of energy flow and bio-geo-chemical cycles would determine the various biotic growth or abiotic recharging functions. The use of natural resources entering in the macro-economic production function is conceived as the market use of natural resources, while the direct use or degradation of such resources by the poor is the direct appropriation of resources outside the market system. Similarly, the growth equation of pollutant stock would show the net growth to be the waste flow both from the market use of natural resources for production and non-market production-cum-consumption use of similar resources by the poor, after subtracting the absorption of wastes by nature due to the degradation of the concerned compounds through the bio-geo-chemical cycles or the weathering process. Waste is considered as a byproduct of the social product of GDP. That is why E and φ functions are determined simultaneously and strictly by a common set of variables K, L, R, P. The structure of E and j function may build in abatement of pollution by technological intervention which is important for facilitating the attainability of the conditions of sustainability by an economic system. The parameters of the functions of F and A would involve assumption about the underlying ecological behaviour.

As it is proposed to use unemployment to represent the extent of poverty the model relates non-market products use and non-market waste products as functions of unemployed labour. The growth of labour force has been influenced by demographic rates of birth and death. The demographic growth of labour force is a function of the size of the labour force assuming that the survivability rate, the age structure and the female fertility rate, etc. to remain unchanged over time. In the labour balance condition the size of the labour force is equated with the labour employed plus labour unemployed. The problem allows for the discounting of time, time being treated as a continuous variable.

The existence and the nature of the optimal path of per capita consumption $(C(t)/L_s(t))$ and well-being u(t) would depend on the preference structure of the representative individual, role of the altruistic concerns as expressed in the rate of time discount, sensitivity of u with respect to the rate of unemployment $(SL_s(t)/L_s(t))$, productivity conditions of the economic system as well as the ecosystem, ecosystem's efficiency to absorb waste to provide life support to living organism, and the resource use related environment degrading impact of poverty or unemployment. If the optimal solution does not satisfy the sustainability condition, in the sense of intergenerational equity condition that

$$\frac{du^*(t)}{dt} \geq 0.$$

where $u^*(t)$ is the optimal u at time t, then there exists no sustainable optimal development path for the economic system. This can happen either because there exists no feasible solution of the problem with

$$\frac{du(t)}{dt} \geq 0.$$

or, the optimal choice does not satisfy the sustainability condition although feasible solutions with non-declining u(t)-paths exist. In the case of infeasibility the productivity conditions of technology and ecosystems, the degrading effect of poverty on nature and the nature's efficiency in handling wastes arising from the economic systems are such that no feasible solution path of the control and state variables exists which would satisfy the monotonic nondeclining feature of u(t). On the other hand, if some feasible solution exists which ensures the feature of nondeclining u(t) over time, but the optimal choice does not ensure the satisfaction of such conditions, one must conclude that the preference structure of the society does not really consider the sustainability to be any consideration of dominant importance in determining the intertemporal social choice. If sustainability is a dominant consideration in the choice of strategy of development, the optimal path would satisfy the required condition of sustainability provided feasible paths of sustainable development exist. This would require certain conditions on the values of rate of time presence ρ and the parameters of u-function (preference structure) to be satisfied. In the other case where no feasible solution exists with the required monotonic nondeclining feature for u, it will be necessary to improve the technological conditions of production and/or reduce unemployment and poverty to abate its degrading effect on nature, and introduce other pollution abatement measures and interventions like recycling of wastes as inputs for production, etc. so that the feasible set of solution paths may contain non-declining u(t). It may be noted here that both the extents of shift of ρ or parameters of u-function, on the one hand, and those of the parameters of φ and E-functions, on the other, would be relative to the productivity and the reforming ability of the nature—i.e., the parameters of F, G and A functions. It is the interaction of the ecological and the economic forces which would characterize the adoption of policy measures in a given context which would ensure the sustainability of development.

The capital theory model approach as described above also yields estimates of valuation of all kinds of stocks whether manmade or natural or human capital or stock of pollutants. The solution of time paths of the dual variables (Lagrangians) will give the respective prices and the following current value Hamiltonian of the problem (p) will yield the estimate of current value of national income in period t.

National Income (normalized to per capita)

$$= u + \lambda_1[\varphi - c - \delta k] + \lambda_2[F - R - RNM] + \lambda_3[E + ENM - A] + \lambda_4 G$$

$$= u + \lambda_1 \dot{\kappa} + \lambda_2 \dot{N} + \lambda_3 \dot{P} + \lambda_4 \dot{L}$$

λ_1, λ_2, λ_3 and λ_4 are the current shadow values of manmade capital, natural capital, stock of pollutant and stock of population, respectively. The per capita national income is the optimized current value of consumption plus investment in all those stocks in terms utility numeraire in any period. In a situation of adverse effect of unemployment on environment λ_4 is expected to be negative, while λ_1 and λ_2 would assume positive values. λ_3 would be negative in view of the expected sign of partial effect of any change in p in the concerned functions of the model. Such an estimate of national income would take the impact of growth or degradation of natural resources and environment and the growing over population and represent measure of national income as per the rules of sustainable accounting. The value of the objective function of our problem (p) would give a measure of per capita wealth of the nation represented by the physical endowments of the stocks in terms of their potential contribution to the optimized stream of utility of a representative individual over the time horizon. With the passage of time as stocks grow or change, the wealth of the nation would change. An alternative way of defining the notion of sustainability would be to stipulate the requirement of measure of per capita wealth U_T to be non-declining over time. In other words, this requirement implies that the normalized per capita measure of the national wealth as given by the optimized value of U_T should be non-declining with T, where

$$U_T = \int_T^\alpha u\,e^{-\rho(t-T)}\,dt$$

for given constraints and endowments of stocks at the time T. While such a translation of the concept of sustainable development harks back to the world of Adam Smith where the wealth of the nation was considered as the measure of the index of development, it does not necessarily stipulate that all the individual stocks of natural or manmade resources and pollutant stock should move favourably allowing the calculus of trade off to play its own role in the determination of the time paths of the individual stocks. Finally, what is important here in the context of sustainability is that Smith's concept of wealth of nation should include the state of the natural resource and environment and take due account of the interaction between ecosystem and economy interaction in influencing the levels of the stocks.

At the sectoral or micro level, one can formulate similar ecological models of sustainable development where the feed back effect of the waste flows or resources overuse is internalized in the problem of intertemporal choice of development; for example, agricultural farm using various organic inputs, chemical fertilizer, pesticides, etc. with integration of the negative feed back effect of pollution on the productivity of the ecosystem and particularly of the farm land. Such models may examine the conditions of agricultural practices or choice of technology which would ensure the optimal path of agrarian productivity to be nondeclining over time. The interactive problem of agricultural development using phosphorous fertilizer can be considered leading to lake eutrophication and having negative externality (unidirectional) for the aquaculture in the lake. Appropriate conditions can be found for the joint optimum development of the agricultural farm and the fishery and should satisfy in order to ensure sustenance of growth of both agricultural and fishery output.

But, is sustainable development a viable process in the light of the discussion in the last few chapters? While the role of ecological factors points to the pessimism of stationary state in the long run, the scope of policies for ensuring some development in human time scale exists. The extent of scope would, however, depend on the accepted notion of development. If the index of development is a combination of the level of well-being of a typical individual of society and the distribution of well-being among the individuals of a society, the same level of social product can provide a higher level of social well-being if:

(a) the population size to share the product is lower;

(b) a more equitable intertemporal redistribution can improve the well-being index and warrant composition of social product (including infrastructure) that would create less stress on the environment and resources (refer to the objective function of our problem (p));

(c) technical change can ensure higher efficiency of use of resources (for example, refer to the energy or matter conserving shifts in φ function of our problem (p));

(d) change in human value system pertaining to the notion of well-being causes shifts in the preference of individuals of society so that they demand less of constraining natural resources and environmental services for remaining at the same level of utility (refer to the appropriate shifts in the parameters of u-function or ρ in problem (p)).

The dynamics of population, income distribution, technology and human values can thus create some space for the human well-being index to improve. Alternatively, the maximum number of people which can be supported at a given level of per capita well-being by the resources of an ecosystem, called environmental carrying capacity can be raised by such changes. Such estimates of carrying capacity can be obtained from the solution of the following problem, say $\bar{L}_s$ where $\bar{L}_s$ solves the following problem:

max L_s

S.t. all the constraints of (p) except the dynamic condition

involving $L_s(t)$, which is to be replaced by $\overset{o}{L}_s(t) = 0$, and

initial condition $L_s(o) = \bar{L}_s$ which is not given as fixed and the additional condition u(t) non-declining or U_τ non-declining.

Policy Approach of Sustainable Development

Role of Technology and Human Values

How can technology relax the biophysical limits on economic processes and create space for a sustainable upward movement of economic well-being index in the face of growing human population? Technological developments need to relax the constraints imposed by the ecological principle to the functioning of the human economy through appropriate interventions. The development of the knowledge base for such technical change has to take due account of the ecological principles that govern the ecosystems interfacing the economy. By considering the limitedness of resources of the earth and the problem of manmade wastes, the technological concerns should broadly aim at the following:

(a) dematerialization of economic process;

(b) decarbonization of energy;

(c) increasing substitution of nonrenewable resources by renewables;

(d) recycling of waste by converting it into a manmade resource;

(e) non-recyclable waste treatment before disposal;

(f) enhancement of primary productivity of biospheric space in ecosystems;

(g) facilitation of the redistribution process of income by increasing the productivity of wage goods and creating more employment opportunities.

Dematerialization requires higher efficiency of material input use per unit of GDP of a society. Recycling of material waste can also reduce the material flow from nature into economy and dematerialize the net aggregate impact of economic process on such flow. Hypothetically if the entire waste could be recycled, the economy would operate like a spaceship and all the waste would have been converted into resources . However, no recycling is 100 per cent efficient, not all wastes are usable in the production system in cost effective manner. The non-recyclable waste needs attention and action for being converted into at the least as harmless chemical compounds. The test criterion for safety of waste disposal should be based on life support system and taking due account of the ecological principles. The sustainable strategy of material management is thus minimization of the flow of material resources into the economic system and the reverse flow of difficult waste and, at the same time, the maximization of the flow of use and circulation of material resources within the economic system as a sustained process (see Erkman 1999).

On the energy front the challenge for sustainability is greater because recycling of energy is not possible due to the entropy law. Besides, our current energy resource is either fossil fuel or biomass, while the former is exhaustible, the latter is bounded in supply due to the photosynthesis limits. Although primary electricity resources like hydel or solar PV cells have their respective environmental problems, their renewable character can at least ensure sustained flow from nature. Dams have their well known environmental effects stemming from the submergence of land and forests. The manufacture of PV cells involves serious problems of chlorine pollution. While energy conservation through higher efficiency of use is of paramount importance, the decarbonization of energy needs to be targetted to circumvent the problems of pollution and exhaustibility of fossil fuels and to reduce the pressure on land created by the use of plant biomass for energy by a growing population.

Progress of science and technology is a major source of optimism for the possibility of sustainable development as an indefinite process over time. In economic terms this implies the assumption of productivity of investment in R&D activities. In spite of the uncertainty of success of an individual effort in R&D, estimates can be obtained for the expected pay off of an investment in such activities as it is possible to postulate the probability distribution regarding the outcomes of R&D effort. If the costs and the benefits of R&D investments are ascertainable, technology can be conceived as a reproducible item. Every technology involving the use of a nonrenewable or renewable resources can be considered as a part of an organic system in which a technology gives birth to a new technology. The Hotelling rent that arises from the use of any scarce resources (particularly exhaustible) can be used for financing R&D activities to discover and upgrade the backstop technology which would be competitive and would replace the existing technology. Just as capital gives rise to profit and profit is again employed to augment capital base, natural resource when exploited with the help of a technology gives rise to surplus in the form of rent in a capitalist system which needs to be mobilized and invested to develop new resource and technology. Like an organism, capital and technology can thus reproduce themselves. Profits on capital when reinvested result in new capital formation which can be conceived as offsprings of the original manmade capital, rental income of nature resources and when mobilized for R&D activities would result in the emergence of new technologies which can be deemed to be as the offsprings of the earlier technology. Like organisms of a species some of the new capital or technology may die or become unproductive due to obsolescence due to unforeseen changes in market, consumer tastes, and competing technology. Such biological behaviour of the constituents of the economic system provides the basis of optimism regarding the viability of a sustainable development process.

According to the school of thought which considers the conflict between growth and environmental quality to be a non-issue, the environmental quality may suffer with industrialization and growth only temporarily in the initial phase of development. Economic growth and environmental cleanliness would move together in the same direction beyond a threshold of development and is supported both by the demand and supply side arguments. On the demand side the environmental quality is considered as a normal good with positive income effect (i.e., the people demand higher environmental quality as their income increases). As environmental quality is often a nonmarketed service, the preference for it would get reflected in the stringency of environmental regulation implemented through various instruments like pollution tax, etc. On the other hand, industrialization in developing countries leads to the rise in the overall energy intensity of GDP and in the hazardous waste output because of the rising share of the secondary sector in the GDP of the economy. Such a feature of sectoral share movement very often leads to increase in the weightage of processing of minerals as well as biomass, production of chemicals and other industrial materials, machinery and equipment, etc. As industrialization leads to urbanization and the accompanying explosion of traffic movement, the total direct and indirect pollution intensity of GDP goes up. This output composition effect pushes the distribution of value added as per pollution intensity in production away from ecofriendliness. However, at a later, mature stage of capitalist development the share of service sector in GDP goes up at the cost of industry which contributes to the lowering of the pollution intensity of the social aggregate product because of the nature of demand composition and product preferences. The income-elasticity of demand for environmental services would also influence the emergence and the weightage of some of the ecofriendly products in the economy and the market. It is, therefore, often contended that as a result of the scale, technique and output composition effect growth in a closed economic system will first cause a rise in environmental stress followed by a decline after reaching a threshold level of per capita income. Such a pattern as represented by the environmental Kuznet's Curve is illustrated in Figure 7.1 (see World Bank 1992; Grossman *et al.* 1995).

The threshold level of income or the peak value of stress need not be identical for all the countries. While empirical observations do not always convincingly establish such a relationship, resource endowment, preference pattern and technology access determine the actual position and shape of the curve for a country, whatever shape it may be. While the actual shape of such relationship is a subject of debate one important implication of environmental Kuznet's curve in the case of its validity is the assurance of

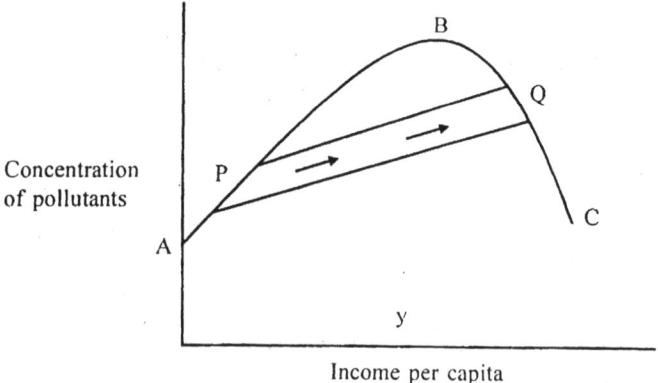

Figure 7.1 Environmental Kuznet's curve.

emergence of environmentally friendly products and higher level of availability of environmental services at a higher level of development. This also means that a faster growth of market of ecofriendly products and technology would require a faster development process, so that a country crosses the threshold level quicker and expands quickly the demand for environmental services. New paths of development for the newly industrializing countries need to be identified which may enable them to avoid the dirty phases of development as experienced by the early industrializing economies, by adopting cleaner technology and growth strategy from the beginning. Such an economy can follow a tunnel like PQ instead of a path like ABC (in Figure 7.1). While this would ensure faster development and market accessibility for ecofriendly products, processes and technology, such a strategy would however involve imposition of stringent environmental regulations by taking appropriate policy initiatives. Only a shift in the basic preference structure would alter the income-environmental quality relationship and result in the political economic feasibility of such tunnelling as outlined.

While the control of population growth and development in science and technology commonly constitutes the basis for optimism regarding viability of economic development as a sustainable process appropriate human values are equally important in defining the space for further development at each stage of the development process. Conventional economics assumes preferences of individuals as given and visualizes social well-being as a result of aggregation of fixed individual preferences. These preferences are postulated to be independent of all other relevant variables in any model of development. However, preferences of people can be manipulated by technological changes, by creating new wants through advertisement in a consumerist culture which can offset part of the benefit of population control. The information as well as the knowledge base of people especially regarding the consequences of their preferences on the ecosystem can influence their preferences themselves. Like technology, the notion of well-being changes over time depending on the realization of the people regarding the role of various factors including the ecological ones in determining the quality of life. Human values as reflected in enlightened preferences should enable the economic development process to find some space for itself in the human time-scale. Technology and human values need to develop in order to resolve the conflicts between conventional economic and ecological principles and between the human and the natural systems.

The conflict between economic and ecological principles is an issue of ethics relating to how the natural world is valued in which human beings evolved and reached the present stage of civilization (Ehrlich 1988). The drive towards indefinite personal freedom is considered basic to human spirit, in order to rationalize capitalism and apparent human success of creating indefinite new options in spite of all obstacles posed by nature and social order. However, in order to sustain the free spirit human being requires the resolution of its conflict with nature. Biodiversity preservation which acknowledges the right of other species to live in this planet, serves the long term interest of human beings to survive. However, human nature as conditioned by the economic existence of capitalist society, is guided more by the short run instead of long run gains and losses. Neoclassical Economics has unfortunately conceived the man's essence at an individual level to be one of self interest maximization in a conflict situation with nature and of competition with others in society. Sustainability of human well-being requires that man's essence should the spirit of individual's co-operation with nature and society. A new paradigm and analytic framework needs to emerge for the analysis of human economic development which would adopt a transdisciplinary approach to handle issues relating to demographic movements, technological advance and human values. Only then economics and ecology can be combined in an appropriate manner to generate the right policies for sustainable development.

Management of Sustainable Development and Institutions

At the beginning of this Chapter it was pointed out what should characterize sustainable development condition for an economy. While the capital theoretic normative approach as formulated in the preceding sections of this chapter may help in identifying the optimal sustainable path of development for a society, there·

remains a big question of managing the economy to ensure its movement along the sustainable path. In order to make the results of such models as structured for macro level or sectoral micro level for any specific region operational, some appropriate institutional mechanism is required. If a perfectly competitive market arrangement would fit the theory of environmental sustainability of the development process, then moving towards a perfectly competitive market arrangement would have solved the problem as Adam Smith's invisible hand would have appropriately coordinated the actions of the players in the game of development process. However, some of the major problems of resource and environmental management arise from the problem of market failure. The common property character of many of the resources of nature (for example, common pasture land, forest, water bodies, etc.) often contribute to environmental externality as the private cost of use of the resource being less than its social cost leading to its over exploitation and ecological degradation. Nature as a sink is used as a non-market public good causing a similar divergence between the private and the social cost and the generation of adverse effects of externalities. As most of the ecoservices of nature do not flow through the market, the incentive of preserving the regenerative power of ecosystem is absent in a market based socio-economic order of management of resources. The externality generating and public good character of common resource has often led to a situation of prisoners' dilemma game among the users of these resources resulting in sub-optimal equilibrium with complications of environmental degradation (see Bardhan and Udry 1999).

The standard neoclassical prescription to problems of resource or environmental management has been in terms of social intervention by using market based instruments of Pigovian tax or tradeable permit so that the market prices can be brought in line with the social cost of use of environmental resources. However, the manner in which shadow prices are often calculated they reflect mostly the direct use values, and not properly the loss of option values due to irreversible changes caused by resource use. It is difficult for market based instruments to resolve the problem of externalities unless the non-market services of ecosystem are correctly evaluated by the regulating authority which decides the level of quota or tax. The quality of outcome of use of such instruments would depend on the reliability of perception of the problems and policy decisions by the centralized regulating authority. The transaction cost of carrying out efficiently such business by such authority may in fact erode the relative efficiency of such instruments.

However, another approach to solve the problem of sub-optimal use of common property resources has been the defining of property rights on resources by privatization and then leaving the use of resource system to the process of market transaction and private bargaining (Coase 1960). Such an approach is expected to generate incentives for greater internalization of externalities and careful husbanding of resources by private owners. However, straight forward privatization of common property resources often has serious distributional implications, particularly in the form of marginalization of the poor. This is a serious problem as the different stakeholders involved in the changes involved in privatization have been very asymmetrically situated with reference to the endowment of commandeered socio-economic and political power. From the experience of the enclosure movement in the eighteenth century England to the present day appropriation of forests and grazing land by timber merchants or cattle ranchers in developing countries, it has been the same unfortunate story of the poor with reference to their receipt of compensation as previous users of the common property. Even with increased efficiency of management, lower rate of harvesting of the resource and positive profit the earlier user's present receipt as wage earners constitutes a lower share in income generated in comparison with the earlier benefit derived as user of the common property.

Even from the efficiency point of view it is not clear for several reasons if privatization would lead to better use of the vulnerable environmental resources. First, of all high time preference of the private owner may induce higher rate of harvesting offsetting at least partially the benefit of controlling over use due to the earlier open access arrangement. Secondly, the tradeability of property rights makes the long-term relationship among beneficiaries of a resource less reliable and this may lead to inadequate concern and investment for proper maintenance and preservation of resources. Besides, the enforcement of private property rights often weakens the implicit cooperative relationship of the earlier beneficiary users of the resource, leading to irresponsible and destructive practices, particularly if privatization is perceived as violating the norms of fairness and equity resulting in a state where everybody is worse off.

An alternative to privatization may be offered either in terms of nationalization of local common property or to the local level management by community organizations. The former option has its serious limitations in terms of the well known reasons of government failure due to both inefficiency and inequity due to ineffective or corrupt government supervision replacing traditional control structure. However, the second option deserves some serious attention and consideration for analysis. A model of cooperation on common property with well-defined property rights at community level (absence of open access) may be able to resolve the problem of conflicts and disputes regarding the purpose and manner of resource utilization and enable systems to attain a cooperative solution which is Pareto optimal from the point of view of resource allocation or at least definitely superior to the non-cooperative equilibrium. Since local level community management through cooperation, places decision-making in the hands of people who have indigenous knowledge regarding local ecological system, information, and motivation, that would be lacked by outsiders (private merchants or state bureaucracy). Cases of both success and failure exist in local level common property management in different parts of the world today (see Baland and Platteau 1996; Bardhan *et al.* 1999; Chopra *et al.* 1989; Dasgupta *et al.* 1997). Study of these cases is important for arriving at the conditions of success of such institutional arrangement which would depend on how the community decides the benefit sharing arrangement and sanctions for violating rules, while taking account of the possibility and circumstances inducing strategic behaviour by the individual players. The game theory literature on such models of cooperation has been useful in arriving at conditions of feasibility and chances of success of cooperation. It appears that human society has to come to terms of co-operation at the organizational level of planning for local resource use without opting for destructive competitive sharing in the use of natural resource whether intra-temporally or inter-temporally. This would not, however mean denying the necessity of the institution of market transaction for matching demand and supply of commodities and services which would induce the forces of competitive efficiency to influence decision-making at all stages including the local community. In terms of institutional arrangement what is thus important for interdependent ecological and social sustainability of development process is the definition of property rights and obligations relating to the use of natural and environmental resources without necessarily meaning their privatization, and a rightly balanced role of local community organization and market to combine efficiency and equity in both economic and ecological sense.

If sustainability of economic well-being of human society demands not only eco-restructuring of technologies, but also similar restructuring of the human values and the institutional and legal arrangement for the functioning of the economy, then conventional economics is required to undergo changes in its framework and method of analysis. The inevitable institutional restructuring due to new eco-principles and eco-restructuring of human values would require economics to accommodate the need of transdisciplinary approach and admit the influence of science and ecology not only on the supply side laws of economic system but also on the demand side and on the institutional rules of the game to ensure the meeting of demand and supply. The movement of ecological economics is to target such reorientation of conventional economics so that it can provide the right framework and methodology for analysing the process of sustainable development of mankind.

Annexe ═══════════════════════

INDIA'S AGRO-ECOLOGICAL
REGIONS

An important component of development plan of an over-populated country like India has involved careful planning of the use of land and associated natural resources in different parts of the country taking account of their respective ecological characteristics. As agriculture provides the life support to human being, consideration of land use for agriculture has dominated the classification of land resource and land use planning. Land is mostly classified into agro-climatic zones, each zone being characterized by its major climatic feature and a range of length of growing period. The growing period is defined to be the duration in which the moisture of soil is enough to provide support to plant growth. However, an ecological classification of the regions of a country would depend on the nature of ecological response to climatic condition in terms of vegetation, fauna, micro-organisms in soil, aquatic organisms, etc. The nature of these responses to a given climatic condition depends again on soil characteristics—its organic and inorganic constituent chemical compounds as well as landform or topography. Soil is the outcome of a combined action of climate and vegetation on parent rock as conditioned by topography over a period of time. The vegetation is an ecological response of climate in a given topography and soil. It has a feed back effect on soil by influencing its organic composition. While the parent rock is the source from which soil derives its mineral contents, a great variety of soil in terms of depth of cover of soil, its texture, organic and mineral content are formed depending on the variation in the soil forming factors or processes. These characteristics influence water holding capacity of soil among others which is of great significance for land use planning. The National Bureau of Soil Survey and Land Use Planning has therefore classified India into agro-ecological regions based on the combinations of the following basic factors:

(a) physiography of a region which influences soil development and climatic condition of a region, for example, plain, hills, plateau, coastal plain, etc. for India (see Table A1);

(b) soil characteristics such as red, black, green, brown, coastal alluvium, lateritic, desert (saline), sandy, littoral, etc. (see Table A2);

(c) bio-climatic factors like rainfall, temperature, altitude, vegetation, potential evapo-transpiration, limits describing the climatic types like per humid, humid, sub-humid, semi-Arid, and Arid (see Table A3 for Indian condition). The soil moisture and soil temperature as determined by such climatic condition would greatly influence the biotic activities of the plants and the availability of water and nutrients for them;

(d) length of growing period (LGP), that is, the period when the moisture in soil is adequate to support plant growth, is dependent on the time distribution of precipitation vis-à-vis potential evapo-transpiration. There is also correlation between the bio-climatic types and the length of growing period. Table A4 shows the correspondence between the bio-climatic classification and the LGP under Indian condition.

India's total land area has been divided into 19 physiography units. India's soil resources have been classified into 16 categories. Combining the physiographic units and the soil categories one can identify 24 widely distributed soilscape regions which India's total land area would comprise. The bio-climatic conditions of the different regions can be classified into 5 broad climatic categories and also into 5 ranges of LGP. Combining 5 broad bio-climatic types and 5 LGPs, 18 moisture availability regions are identified of which 9 are widely different. These 9 bio-climatic-cum-LGP combinations when superimposed on 24 soilscape regions provide us 24 broad agro-ecological regions which can be further aggregated over minor variations in agro-ecological condition and generalized into 20 agro-ecological regions.

The Agro-Ecological map of India as per such classification is given at of (see Figure A1). The map conveys some idea about primary productivity of the different ecological regions and the nature of vegetation and land use in India. The map further gives us the land utilization and forest type for each of these agro-ecological regions of India. Such a description of India's agro-ecosystem of the different regions points to the interface relation between India's ecological conditions and the regional pattern of India's economic activities in the primary sector. The ecological classification of the regions as referred to in this section would provide the ecological basis for land use planning for regional development so as to optimize agrarian growth without violating the condition of balance of agrarian and non-agrarian land use requirements and that of conservation of the ecological balance of each of the concerned regions.

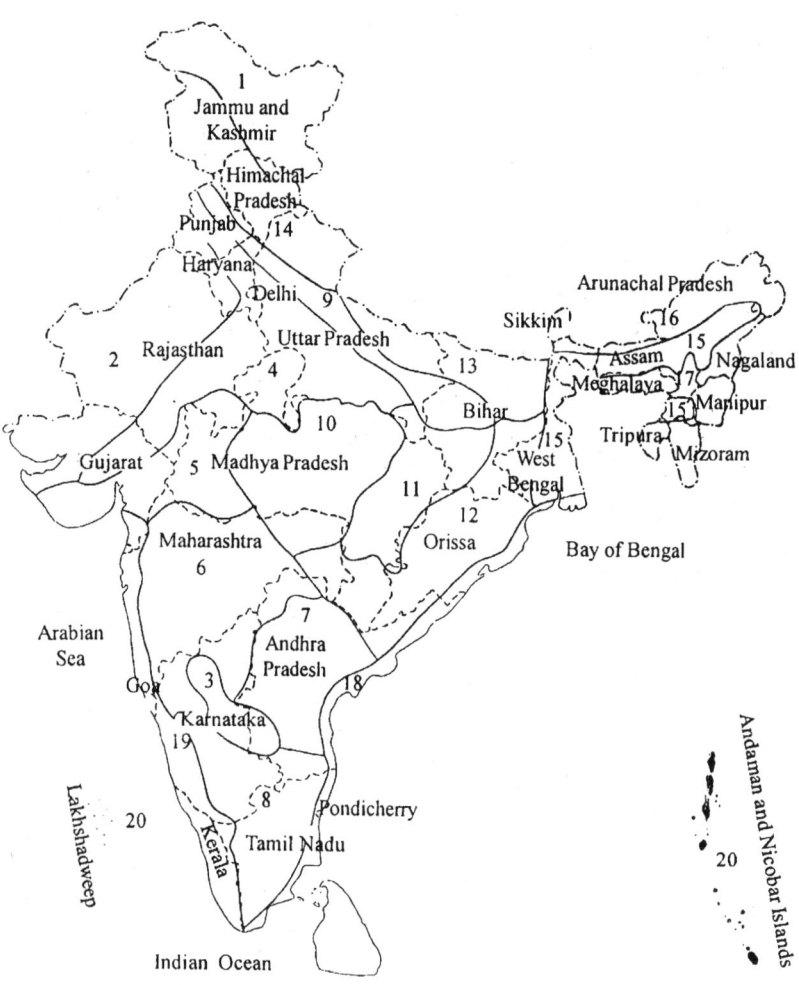

Figure A1   Agro-ecological regions of India

Notes to Figure A1
Agro-Ecological Regions of India

Arid Ecosystem

1. Western Himalayas, cold arid ecoregion, with shallow skeletal soils and length of growing period (GP) <90 days
2. Western Plain, Kachchh and part of Kathiawar Peninsula, hot arid ecoregion, with desert and saline soils and GP <90 days
3. Deccan Plateau, hot arid ecoregion, with red and black soils and GP <90 days.

Semiarid Ecosystem

4. Northern Plain and Central Highlands including Aravallis, hot semi-arid ecoregion, with alluvium-derived soils and GP 90–150 days
5. Central (Malwa) Highlands, Gujarat Plains and Kathiawar Peninsula, hot semi-arid ecoregion, with medium and deep black soils and GP 90–150 days
6. Deccan Plateau, hot semi-arid ecoregion, with shallow and medium (with inclusion of deep) black soils and GP 90–150 days
7. Deccan (Telangana) Plateau and Eastern Ghats, hot semi-arid ecoregion, with red and black soils and GP 90–150 days
8. Eastern Ghats, TN uplands and Deccan (Karnataka) Plateau, hot semi-arid ecoregion with red loamy soils and GP 90–150 days

Subhumid Ecosystem

9. Northern Plain, hot subhumid (dry) ecoregion, with alluvium-derived soils and GP 150–180 days
10. Central Highlands (Malwa, Bundelkhand and Eastern Satpura), hot subhumid ecoregion, with black and red soils and GP 150–180 (to 210) days
11. Eastern Plateau (Chhattisgarh), hot subhumid ecoregion, with red and yellow soils and GP 150–180 days.
12. Eastern (Chhotanagpur) Plateau and Eastern Ghats, hot subhumid ecoregion, with red and lateritic soils and GP 150–180 (to 210) days
13. Eastern Plain, hot subhumid (moist) ecoregion, with alluvium-derived soils and GP 180–210 days
14. Western Himalayas, warm subhumid (to humid with inclusion of perhumid ecoregion with Brown forest and Podzilic soils and GP 180–210+ days

Humid-Perhumid Ecosystem

15. Bengal and Assam Plain, hot subhumid (moist) to humid (inclusion of perhumid) ecoregion, with alluvium-derived soils and GP 210+ days

16. Eastern Himalayas, warm perhumid ecoregion, with brown and red hill soils and GP 210+ days

17. North-eastern Hills (Purvanchal), warm perhumid ecoregion, with red and lateritic soils and GP 210+ days

Coastal Ecosystem

18. Eastern Coastal Plain, hot subhumid to semi-arid ecoregion, with coastal alluvium-derived soils and GP 90–210+ days

19. Western Ghats and coastal plain, hot humid-perhumid ecoregion, with red, lateritic and alluvium-derived soils and GP 219+ days

Island Ecosystem

20. Islands of Andaman-Nicobar and Lakshadweep hot humid to perhumid island ecoregion, with red loamy and sandy soils and GP 210+ days

Source: National Bureau of Soil Survey and Land Use Planning (ICAR), *Agro-Ecological Regions of India,* Publication No. 24.

Table A1
Physiographical regions of India

A Western Himalayas: includes Ladakh Plateau, Kashmir Himalayas, Punjab Himalayas and Kumaun Himalayas of Uttar Pradesh

B Central Himalayas: includes mainly Nepal Himalayas and foot-hills of U.P. Himalayas

C Eastern Himalayas: includes Arunachal Pradesh, Sikkim and Darjeeling Himalayas

D North-Eastern Hills: includes Meghalaya Plateau, hills of Nagaland, Manipur, Mizoram and Tripura

E Eastern Ghat: includes northern, central and sourthern Sahyadris, including Western Coastal Plain

H Eastern Ghats and Tamil Nadu Uplands: includes Tamil Nadu Upland, Eastern Ghat ranges and parts of Karnataka Plateau

I Central Highlands: includes Malwa Plateau, parts of Bundelkhand Upland, Vindhyan Scarplands, Madhya Bharat Plateau, parts of Aravalli Range, Gujarat Plain and parts of Kathiawar Peninsula

J Eastern Plateau: includes Baghelkhand Plateau, Chhota-Nagpur Plateau, Garhjat Hills, northern spurs of Eastern Ghats and Dandakaranya Plateau

K Deccan Plateau: includes Maharashtra Plateau, northern Karnataka Plateau, Telangana Plateau and western spurs of Eastern Ghats

L Kachchh and Kathiawar Peninsula: inclues Peninsular part of Gujarat

M Eastern Plain: includes south-western parts of Punjab and Haryana Plains, Rajasthan Bagar, Marusthali, Kachchh Peninsula (including great Rann of Kachchh and northern parts of Kathiawar Peninsula)

N Northern Plain: includes Western parts of Ganga-Jamuna plains, Punjab Plains, eastern Rajasthan Uplands (including parts of Aravalli Range and Central Highlands)

O Eastern Plain: includes north Bihar Plain and parts of south Bihar Plain and northern parts of Avadh Plain

P Gujarat Plain: includes main lands of Gujarat

Q Bengal and Assam Plains: includes Bengal Basins, north Bengal Plains (Teesta Valley) and Assam Plain (Brahmaputra Valley)

R Western Coastal Plain: includes coastal areas of Saurashtra, Maharashtra, Karnataka and Kerala

S Eastern Coastal Plain: includes coastal parts of Tamil Nadu Plain, Andhra Plain, Utkal Plain and south coastal part of Bengal Basin

T Eastern Island: includes the Andaman and Nicobar group of Islands

U Western Island: includes Lakshadweep group of Islands

Source: National Bureau of Soil Survey and Land Use Planning (ICAR). *Agro-Ecological Regions of India,* Publication No. 24

Table A2
Soilscapes for India

1. Red Loamy Soils: occur in Eastern Himalayas, Eastern Ghats and Tamil Nadu uplands
2. Red and Lateritic Soils: are observed in Eastern plateau, North-eastern hills and Western Ghats and in patches in Eastern Ghats
3. Red and Yellow Soils: are observed in parts of Eastern plateau adjoining the central highlands
4. Shallow and Medium Black Soils (with inclusions of deep phases): occur dominantly in Deccan plateau, including Central Mahatashtra and Karnataka plateau
5. Medium and Deep Black Soils (with inclusions of shallow phases): are observed dominantly in Central highlands and Narmada valley, including Malwa plateau, Bundelkhand upland and Kathiawar peninsula
6. Mixed Red and Black Soils: occur dominantly in parts of Deccan plateau, including Telangana plateau, western part of Eastern Ghats, Bellary and Anantapur region of northern Kamataka plateau
7. Coastal Alluvium-derived Soils: dominantly occur in the eastern coastal plains and in narrow strips along the western coastal plain
8. Alluvium-derived Soils: occur in the western, northern and eastern, including Bengal and Assam plains
9. Desert Soils: dominantly occur in south-western parts of Punjab and Haryana plains, Rajasthan Bagar, Marusthali and Kachchh peninsula
10. Tarai Soils: mainly occur in the foothills of Central and Western Himalayas
11. Brown and Red Hill Soils: occur in association with red loamy soils in parts of Eastern Himalayas
12. Saline and Alkali Soils: occur in Kathiawar peninsula and in the alluvial plain areas of Uttar Pradesh, Haryana, Punjab and Rajasthan
13. Shallow and Skeletal Soils: are observed in Ladakh plateau and rugged ranges of Kashmir Himalayas
14. Grey Brown Soils: occur along the foothills of Aravallis
15. Brown Forest and Podzolic Soils: are observed in the NW Himalayas
16. Sandy and Littoral Soils: occur in Lakshadweep and coastal areas of Andaman and Nicobar Islands

Source: National Bureau of Soil Survey and Land Use Planning (ICAR), *Agro-Ecological Regions of India,* Publication No. 24.

Table A3
Limits of moisture index of various climatic types

Symbol and climate type	Moisture index	Classification
E Arid	-(66.7 to 100)	
D, Semi-arid	-(33.3 to 66.7)	dry
C1, Dry subhumid	-(33.3 to 0)	
C2, Moist subhumid	0 to 20	
B1, Humid	20 to 40	
B2, Humid	40 to 60	moist
B3, Humid	60 to 80	
B4, Humid	80 to 100	
A, Perhumid	> 100	wet

Source: *Agro-Ecological Regions of India,* National Bureau of Soil Survey and Land Use Planning (ICAR), Publication No. 24.

Table A4
Length of growing period

LGP	Climatic condition
< 90 days	Arid
90–150 days	Semi-Arid
150–210 days	Subhumid
> 210 days	Humid and perhumid

Source: *Agro-Ecological Regions of India,* National Bureau of Soil Survey and Land Use Planning (ICAR), Publication No. 24.

References

Ayers, R.U. and A.V. Kneese (1969), 'Production, Consumption and Externalities', *American Economic Review*, Vol. 59, pp. 282-97.

Ayres, R.U. (1978), 'Application of Physical Principles to Economics' in R.U. Ayres (ed.), *Resources, Environment and Economics: Applications of the Materials Energy Balance Principle*, New York: John Wiley and Sons, pp. 37-71.

Ayres, R.U. (ed.) (1998), *Eco-restructuring: Implications for Sustainable Development*, Tokyo: UN University Press.

Baland, J.M. and J.P. Platteau (1996), *Halting Degradation of Natural Resources: Is there a Role for Rural Communities?*, Oxford: FAO of the UN and Clarendon Press.

Bardhan, P. and C. Udry (1999), *Development Microeconomics*, London: Oxford University Press, ch. 13.

Baumol, W.J. and W.E. Oates (1975), *The Theory of Environmental Policy: Externalities, Public Outlays and the Quality of Life*, Englewood Cliffs, New Jersey: Prentice Hall.

Boulding, K. (1966), 'The Economics of the Coming Spaceship Earth', reprinted in A. Markandya and J. Richardson (1992) (eds), *Environmental Economics: A Reader*, New York: Martin's Press, pp. 27-35.

Boulding, K. (1970), *Economics as a Science*, New York: McGraw Hill.

Brandon, C. and K. Homman and N.M. Kishore (1995), 'The Cost of Inaction: Valuing the Economy—Wide Cost of Environmental

Degradation in India', mimeo (paper presented at the UN University Conference on the Sustainable Future of the Global System held at Tokyo in 1995), Washington, DC: World Bank.

Chopra, K., G.K. Kadekodi and M.N. Murty (1989), *Participatory Development: People and Common Property Resources,* New Delhi: Sage.

Coase, R.H. (1960), 'The Problem of Social Cost', in *Journal of Law and Economics,* Vol. 3, pp. 1–44.

Common, M. and C. Perrings (1992), 'Towards an Ecological Economics of Sustainability', *Ecological Economics,* Vol. 7, pp. 7–34.

Conrad, J.M. and C.W. Clark (1987), *National Resource Economics,* Cambridge: Cambridge Unviersity Press.

Costanza, R., J. Cumberland, H. Daly, R. Goodland and R. Norgaard (1997), *An Introduction to Ecological Economics,* Boca Raton, Florida: St. Lucie Press.

Cunningham, William P. (1994), *Understanding Our Environment: An Introduction,* Oxford, England: Wm. C. Brown Publishers.

Dahl, A.L. (1996), *The Eco Principle: Ecology and Economics in Symbiosis,* Oxford: George Roland.

Daly, Herman E. (1991), *Steady State Economics,* Washington DC: Island Press.

d'Arge, R., R.U. Ayres and A.V. Kneese (1970), *Economics and the Environment: A Material Balance Approach,* Baltimore: Johns Hopkins University Press.

Dasgupta, P. (1982), *The Control of Resources,* Oxford: Basil Blackwell.

Dasgupta, P., B. Kriström and K.G. Mäler (1997), The Environment and Net National Product, in P. Dasgupta and K.G. Mäler (eds), *The Environment and Emerging Development Issues,* Vol. 1, Oxford: Clarendon Press, pp. 129–139.

Dasgupta, P. and G.H. Heal (1979), *Economic Theory and Exhaustible Resources,* Cambridge: Cambridge University Press.

Dasgupta, P, and K.G. Mäler (1993), 'Poverty Institutions, and the Environmental Resource Base', in J. Berhman and T.N. Srinivasan (eds), *Handbook of Development Economics,* Vol. IIIA, Amsterdam: North Holland.

Dasgupta, P. and K.G. Mäler (ed.) (1997), *The Environment and Emerging Development Issues,* Vol. 1 and 2, Oxford: Clarendon Press.

Dasgupta, P. and K.G. Mäler (1999), 'Net National Product and Social Well-being', Mimeo.

Datt, Gaurav (1998), 'Poverty in India and Indian States—An Update', FCND Discussion Paper No. 47, Washington DC: International Food Policy Research Institute.

Ehrlich, R.R. (1988), 'The Loss of Biodiversity', in E.O. Wilson (ed.), *Biodiversity*, Washington DC: National Academy Press, USA.

Erkman, Suren (1999), 'Emerging Principles of Industrial Ecology and Cleaner Production: Applicability in South Asia', mimeo, open lecture delivered in IIM Calcutta.

Erwin, T.L. (1983), 'Beetles and Other Insects of Tropical Rainforest Canopies at Manus Brazil, sampled by Insecticidal Fogging', in S.L. Sutton, T.C. Whitmore and A.C. Chadwick (eds), *Tropical Rain Forests: Ecology and Management,* Edinburgh: Blackwell, pp. 59–75.

FAO (1993), 'Forest Resource Document 1990: Tropical Countries', *FAO Forestry Paper 112,* Rome: Food and Agricultural Organization of United Nations.

Georgescu–Roegen, N. (1971a), *The Entropy Law and the Economic Procesess,* Cambridge: Massachusetts, Harvard University Press.

Georgescu–Roegen, N. (1971b), 'The Entropy Law and Economic Problem', reprinted in R. Costanza, C. Perrings and C. Cleveland (eds) (1997), *Developments in Ecological Economics,* Cheltenham: Edward Elgar Publishing Co., pp. 236–47

Government of India, Central Statistical Organisation (1997), *Compendium of Environment Statistics 1997,* New Delhi: Central Statistical Organisation (CSO).

Government of India, CSO (1998), *Compendium of Environmental Statistics 1998,* New Delhi: CSO.

Government of India, Department of Family Welfare (1997), *Family Welfare Programme in India: Year Book 1996–97,* New Delhi: Department of Family Welfare.

Government of India, Ministry of Finance (1996), *Economic Survey 1995–96,* New Delhi: Ministry of Finance.

Government of India, Ministry of Finance (1999), *Economic Survey 1998–99,* New Delhi: Ministry of Finance.

Government of India, Planning Commission (1992), *Eighth Five Year Plan 1992–97,* New Delhi: Planning Commission.

Grossman, G.M. and A.B. Krueger (1995), 'Economic Growth and Environment', *Quarterly Journal of Economics,* Vol. 110, pp. 353–77.

Gupta, Avijit and Mukul G. Asher (1998), *Environment and the Developing World,* Chichester: John Willey and Sons.

Gurumurti, K., D.P. Raturi and H.C.S. Bhandari (1984), 'Biomass Production in Energy Plantation of Prosopis Julifflora', *The Indian Forester,* Vol. 110, No. 9, pp. 879–93.

Hanks, Sharon La Bonde (1996), *Ecology and the Biosphere: Principles and Problems,* Delray Beach, Florida: St. Lucie Press.

Hartwick, J. (1994), 'National Wealth and Net National Products', *Scandinavian Journal of Economics,* Vol. 96, pp. 253–6

Hayes, P. and K. Smith (eds) (1993), *The Greenhouse Regime: Who Pays?,* Tokyo: UN University.

Hotelling, H. (1931), 'The Economics of Exhaustible Resources', *Journal of Political Economy,* Vol. 39, No. 2, pp. 137–75.

IPCC (1996), *Climate Change 1995, The Economic and Social Dimensions of Climate Change,* Report of the IPCC Working Group III, New York: Cambridge University Press.

Jindal, R. and J. Singh (1989), 'Toxicity of Pesticides to the Productivity of a Fresh Water Pond', *Indian Journal of Environmental Health,* Vol. 31, No. 3, pp. 257–61.

Khoshoo, T.N. (1995), 'Census of India's Biodiversity: Tasks Ahead', *Current Science,* Vol. 69, No. 1, pp. 14–17.

Koromondy, E.J. (1994), *Concepts of Ecology* (Third Edition), New Delhi: Prentice Hall of India.

Koromondy, E.J. (1999), *Concepts of Ecology* (Fourth Edition), New Delhi: Prentice Hall of India.

Kumar, K.S. Kavi and J. Parikh (1998), 'Climate Change Impacts on Indian Agriculture: The Ricardian Approach', in Dinar *et al.* (eds) (1998), Measuring the Impacts of Climate Change on Indian Agriculture, World Bank Technical Paper No. 402, Washington DC: The World Bank.

Kupchella, Carles E. and Margaret C. Hyland (1998), *Environmental Science: Living within the System of Nature,* Boston: Allyn and Bacon.

Lovelock, J.E. (1988), *The Ages of Gaia,* Cambridge: Cambridge University Press.

Lutz, E. (ed.) (1993), *Towards Improved Accounting for the Environment,* Washington DC: The World Bank.

Malthus, Robert (1798), *An Essay on the Principle of Population,* republished in 1959, K. Boulding (ed.), Ann Arbor: University of Michigan.

Markandya, A. and J. Richardson (eds) (1992), *Environmental Economics: A Reader,* New York: St. Martin's Press.

Marx, Karl, *The Capital,* Vol. 1, (1988), Vol. 2 and Vol. 3, republished Vol. 1 and Vol. 2 (1970), Vol. 3 (1972), London: Lawrence and Wishert.

Meadows, D.H. and D.L. Meadows (1972), *Limits to Growth,* New York: Universe Books.

Meadows, D.H., D.L. Meadows and J. Randers (1992), *Beyond the Limits,* Vermont: Chelsea Green Publishing Company.

Metrick, A. and M.L. Weitzman (1998), 'Conflicts and Choices in Biodiversity Preservation', in *Journal of Economic Perspectives,* Vol. 12, No. 3, pp. 21–34.

Nandan, S.B. and Abdul Aziz (1995), 'Water Quality and Benthic Fauna Diversity of a Polluted Estuary of the South-West Coast of India', in *India Journal of Environmental Protection,* Vol. 16, No. 1, pp. 12–22.

National Bureau of Soil Survey and Land Use Planning, ICAR (1992), *Agro-Ecological Regions of India,* NBSS Publication No. 24, New Delhi: Oxford and IBH Publishing Company.

NCAER (1985), 'Domestic Fuel Survey with Special Reference to Kerosene', Vol. I and II, New Delhi: National Council of Applied Economic Research.

Nordhaus, William D., 'Economic Approaches to Global Warming' in R. Dornbush and J. Poterba (eds) (1992), *Global Warming: Economic Policy Responses,* Cambridge: MIT Press.

Nordhaus, William D. (1992), *Managing the Global Common,* Cambridge, Massachusetts: MIT Press.

Odum, E.P. (1975), *Ecology: The Link between the Natural and Social Sciences,* New Delhi: Oxford and IBH Publishing.

Pachauri, R.K. and P.V. Sridharan (eds) (1998), *Looking Back to Think Ahead: Green India 2047,* New Delhi: Tata Energy Research Institute.

Parikh, K.S. (1991), An Operational Definition of Sustainable Development, DP-2 (Revised), Discussion Paper Series, Bombay: Indira Gandhi Institute of Development Research.

Parikh, K.S., J.K. Parikh, V.K. Sharma and J.P. Painuly (1992), *National Resource Accounting: A Framework for India,* Bombay: Indira Gandhi Institute of Development Research.

Parikh, K.S. and Utpal Ghosh (1991), National Resource Accounting for Soils: Towards an Empirical Estimates of Costs of Soil Degradation for India, DP-48, Discussion Paper Series, Bombay: Indira Gandhi Institute of Development Research.

Pearce, D.W., E. Barbier and A. Markandya (1989), *Sustainable Development: Economics and Environment in the Third World*, Aldershot, England: Edward Elgar.

Pearce, D.W. and R.K. Turner (1990), *The Economics of Natural Resources and the Environment*, London: Harvester–Wheatsheaf.

Petty, W. (1899), *Economic Writings of William Petty*, Cambridge: Cambridge University Press.

Pigou, A.C. (1920), *The Economics of Welfare*, London: Macmillan.

Prasad, D.Y. (1990), 'Primary Productivity and Energy Flow in Upper Lake Bhopal', *Indian Journal of Environment and Health*, Vol. 32, No. 2, pp. 132–39.

Ravindranath, N.H. and D.O. Hall (1995), *Biomass, Energy and Environment: A Developing Country Perspective from India*, Oxford: Oxford University Press.

Repetto, R. (1997), 'Second India Revisited: Population Growth, Poverty and Environment Over Two Decades', in R.K. Pachauri, and L.F. Qureshy (eds) *Population, Environment and Development*, New Delhi: Tata Energy Research Institute.

Ricardo, David (1821), *The Principles of Political Economy and Taxation*, later republished in Sraffa P. (ed.) (1951), as *The Works and Correspondences of David Ricardo*, Vol. 1, London: Royal Economic Society.

Sengupta, Ramprasad (1997), 'Energy and Development. Some Macroeconomic Constraints for Energy Planning in India', in A. Bose, M. Rakshit and A. Sinha (eds), *Issues in Economic Theory and Public Policy*, Delhi: Oxford University Press.

Sharma, S.C. and V.K. Srivastava (1984), 'Biomass production in an Age Series of Pinus Patula Plantation in Tamil Nadu', *The Indian Forester*, Vol. 110, No. 9, pp. 915–30.

Singh, L., K.P. Singh and J.S. Singh (1992), 'Biomass, Productivity and Nutrient Cycling in Four Contrasting Forest Ecosystems of India', *Tropical Ecosystems: Ecology and Management*, New Delhi: Wiley Eastern Ltd.

Smith, Adam (1776), *An Inquiry into the Nature and Causes of the Wealth of Nations*, republished (1976), Campbell R.H. and Skinner A.F. (eds), Oxford: Clarendon Press.

Smith, Kirk (1993), 'The Basics of Green House Gas Indices' in P. Hayes and K. Smith (eds), *The Greenhouse Regime, Who Pays?*, Tokyo: UN University.

Solow, R. (1974), 'The Economics of Resources and Resources of Economics', reprinted in R. Dorfman and N. Dorfman (eds) (1977), *Economics of the Environment: Selected Readings*, New York: Norton.

Stockholm Enviornment Institute (1997), *Comprehensive Assessment of the Fresh Water Resources of the World*, Stockholm: World Meteorological Organization.

Tata Energy Research Institute (1998), *Tata Energy Data Directory and Year Book 1998–99*, New Delhi: Tata Energy Research Institute (TERI).

UNDP (1999), *Human Development Report 1999*, New York: Oxford University Press.

UNEP, *Environmental Data Report*, Oxford, Basil and Blackwell Ltd., published annually.

Vitousek, P.M., P.M. Ehrlich, A.H. Ehrlich, and P.M. Matson (1986), 'Human Appreciation of the Products of Photosynthesis', *Bioscience*, Vol. 36, No. 6, pp. 368–73.

Wilson, E.O. (1987), 'The Arboreal Ant Fauna of Peruvian Amazon Forest: A First Assessment', *Biotropica*, Vol. 2, pp. 245–51.

Wilson, E.O. (1988), 'The Current State of Biological Diversity', in E.O. Wilson (ed.), *Biodiversity*, Washington DC, National Academy Press, USA.

World Bank (1992), *The World Development Report 1992*, New York: Oxford University Press.

World Bank (2000), *The World Development Report 1999–2000*, New York: Oxford University Press.

World Commission on Environment and Development (1987), *Our Common Future*, Oxford: Oxford University Press.

World Resources Institute, UNDP and UNEP (1994), *World Resources 1994–95*, New York: Oxford University Press.

World Resources Institute, UNDP and UNEP (1998), *World Resources 1998–99*, New York: Oxford University Press.

INDEX

abiotic environment 27, 29
    conditions of 30
    organic compounds of 29
abiotic segment 27
absorption, of light energy 26, 49
accumulation, of manmade capital
    109, 134
acid land, and aquatic system 31
acid rain 31, 81, 86, 90, 183, 200–1
    and damage to biotic
      regeneration 201
    and phosphorous loss 85
age, distribution 92, 100
    structure of population 95, 106
aggregate population size 96
agriculture (agrarian) 235
    and deforestation 160
    and degradation of forest area
      162
    climatic change and 210
    development of 223
      and loss of forest area 157
      and population growth 100
      process of 36
    growth 237
    holdings in India 126
    land, loss of 140
    nitrogen support to 79–80
    output 138

practices, unsustainable 116
product-mix 33
production, conditions of 31
run-off, and water pollution 155
technology use in 125
agro-climatic and agro-ecological
    conditions 43
agro-climatic zones 235
agro-diversity 171
agro-ecological regions, India's 43,
    238–40
agro-ecological zoning 73
agro-economic system 37
    fuel subsidization 36
air pollution 90, 183–4
    from oil cycles 182
    sulphur and 86
algae 153, 168
alkalization, of soil 143
ammonia 78
animal species *see* fauna
animalia 168–9
annual energy flow 37
aquatic organisms, and detritus
    food chain 63
aquatic ecosystems, terrestrial and
    30
aquatic system, acid land and 31
aquifer reserves 9